Qualitative Networks

How do we interact with people in our everyday life? Who are the people we are connected to? What are the consequences of overlapping social circles and how people deal with the potential emerging conflicts? What are the structural and cultural mechanisms that regulate social worlds? Network science is a scientific approach to the study of network dependencies and associations which tries to answer these and many other questions. This book explores the underlying mechanisms that regulate social life as they are produced, reproduced, modified and abandoned in the spatial and temporal patterns of interactions. The mixed methods approach, that combines formal network analysis with qualitative materials and statistical tools, shows the importance of contextualising structural mechanisms in their social and cultural environment, and allows overcoming the traditional methodological boundaries that shape the field of social sciences.

Elisa Bellotti is Lecturer in Sociology at the University of Manchester and a member of the Mitchell Centre for Social Network Analysis. Before arriving in Manchester in 2008, she worked as Research Fellow at the University of Turin and the University of Bozen, Italy. She completed a PhD in Sociology and Methodology of Social Research in 2006 at the Catholic University of Milan. She publishes in international peer reviewed journals. Among her recent publications are: 'Getting funded: Multi-level networks of physicists in Italy' (*Social Networks*, 2012) and the monograph *Amicizie. Le reti amicali dei giovani single* (Milan: Franco Angeli, 2008).

Social Research Today
Edited by Martin Bulmer

The *Social Research Today* series provides concise and contemporary introductions to significant methodological topics in the social sciences. Covering both quantitative and qualitative methods, this new series features readable and accessible books from some of the leading names in the field and is aimed at students and professional researchers alike. This series also brings together for the first time the best titles from the old *Social Research Today* and *Contemporary Social Research* series edited by Martin Bulmer for UCL Press and Routledge.

Other series titles include:

Charles Seale-Hayne Library
University of Plymouth
(01752) 588 588
LibraryandITenquiries@plymouth.ac.uk

An Introduction to the Philosophy of Social Research
Tim May and Malcolm Williams

Research Social and Economic Change
The uses of household panel studies
Edited by David Rose

Introduction to Longitudinal Research
Elisabetta Ruspini

Researching the Powerful in Education
Edited by Geoffrey Walford

Researching Race and Racism
Edited by Martin Bulmer and John Solomos

Statistical Modelling for Social Researchers
Principles and practice
Roger Tarling

The International Social Survey Program, 1984–2009
Charting the globe
Edited by Max Haller, Roger Jowell and Tom W. Smith

Models in Statistical Social Research
Götz Rohwer

Managing Social Research
A practical guide
Roger Tarling

Contemporary Critical Theory and Methodology
Piet Strydom and Gerard Delanty

Surveys in Social Research (sixth edition)
David de Vaus

Qualitative Networks
Mixed methods in sociological research
Elisa Bellotti

Martin Bulmer is Professor of Sociology at the University of Surrey. He is Director of the Question Bank (a WWW resource based at Surrey) in the ESRC Centre for Applied Social Surveys (CASS), a collaboration between the National Centre for Social Research (NatCen), the University of Southampton and the University of Surrey. He is also a Director of the department's Institute of Social Research, and an Academician of the Academy of Learned Societies for the Social Sciences.

Qualitative Networks

Mixed methods in sociological research

Elisa Bellotti

Routledge
Taylor & Francis Group

LONDON AND NEW YORK

First published 2015
by Routledge
2 Park Square, Milton Park, Abingdon, Oxon OX14 4RN

and by Routledge
711 Third Avenue, New York, NY 10017

Routledge is an imprint of the Taylor & Francis Group, an informa business

© 2015 Elisa Bellotti

British Library Cataloguing-in-Publication Data
A catalogue record for this book is available from the British Library

Library of Congress Cataloguing in Publication data
Bellotti, Elisa.
  Qualitative networks: mixing methods in social research / Elisa Bellotti.
    pages   cm – (Social research today)
    1. Social networks–Research–Methodology. 2. Sociology–Research–Methodology. 3. Social sciences–Network analysis. 4. Social sciences–Research–Methodology. I. Title.
  HM741.B457 2014
  302.3–dc23
  2014006878

ISBN: 978-0-415-60086-6 (hbk)
ISBN: 978-0-203-83712-2 (ebk)

Typeset in Times
by Out of House Publishing

MIX
Paper from
responsible sources
FSC   FSC® C013604
www.fsc.org

Printed and bound by CPI Group (UK) Ltd, Croydon, CR0 4YY

**To Russ Bernard
and Anuška Ferligoj**

Contents

Figures

Tables

Acknowledgements

We must go about our work and meet 'the challenges of the day'
both in our human relations and our vocation.
But that moral is simple and straightforward
if each person finds and obeys the daemon that holds the thread of his life.

(Weber 2004 [1917]: 31)

This book contains the materials and reflections that I have collected and elaborated since the beginning of my career as a sociologist and as a social network analyst. The interest in the first sprang out of the passion for the second, which I still like to consider like a colourful box of crayons. Many years have passed since I first got introduced to social network analysis by Steve Borgatti at Essex summer school. I was fascinated by this incomprehensible world: I could not understand what a standard deviation was, but the colouring of structural equivalence convinced me that I had found my daemon, the vocation in life that Weber refers to in the epigraph. At Essex I also met Martin Everett, who has been a teacher, a mentor and a good friend since. I am indebted to him for everything I know about this fascinating field, for the invaluable advice, for many years of support and encouragement and for many bottles of wine (that he obviously paid for).

Martin is now a colleague at the Mitchell Centre for Social Network Analysis. Having actively participated in the birth and growth of the Centre has been an incredibly exciting experience that has massively boosted my knowledge and has given me the opportunity to invite and meet many network scholars. I am grateful to Nick Crossley and the Department of Sociology at Manchester for envisaging and engineering the return of social networks to Manchester, and continuing the prestigious tradition of the Manchester School. Together with Martin and Nick, all my colleagues at the Mitchell Centre are a daily source of inspiration and support: Gemma Edwards, Susan O'Shea, Kathryn Oliver, Mark Tranmer and Daniel Tischer are some of them, together with all the PhD students and the seminar speakers and attendees who have gravitated around the Centre in the last five years. I am especially grateful to Johan Koskinen who has dramatically improved my statistical knowledge, even if I never understand anything of what he says. A blessing and a curse.

I would like to thank Wendy Bottero, Sue Heath and Roy Greenhalgh for reading and commenting on chapters of this manuscript; Nick Crossley and Martin Everett for reading the whole draft and providing great feedback; and Russ Bernard for the meticulous work of reviewing the book. Reading Russ's comments has been like having him sitting next to me to remind me how to systematically avoid armchair speculation. I am not entirely sure I have achieved this ambitious goal, but I did my best and I can always improve in the next book. I am also grateful to my department and in particular to Brian Heaphy for giving me the time to write this book.

I would like to thank Carole Bernard for editing and proof reading the book and for the support and affection that she always shows me.

A special acknowledgement goes to my good friend and colleague David Evans, who is always there to hold me when I fall (from water slides): I promised him this book would contain the word 'banana'. Here we go, printed in black!

To Emma Shearer, Siobhan Donohoe, Mike Tong and Ben Warren: I am very lucky to have you as my friends. I would have never managed to do this without you.

Alla mia famiglia vanno i miei piú caldi ringraziamenti, per l'amore e il supporto che mi dimonstrano ogni giorno anche nella distanza. Non avrei mai combinato nulla se non fosse per voi.

Finally, to my mountains. To the forest and the rocks and the animals and the people there, who remind me how to live in a place where silence is the rule.

1   Introduction

Every snowflake is unique, as is every wave in the sea.
Yet all snowflakes, like all waves,
are governed by the same immutable laws of nature.
Human beings are like this too.

(Marinoff 2003)

In social science, a longstanding debate has developed around the methodological choices that drive empirical research, as Marinoff's epigraph poetically evocates (Marinoff 2003). Much has been written about what should be considered the realm of observations, what constitutes a unit of analysis, how we should measure it, how to abstract these measurements in formalised schema that can represent social reality, and how to build theories that can be transposed across settings and explain or predict social phenomena. Luckily for someone who wants to write a book about mixed methods, these problems are far from being solved, giving space for more discussion and possibly a small step in advancing the debate. Unluckily for science though, the argument has also witnessed some harsh and fiery moments, building boundaries around methods and disciplines that are sometimes so hard to cross that they seem more like solid walls than matters of scientific discussion.

Network science has always spanned boundaries, both disciplinary and methodological. Despite its stereotyped perception as a hard, mathematical, arid and abstract quantitative approach, or alternatively as a fancy way to visualise data, this unique perspective has long proved to be fertile and versatile in many fields and in combination with many methods.

Network science is a scientific approach with clear definitions of what needs to be studied and how to study it: it is defined by the type of data that it aims to analyse (Brandes *et al.* 2013) in order to discover the mechanisms that regulate empirical phenomena. Being empirical, network science is not simply an abstract and formal exercise of logic and mathematical thinking: it produces theories, but these emerge from observations and are conversely tested against them. And the work of observations and abstraction, especially when dealing with the complexities of the human world, is a challenging task. Sometimes it observes empirical objects with definable properties, for which the process of formalising and testing theories is relatively straightforward. But more often, social scientists do not know much about the phenomena they want to explain; they thus need to dedicate hard and detailed work to describe such phenomena before they can attempt any measurement and formalisation.

As such, network science is not different from any other science. In a similar way, physics needs to dedicate many resources to measure the trajectories of invisible particles; astronomy requires many hours to observe untouchable objects; and archaeology has to deal with sparse and incomplete sources of information. Once they have robust observations, they can build theories, and once they have theories, they have to empirically prove that they can stand up against falsifications.

Thus, what is unique to network science is not its method of enquiry but the specific type of assumptions that define the field and the type of empirical data to be observed. That is, network science is interested in studying associations, dependencies and relations. Regardless of the kinds of phenomena it wants to explain, the foundational elements that characterise such phenomena need to be related to each other, where the pattern of relations is what distinguishes them and what is interesting to study (Brandes *et al.* 2013). Defining, observing, measuring and modelling associations and dependencies is not an easy task. But the main implication of this assumption is that we cannot consider the world (any kind of world—the physical and the social, the past and the present, the one we can directly observe and the one we can only indirectly assume) as a linear aggregation of independent elements whose properties sum up in a meaningful whole. Meaning emerges from the relational texture, and we need theories and methods that allow us to explain such texture.

Defining associations and dependencies entails taking into account that elements are interlocked in a spatial way, which means that they form networks of relationships by virtue of being connected with each other synchronically. However, they are also interlocked in a temporal way: what happens in the present is dependent on what happened in the past and influences what will happen in the future. Therefore, interlocking mechanisms are highly contextual. Despite their localised nature, quantitative research in social science generally tends to study mechanisms by developing either formal models that are too generic to take into account context dependencies or statistical approaches that try to fit data obtained from several contexts into a single model at a time (Edmonds 2012). Against these tendencies, qualitative research has had the invaluable merit of bringing local properties into focus. However, as we will see in the Chapter 2, the fruitful debate between general models and contextualised observations has historically drifted toward a paradigmatic opposition that claimed the ontological, epistemological and methodological incompatibility between natural and social sciences on the one hand and between quantitative and qualitative methods on the other.

This book has the ambitious aim of overcoming this unfruitful drift. Instead of simply discussing the technical requirements that are needed when methods are mixed in social research, it does so by rejecting incompatible paradigmatic stances and by looking at the peculiar ontological, epistemological and methodological dimensions of network science. It does so by starting from the observation that network analysis is not a quantitative method strictly speaking. Although it formalises data into numbers, it radically departs from the classic statistical approaches of categorical and variable analysis, with their foundational assumption of the independence of the units of observation.

Network science, conversely, starts precisely from the observation that actors, however defined, are always entangled in meaningful relations in contextualised settings, and the patterns of such entangled ties are produced by, and conversely shape, structural and cultural mechanisms that regulate social phenomena themselves. Network analysis, by offering analytical tools to measure and model relational patterns, is thus a very useful method for studying social phenomena. But as a method that looks at associations and dependencies, network analysis is highly contextual, as it formalises specific networks whose characteristics are not generalisable via design-based inferences (Snijders and Bosker 2012). This type of inference, very common in statistical analysis, is based on the assumption that it is possible to generalise results obtained for a probability sample to a finite population from which the sample is extracted. In network science, populations are not normally sampled (apart from the specific cases of egonetwork studies, as I discuss in Chapter 3). Each study observes a specific network, and the aim of the research is not to extend contextual characteristics to other networks but to discover social mechanisms that may function across various case studies.

To achieve these goals, network analysis can be equally mixed with qualitative methods as well as statistical tools. The flexibility and thick description of qualitative methods can illustrate the relational work that actors in networks engage with in defining identities, interactions and network structures, in negotiating cultural conventions, and in exchanging symbolic and material resources. I use the term 'symbolic' to refer to the contextual meaning that a specific set of resources would assume in a social world, defined as 'the form that one or another of capital species [economic, cultural and social capital] takes when it is grasped through categories of perception that recognise its specific logic or, if you prefer, misrecognise the arbitrariness of its possession and accumulation' (Bourdieu 1992: 119). Implicit in this definition is the acknowledgement that a resource can assume various symbolic meaning depending on the social world in which it circulates. I will return to this topic in more detail in Chapter 5.

Statistical analysis, on the other hand, is extremely useful in modelling network structures and their dynamics to observe commonalities and differences across networks. Examples of these families of statistical models are exponential random graph models (ERGM), which infer the probability of some basic and foundational properties of network structures to be found in empirically observed networks (Robins *et al.* 2007). Similarly, Siena models look at the dynamics of networks over time (Snijders *et al.* 2010). They can provide insights of how structural mechanisms work, by either showing how they are perceived and enacted by actors or how they are unconsciously reproduced in interaction.

This book does not cover these areas of research. For those interested in the advanced statistical modelling techniques of social networks, other references are available (e.g. Lusher *et al.* 2012 for ERGM models and the review article by Snijders *et al.* 2010 for network dynamics). Whilst the discussion around the development of statistical tools for the analysis of network structure is relatively ordinary in network science, recently an argument has emerged that specifically looks at the contribution of qualitative methods. Within this debate, researchers have often complained about the unbalanced ratio between the use of quantitative and qualitative tools in network studies, claiming that the discipline has favoured the development of highly sophisticated formal methods at the expense of the detailed and rich descriptions of social networks and calling for a more systematic (re)introduction of qualitative methods (Brint 1992; Emirbayer 1997; Emirbayer and Goodwin 1994; Mische 2003; Crossley 2010).

Without denying the ethnographical origins of the disciplines (Mitchell 1969), a new generation of network scholars has dedicated effort to reintroducing the importance of culture and discursive foundations in social network analysis (Knox *et al.* 2006). The recognition of an unbalanced production of quantitative papers compared to qualitative works is not completely unfounded. In the past 30 years, a large proportion of publications has been dedicated to the development of robust methods of analysis, which is required by any discipline building its toolkit for empirical work (McCarty 2010). However, once the methodological tools have been put in place, network science has spread across many substantive fields, where the interest is less in developing analytical methods and more in using them to answer specific theoretical questions. When applied in different contexts, network analysis undoubtedly benefits from a combination of formal models and qualitative accounts that enlighten each other and illustrate contextual mechanisms (McCarty 2010).

In these situations, many researchers have used qualitative techniques to locate and understand formal networks in their social and cultural contexts. Some of these works have explicitly discussed the adoption of mixed methods in network research as a way to overcome parts of the limits of single methods in their respective fields of analysis (Jack 2005; Lubbers *et al.* 2010; Martinez *et al.* 2003; Mische and White 1998; Woo Park and Kluver 2009). Others, given their substantive focus on some specific research topics, have not stressed the accent over the mixed methods aspects, possibly producing the perception of a less common adoption of qualitative methods in network research.

One study that has qualitative methods is the article by Lazega *et al.* (2008). In this study, the network of collaborations between French cancer researchers has been investigated by mapping several kinds of relations between individuals and between organisations. The network was obtained via qualitative interviews, although the use of mixed method research strategy is not highlighted in the keywords or in the abstract. Similarly, in the article by Bodin and Tengö (2012), the relationships that link local tribes in Madagascar and their use of ecological resources are investigated via ethnographical methods. Again, the combination of qualitative observation and social network analysis is not the main scope of the article and therefore is not mentioned in the abstract and keywords.

Conversely, a general lack of interest from qualitative researchers in approaching and adopting a network perspective has been noted (Kirke 2010), which is again likely to be responsible for the perceived marginalisation of qualitative methods. The mainstream trends of qualitative research, especially in their methodological discussions, have been predominantly engaged in paradigmatically rejecting any kind of data formalisation and have therefore avoided any consistent contribution to network science. This book is intended to regain their attention and convince them of the need of rebalancing their input.

Some conceptual clarifications are required at this point. So far, I have used the terms 'network science', 'network analysis', 'social network analysis' and 'social networks'. These are not interchangeable. By network science, I mean the scientific approach to the study of network dependencies and associations. Network analysis is the methodological tool that lies at the core of network science studies: it consists of the application of graph theory to the study of relations among a set of items, whether animate (humans, apes, etc.) or inanimate (countries, organisations, words, blogs, etc.). Social networks are the empirical phenomena of interconnected patterns of relations among living organisms, and social network analysis is the application of network analysis to the study of those patterns. In the social sciences, specifically sociology, the substantive discipline that defines the framework of this book, network studies normally deal with either individual or collective human actors, like firms, organisations, political parties, informal groups and the like. However, nodes and ties can represent virtually anything that has some sort of connection; therefore, network analysis has been applied, for example, in studies of semantic networks, transport networks and patterns of scientific citations.

The aim of this book is to illustrate how to mix network analysis with qualitative methods in sociological research. Overall, I define qualitative networks as network studies with a qualitative component, in the collection and/or the analysis of the data. I do not simply discuss the technicalities about how to mix various methodological tools. I justify the use of qualitative networks ontologically, epistemologically and methodologically; in so doing, I hope to convince the reader of the robustness of an approach that can contribute to the development of network science.

This is not an introductory book on qualitative methods or on network analysis. Although no advanced methodological and analytical skills are required when reading it, the book presupposes some basic knowledge of standard qualitative tools. When used in the empirical examples, qualitative methods are defined and described in detail, but the book does not provide any general discussion of these methods or any review of how they have been applied in other contexts where they were not mixed with network analysis. Similarly, when basic descriptive statistical analysis is adopted in the book, it is assumed that the reader will be familiar with it. For the network terms, I provide a brief guide of definitions in the next section to familiarise the reader with the measures that have been used for the analysis of the empirical material.

Readers who want to improve their skills in either qualitative research or social network analysis should refer to other works, as the main focus here is to understand how the two approaches can be combined together. There are numerous textbooks dedicated to both qualitative methods and social network analysis. Although this is not the place to review all of them, some references may be useful. For qualitative methods, an excellent introduction to the range of techniques for both data collection and analysis is the book by Bernard and Ryan (2010). A clear and detailed handbook for analysis of network data is the one by Borgatti *et al.* (2013), whilst more general introductions to the whole social network perspective are the classic book by Scott (1991) and the recent one by Prell (2011). Wasserman and Faust (1994) is probably still the most comprehensive review of social network methods, and Hennig *et al.* (2012) offer a detailed and useful description of how to conduct empirical research in network science.

A brief introduction to social network analysis

One of the most powerful aspects of social network data is that they can represent social relationships in a formal and comparable way. Relational matrices abstract from the hustle and bustle of everyday interaction and systematise information in terms of presence or absence of ties, expressing them in a directed or undirected, binary or valued form. Regardless of the substantive context in which it is applied, network analysis is grounded in the mathematical realm of graph theory. In graph theory, data can be represented in adjacency matrices (i.e. grids of rows and columns that contain relational information in cells). All networks are comprised of two elements: nodes, which in the adjacency matrix are represented in the rows and columns, and relations between nodes, which are represented by values in the cells' linking rows and columns. Additionally, we might also have some actors' attributes, which can be represented in standard vectors; actors in rows; and attributes in columns, with the (i,j) cell giving the value of actor i's jth attribute (e.g. age, ethnicity or gender).

The following glossary is not intended to be an exhaustive review of the concepts and measures in network analysis but is a brief guide to introduce the network terms that will be used in the book. Readers unfamiliar with the topic should use it as a point of reference to go back to every time they meet a network term that they do not know. Readers with a basic or advance knowledge in network analysis can skip this part and move to the next.

Glossary

Node: A node is the first basic element of networks; it represents the unit of analysis or actors in the network. It is also called vertex.

Relation: Relation is the second basic element of networks; it represents the tie that connects two nodes. It is also called an arc or edge. We say an edge is incident to a node if it is connected to that node.

Graph: A graph is the third basic element of networks; it consists of a set of nodes and a set of relations connecting them.

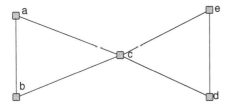

Figure 1.1 Graph

Matrix: A matrix is a grid with rows, columns and values in cells.

Square matrix: A matrix is square when the nodes in the rows are the same as the nodes in the columns. An adjacency matrix is a square matrix, sometimes referred to as a one-mode matrix.

Table 1.1 Square matrix

	a	*b*	*c*	*d*	*e*
a	0	1	1	0	0
b	1	0	1	0	0
c	1	1	0	1	1
d	0	0	1	0	0
e	0	0	1	1	0

Rectangular matrix: A matrix is rectangular when nodes in rows are different than the nodes in the columns. It is also called an affiliation or incidence matrix or a two-mode network, where nodes of one mode (rows) can only relate to nodes of the other mode (columns).

Table 1.2 Rectangular matrix

	1	*2*	*3*
a	1	1	0
b	0	1	0
c	0	0	1
d	0	0	1
e	1	0	1

Projecting two modes into one mode: A rectangular matrix can be transformed into two square ones by matching rows and columns. The routine transforms the rows-by-columns matrix into either a row-by-row matrix or a column-by-column one. For example, if rows are actors and columns are events, the results of the projection will be an actors-by-actors matrix, where the cells give the number of events actors have in common, and the corresponding events-by-events matrix, where the cells give the number of actors events have in common.

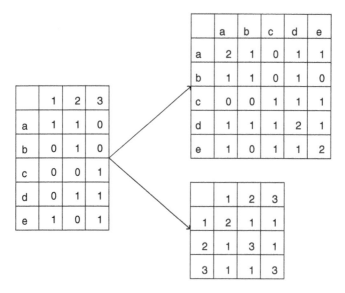

Figure 1.2 Projecting two modes into one mode

Symmetric matrix: A matrix is symmetric when the cell that represent the relational information between node A and node B has the same value of the cell representing the relational information between node B and node A. It is symmetric because the top right triangle of the matrix is equal to the bottom left one. A symmetric matrix represents an undirected graph.

Table 1.3 Symmetric matrix

	a	b	c	d	e
a	0	1	1	0	0
b	1	0	1	0	0
c	1	1	0	1	1
d	0	0	1	0	1
e	0	0	1	1	0

Asymmetric matrix: A matrix is asymmetric when a cell that represent the relational information between node A and node B can have a different value of the cell representing the relational information between node B and node A. It is asymmetric because the top right triangle of the matrix is different to the bottom left one. It is used to represent the direction of relations and is therefore a directed graph. Note that the direction is from the row to the column; hence in the example below, the connection is from a to b but there is no connection from b to a.

Table 1.4 Asymmetric matrix

	a	b	c	d	e
a	0	1	1	0	0
b	0	0	1	0	0
c	1	0	0	1	1
d	1	1	0	0	1
e	1	0	1	0	0

Symmetrise: To symmetrise a matrix means to transform an asymmetric matrix into a symmetric one. This can be done in various ways; for example, by substituting the values of both cells with the highest value between the two, or the lowest, or the sum, difference, product, division, or average of the two. Other computational methods are also available. In the example below, the method adopted uses the lowest value between two cells.

	a	b	c	d	e
a	0	1	1	0	0
b	0	0	1	0	0
c	1	0	0	1	1
d	1	1	0	0	1
e	1	0	1	0	0

	a	b	c	d	e
a	0	0	1	0	0
b	0	0	0	0	0
c	1	0	0	0	1
d	0	0	0	0	0
e	0	0	1	0	0

Figure 1.3 Symmetrise

Binary matrix: A matrix is binary when it only has values of 1 or 0 in the cells.

Table 1.5 Binary matrix

	a	b	c	d	e
a	0	1	1	0	0
b	1	0	1	0	0
c	1	1	0	1	1
d	0	0	1	0	1
e	0	0	1	1	0

Valued matrix: A matrix is valued when values in cells can be different than 1 and 0. It is used to represent the strength of relations.

Table 1.6 Valued matrix

	a	b	c	d	e
a	0	3	5	6	2
b	3	0	1	1	5
c	5	1	2	4	6
d	6	1	4	3	3
e	2	5	6	3	1

Dichotomise: To dichotomise a matrix means to transform a valued matrix into a binary one. This can be done by selecting a specific threshold (e.g. greater or less than, equal to). In the example below, the method adopted uses the threshold of numbers strictly bigger than 3.

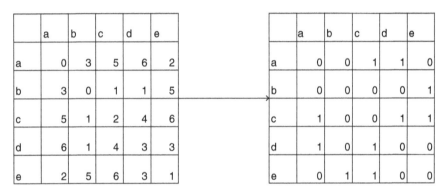

Figure 1.4 Dichotomise

Diagonal: The diagonal represents the values in a square matrix contained in the cells that connect each node with itself. The value is often 0, but can also be valued. For example, in the row projected of actors by events, the diagonal value represents the number of events each actor has attended.

Table 1.7 Diagonal

	1	2	3
1	2	1	1
2	1	3	1
3	1	1	3

Whole network: In a whole network, a relevant population of nodes is identified and information is collected for all of them, seeking to establish the existence or not of a relevant relation between each pair of nodes in that population.

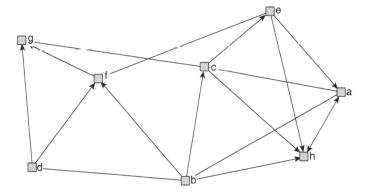

Figure 1.5 Whole network

Egonetwork: In an egonetwork, or personal network, or actor-centred network, information is collected only for a single node, asking to report about her relations with a set of others (alters) she herself identifies as relevant. Sometimes alters' attributes are also collected. In the following three examples, ego is represented as a black node.

Star: A star is defined as the set of ego, alters and ego–alter ties

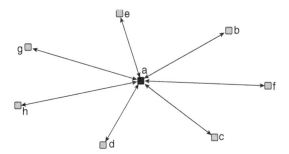

Figure 1.6 Star

First zone: In an egonetwork, a first zone is defined as a star (the set of ego, alters and ego–alter ties) plus the alter–alter relations (Barnes 1972). This is also known as a local neighbourhood.

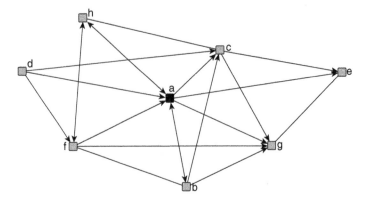

Figure 1.7 First zone

Second zone: A second zone comprises alters that are connected to a first zone set of nodes and relations between these additional alters (Barnes 1972). It is also known as a two-step local neighbourhood.

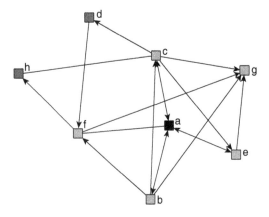

Figure 1.8 Second zone

Local neighbourhood: See first zone.

Target, concentric circles: The target is a sociometric tool to collect egocentric data. It consists of a number of concentric circles (six is a popular choice), where ego is located in the middle and she is asked to name alters and place them in the surrounding circles. The closer the alter is to ego, the stronger the relationship with her (Kahn and Antonucci 1980).

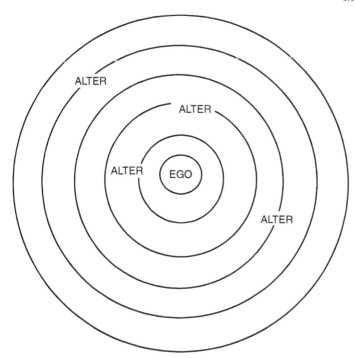

Figure 1.9 Target, concentric circles

Dyad: A dyad consists of two nodes and the relation that links them. It can be null (no relation), directed (with a relation that links one node to the other but not the other way around), reciprocal (with two relations linking one node to the other and vice versa), and symmetric (where the direction of the relation is meaningless).

Figure 1.10 Dyad

Triad: A triad consists of a set of three nodes and the relations that may connect them. The triad census identifies 16 possible configurations for directed data (Davis and Leinhardt 1972; Holland and Leinhardt 1970).

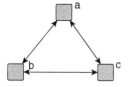

Figure 1.11 Triad

Size: The size of a network consists of the number of nodes belonging to it (see also degree centrality for egonetwork size).

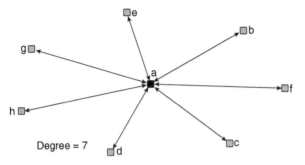

Figure 1.12 Size

Average distance: The length of a path is the number of ties it contains. The distance between two nodes is the length of the shortest path. The average distance is the average value of all the shortest paths in a network.

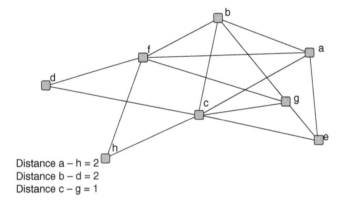

Distance a – h = 2
Distance b – d = 2
Distance c – g = 1

Figure 1.13 Average distance

Degree centrality: Degree centrality is defined as the number of alters adjacent to a node. In an egonetwork (with ego not represented), this represents its size (see also size). In an asymmetric matrix, we distinguish between in-degree (the number of ties received by that node) and out-degree (the number of ties initiated by that node). In a valued matrix, degree is the sum of the values of all the ties incident to a node.

Density/average degree: The density of a binary network is the total number of ties divided by the total number of possible ties. For a valued network, it is the total of all values divided by the number of possible ties, which is equal to the average degree.

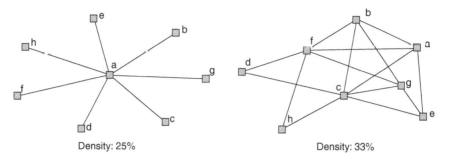

Figure 1.14 Density/average degree

Components/main component: In an undirected graph, two nodes are members of the same component if there is a path connecting them. In a directed graph, components can take into account the directions of the ties to establish if there is a connecting path. The largest component is called the main component. In a network, components are parts of the network that are not connected to each other. In the following example, there are four components, and (a, b, c, d) represents the main one.

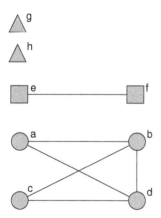

Figure 1.15 Components/main component

Clique and *n*-clique: A clique is a maximally complete subgraph. It is complete because every node in the clique is adjacent to every other. It is maximal because we cannot increase its size and still have it be complete. An *n*-clique defines the minimum number of nodes (*n*) to be included in a clique.

Core–periphery, categorical and continuous: A core–periphery structure is defined by a highly connected central set of people (the core) and some peripheral people

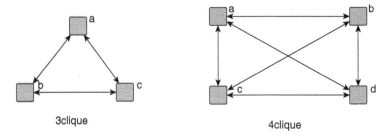

Figure 1.16 Clique and *n*-clique

connected to the core but not to each other. The distinction can be categorical, with a binary distinction between core and periphery (nodes in the core are given a value of 1; nodes in the periphery a value of 0), or continuous, with a range of values from 0 to 1 that indicate the coreness of each node (how much a node belong to the core).

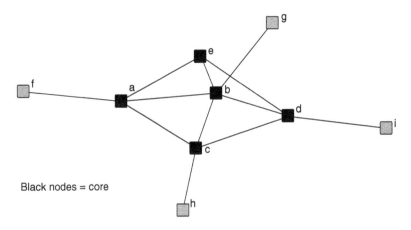

Figure 1.17 Core–periphery, categorical and continuous

Structural hole: A structural hole consists of the lack of a direct connection between two nodes, which are both connected to a common third actor (a broker, see brokerage).

Brokerage: A brokerage position is defined as the number of times ego lies on the shortest path between two alters separated by a structural hole (i.e. the number of pairs of alters that are not directly connected). The normalised version of this measure consists in the number of brokerage opportunities divided by the egonetwork size.

Cutpoint: A node is a cutpoint if it connects two otherwise disconnected components.

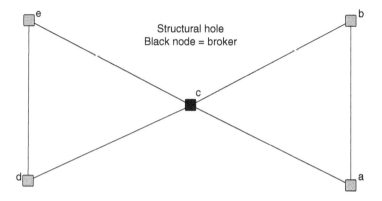

Figure 1.18 Brokerage

Pendant: A pendant is a node connected to a network via only one tie.

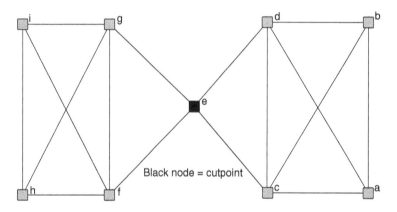

Figure 1.19 Cutpoint

Structural equivalence: Two nodes are structurally equivalent if they are linked to the exact same sets of nodes.

Regular equivalence: Two nodes are regularly equivalent if they relate to similar set of actors. Equivalent actors has the same types of relations with equivalent others, but not necessarily the same others.

Spring embedder: Spring embedder is a visualisation method in which the nodes in the graph are like similar poles of a magnet and the edges are like springs. Nodes repel each other but the edges pull them together. Spring embedders arrange the nodes in a way that reduces the overall stresses of pulling and pushing.

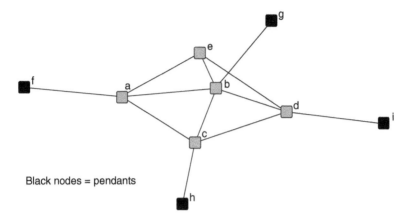

Black nodes = pendants

Figure 1.20 Pendant

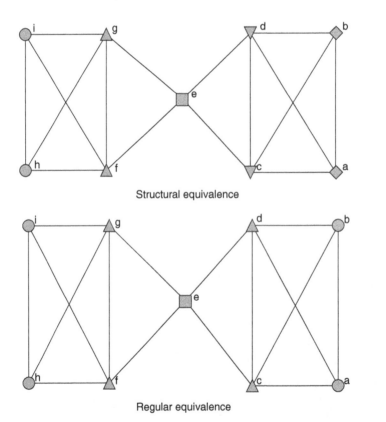

Structural equivalence

Regular equivalence

Figure 1.21 Regular equivalence

Outline of the book

The next chapter (Chapter 2) is an overview of the historical emergence of the so-called paradigm war, and its sometimes irreducible opposition between qualitative and quantitative methods. The review of the longstanding debate between quantitative and qualitative researchers is necessary because such opposition has generated a general lack of interest from mainstream qualitative researchers in approaching and adopting a network perspective (Kirke 2010).

In Chapter 2, the paradigmatic stances of qualitative research against quantitative methods are relocated within their original reaction to the domination of structural functionalism and its use of inferential statistical analysis in social sciences, especially sociology. By putting the debate into its historical perspective, the chapter challenges the thesis of the ontological and epistemological incompatibilities and explores some theoretical and methodological approaches that have attempted to overcome this unfruitful opposition. In particular, the perspectives of pragmatism and critical realism are reviewed, together with their implications for mixed methods studies. These perspectives have been selected for discussion as pragmatism is adopted by the mixed method approach, which probably constitutes the most common epistemological justification in discussing the mix between qualitative and quantitative data. Critical realism instead presents interesting similarities with network science in acknowledging the ontological and epistemological foundations of social sciences.

Chapter 3 gets to the core topic of this book by looking at the peculiarities of network science and the definition of the foundational elements of network studies. It does so by looking at the ontological properties of actors, relations and networks, which are considered the foundational bricks of social phenomena. I review the positions of analytical and relational sociology, which have deeply engaged with the discussion of the characteristics that define these foundational elements, and I highlight similarities and differences between the two perspectives. I then discuss the implications of the theoretical definition of actors, relations and networks for the study of mechanisms that underlie the dynamics of social phenomena. I compare the epistemological positions of critical realism with those of network science: structural configurations and cultural formations are defined as the two ontologically indivisible aspects of any social phenomena, which require methods for analysis of formal properties as well as contextual meanings. The chapter concludes with a general introduction to social research that combines mixed network analysis with qualitative techniques, specifically in interviews, ethnographic observation and archival material.

Chapters 4, 5 and 6 illustrate three empirical examples in which network analysis has been mixed with these qualitative methods. The three cases cover research projects I have been involved with over the last ten years. The first example, in Chapter 4, combines social network analysis with in-depth interviews in the collection of the egonetworks of 23 men and women living in Milan, Italy. I conducted the research in 2005 and focused on the structure and meaning of friendship: a classic version of name generator, which collected information on the names of each interviewer's friends, their personal characteristics, and the relationships between all the named friends was matched with an in-depth interview that explored the content, meaning, history and dynamics of friendship ties. I analysed the data by combining both the network information and the narrative accounts, following a mixed method research design where methods are equivalent and simultaneously used in both data collection and analysis (Tashakkori and Teddlie 1998). The example illustrates how actors' identities are defined and emerge out of interactions and relationships and how these relations overlap in local networks. The interwoven nature of friendship ties is described in its temporal dynamics and its structural patterns in accordance with the theoretical requirements presented in Chapter 3.

Chapter 5 enlarges the perspective from individually centred local structures to overlapping networks by looking at various social circles in which individuals are embedded and at symbolic and material resources that circulate within and across them. It does so by looking at the social relations of two street groups involved in illegal activities, again in Milan. I collected data ethnographically by conducting moderate and fully participant observations (Spradley 1980) over an extended period of time in 2000 and 2001 and I used unstructured interviews, in-depth interviews and a focus group. The research design in this case was predominantly qualitative: I collected and analysed data via qualitative methods and used social network analysis only descriptively to formalise the structure of relationships that street groups activate with other groups and other significant people. A comparison with the theory of social fields proposed by Bourdieu (1992) is presented to show how social relations should not be conceptualised as a form of capital that can be accumulated over time and summed up with other types of capital; rather, they constitute the relational infrastructure in which other resources (economic, cultural) circulate and become symbolically meaningful.

Chapter 6 describes the social world of philosophy in Italy by looking at the research collaborations that academics have established over a decade. I collected data using the archives of the Italian Ministry of University and Research, particularly by looking at all the research projects of National Interest (PRIN) funded for philosophy from 1997 to 2006. The formal structure of the network of research collaborations is first described and then statistically modelled to reveal the social mechanisms that facilitate or hamper the process of institutional research funding. Such mechanisms are then qualitatively explored by looking at the content of the projects and then at a description of the individual researchers' tasks and duties. Research topics and interests, together with rules and conventions of collaborations and symbolic and material resources exchanged across research groups, illustrate the structural and cultural features of the academic field, which can be classified as a social world in the acceptance used by symbolic interactionism in the first place (Becker 1982) and subsequently adopted by relational sociology (Crossley 2011).

In this last empirical example, I adopted a research strategy using a sequential mixed method approach (Tashakkori and Teddlie 1998), with the quantitative component preceding the qualitative one both in terms of data collection and analysis. The two approaches are equivalently mixed in the interpretation of results, as they both produce insights on the social mechanisms that regulate research funding.

2 Paradigm war and the roots of social networks

There has been growing interest recently in the debate around mixing formal social network analysis with qualitative methods. The practice has always been a feature of social network studies (see, for example, the seminal work of the Manchester School of Anthropology, Mitchell 1969), but the reasons why we need to mix and how we mix the two approaches along with the epistemological foundations of a mixed methodology have become the focus of renewed attention (Bellotti 2010; Crossley 2010; Edwards 2010; Fuhse and Mützel 2011; Hollstein 2011).

Despite its importance in the social sciences in general, the debate around qualitative and quantitative approaches can only partially be applied to social network analysis. That is because this perspective, from its very beginnings until today, has been about both the formalisation of structure, based on graph theory, and the study of structure ethnographically. Nevertheless, it is useful to review the mixed methods debate to understand the peculiarities of traditional quantitative (as in statistical) and qualitative (as in hermeneutic) approaches and how they can be reconciled in combination with social network analysis; it also introduces important elements of discussion in terms of definitions of cases and units of analysis, interdependency of observations, and ways to link micro and macro levels of analysis.

The position advanced here is that the dichotomy between quantitative and qualitative methods is embedded in two different levels of discussion. On the one hand, the debate is located within specific historical scientific communities competing for reciprocal validation. It is only by looking at the dominance of certain kinds of sociological theories (in particular, structural functionalism) that we can understand why there has been a reaction against the quantification of the way of observing and interpreting society, which led to a paradigm war. On the other hand, the contextualised characters of the discussion between competing stands are useful to highlight different philosophical foundations, which, although not incompatible, are at least in opposition.

These philosophical foundations have implications for the practice of research— not in preventing the mixing of different methodological tools, but in bringing the object of study into focus. By observing social reality from different distances— focusing, for example, on individuals, groups, organisations, countries and the like—we need to adapt the magnifying lens and bring into focus the whole picture of what we are trying to study: social networks are a valid attempt to connect different and nested levels of interactions, assuming a detailed conceptualisation of what these levels are (Bellotti 2012). Maintaining consistency between the different scales of observations in terms of coherence and integration of theoretical and methodological concepts is not a trivial task, but it is not an unreachable (or philosophically impossible) one (Crossley 2011: 181).

This chapter starts with the former position, revising how the so-called paradigm war was declared by certain groups of qualitative researchers by constructing a definable enemy via the redefinition of some characteristics of quantitative approaches. We will see how some scholars, reacting to the marginalisation in which the qualitative tradition was constrained by specific streams of quantitative research, reframed the latter by distorting some of the elements that were believed to characterise natural sciences. Whilst the overall battle between qualitative and quantitative approaches is contextualised within the historical conditions in which it emerged, some useful elements of the debate can be extrapolated. In particular, mixed methods studies on one hand and critical realism with its methodological tool of configurational comparative studies on the other, are discussed as two interesting attempts to overcome the drifts of the paradigm war. These two perspectives have been selected because of their centrality within the debate around mixing qualitative and quantitative methods and because of their different positions toward it.

Mixed methods studies focus on the methodological implications of merging qualitative and quantitative data and offer some useful categorisations of the various ways these studies can be conducted (Tashakkori and Teddlie 1998). However, they can be evaluated in critical terms for their reduction of the discussion to a practical set of technicalities. Critical realism deeply engages with the ontological and epistemological foundations of social sciences and presents some commonalities with the core elements of network sciences. As such, it offers a robust framework on which to ground a mixed methodology, although with some limitations.

Paradigm war? On the rhetoric of polarisation

It is difficult to attribute the declaration of war between different perspectives in social research to a single paper, but there is little doubt that the battle is real and that it has been framed mainly by qualitative researchers. A good starting point is the work of Lincoln and Guba (1985) and Guba and Lincoln (1994), where the differing perspectives are expressed in terms of irreconcilable paradigms. One of those perspectives is that of natural science, where ironically the dispute has never occurred.

In their 1994 chapter, Guba and Lincoln describe the opposition of the qualitative and quantitative *paradigms*, in Kuhn's (1970) sense of that term: a set of shared beliefs among members of a speciality area,[1] where interests converge around a specific set of problems identified as significant for the advancements of knowledge. By supporting the same paradigm, researchers also share specific understandings of which research techniques are appropriate for investigating

Table 2.1 Differences between quantitative and qualitative paradigms

	Positivism and post-positivism	*Critical theory and constructivism*
Ontological assumptions	Existence of an external objective reality	Reality is socially constructed and therefore varies according to different observers
Epistemological assumptions	What is observed is independent from who is observing it	What is observed is never independent from who is observing it
	Empirical observations are independent from theoretical conceptualisation and are value free	Denial of theory and value independence
Methodological assumptions	Search for universal causal laws	Denial of the existence of universal causal laws in social reality
	Use of deductive logic and falsifiable hypotheses	Use of inductive logic (not originally in Lincoln and Guba [1985] or Guba and Lincoln [1994] but suggested by many authors, and included in the list by Tashakkori and Teddlie [1998])
	Use of large generalisable samples	Use of small, non-representative samples

these problems and a sense of identity that is constructed via interpersonal networks and the processes of information sharing. They can therefore be identified in observable research communities (Kuhn 1970: 176–83), alternatively defined as communities of practice (Denscombe 2008). The search for observable communities of practice has a long history in the sociology of science, from the identification of invisible colleges (Crane 1972), to the recent analysis of citation networks and authorship paths (Burt 1978/79; Hummon and Carley 1993; Hummon and Doreian 1989; Liberman and Wolf 1998; Lievrouw *et al.* 1987).

Guba and Lincoln (1994: 107) shift the debate from Kuhn's definition of communities of practice to a profound opposition of ontological and epistemological positions within four competing paradigms: positivism, post-positivism, critical theory and constructivism. They accuse the former two of dominating and rejecting the latter two. Qualitative researchers generally agree on the claimed differences between the paradigms (Bergman 2008; Guba and Lincoln 1994), which are summarised in Table 2.1.

Guba and Lincoln's formulation is constructed around the identification of their opponents as belonging to a coherent philosophical position that they believe was *ipso facto* imported from natural sciences. Although their attempt is to ontologically distinguish the social realm from the natural one, they end up by rhetorically using arguments developed within the debate over the definition of the scientific method, the same one that they are aiming to reject. The problem is that positivism and post-positivism, far from being coherent paradigms themselves, have not been developed within natural sciences strictly speaking, although the Vienna Circle of logical positivism, which largely contributed to the original development of positivism, included physical scientists as well as philosophers and social scientists (Bernard 2000).

The term 'positivism' was initially formulated by Comte (1907 [1830–42]) to avoid the reduction of the social sciences to natural ones, not by rejecting the scientific method, but by distancing the social sciences from the speculative philosophy of the time and the then-current battle between idealism and empiricism. By distorting the original meaning of positivism, and by attacking it with the same logical argument developed within the scientific method, Guba and Lincoln's attack ends up in a weak position where fallacies emerge.

For example, the problem of independence of observations, which challenges the idea of a single objective reality, was addressed in the natural sciences (as recognised by Guba and Lincoln 1994: 107) by Heisenberg's 1927 'uncertainty principle', which states that the very act of observing itself has an effect on what can be measured (Heisenberg 1989: 32–3). Natural scientists might agree on the observability of some objects, like fossils in palaeontology, although they also agree that observations are never independent from the aims of the observer. But they also agree that large areas of empirical research, for example in physics, are based on unobservable entities that are also unpredictable.

We cannot observe particles and we cannot measure their properties simultaneously without interfering in the measurement with the very act of observation (Williams 2000: 42). Therefore, we cannot know the individual motion of a single particle (by identifying a deterministic causal mechanism of movement). But we can still describe it starting from the aggregate level of movement when we reason in terms of probability rather than mechanical determination: once we know the odds, we can mathematically model and simulate phenomena (Williams 2000: 43).

The uncertainty principle has obvious philosophical consequences, as it implies that different observers will produce different observations and measurement of the same phenomenon, thus diminishing the validity of the measurement and the reliability of the data. Reliability refers to the extent to which different measurements of the same phenomenon give similar results. This is only possible if we can assess the validity of the measurement, which indicates the assurance that we are measuring the concept we intend to measure (Kogovšek and Ferligoj 2005). The uncertainty principle diminishes the precision of the measurements, and the same limits apply to the observation of social phenomena. However, this does not exclude a priori the possibility of providing a scientific description of social reality. It only means that scientific descriptions and inferences, rather than mechanically deterministic, are more likely to be probabilistic. In the social sciences, we cannot deterministically predict the behaviour of each individual, just as natural scientists cannot predict the fall of a particular leaf from a tree (Scriven 1964: 171); but according to some statistics, we can give a probability estimate of aggregate behaviours.

The fallacy of Guba and Lincoln's argument rests on the fact that the two authors do not recognise the validity of probabilistic estimations. Although not completely unfounded, as we will see in the next chapter, Guba and Lincoln push the issue to the extreme position from which they challenge the possibility of generalisation altogether, by claiming the inapplicability of general data to individual cases. The example they use states that 'the fact, say, that 80 per cent of individuals presenting given symptoms have lung cancer is at best incomplete evidence that a particular patient presenting with such symptoms has lung cancer' (Guba and Lincoln 1994: 106).

By quoting this example, the authors actually move the debate to the discussion around inferential principles, and to their second fallacy. In the case of lung cancer, what the authors are stating is that the inference does not follow a deductive principle, which would be formulated as follows: 'all individuals with given symptoms have lung cancer'; 'this individual has these symptoms'; hence, 'this individual has lung cancer'. The statement instead is expressed in probabilistic terms: by following an inductive logic, we shall assume that although having symptoms, the individual might be part of the 20 per cent who do not have lung cancer: whilst deductive logic implies mechanical causation, in inductive logic it is not necessarily the case that if the premises are true, then so is the conclusion.

The assumption that science (and consequently social sciences) can only be achieved via deductive logic, mentioned by Guba and Lincoln as the problem of the indetermination of theory (1994: 107), is not a characteristic either of the positivist paradigm or of natural sciences, but instead of the tradition of Cartesianism and rationalism. Deductivism has been subsequently generally adopted by microeconomists, especially econometrics, where the tradition of enquiry is dominated by theoretically formulated hypothesis that are tested against empirical data. Although post-Keynesian macro-economy has reacted to the reductionist principles of deductive logic (Hodgson 2000), parts of economics are still deeply embedded within neoclassic approaches, which have also trickled down into some areas of sociology like rational choice theory. Conversely, positivism, even in its stricter formulation of logical positivism, has always advocated inductionism over deductionism. The principle of verification, as a logical tool to identify statements that are true because they accurately correspond to a state of affairs in the real world, was deeply rooted in inductive logic.

The same inductive logic was proven fallacious by Popper's falsification principle, which also claimed the lack of independence between theory and empirical observation. Popper demonstrated that a theory can never be verified through empirical evidence, as there could always be a contradictory observation in the future that invalidates previous observations. He uses the example of the black swan, which falsifies the theoretical statement that all swans are white, constructed according to previous observations. The consequences for theory validity are that we can never prove a theory to be true, but we can only hold it valid until it is not falsified: therefore, subsequent empirical observations should be directed to see if we can find cases that refute a theory rather than prove it.

More important, the falsification principle also weakens the attempts to discover universal laws that hold true across time and space by simply using the principle of verification. In natural sciences (as well as in social sciences), this does not mean that universal laws do not exist but simply that we cannot prove them true; we can only affirm that we have not yet found any empirical evidence that proves them false. The consequences of the falsification principle, however, are not that we should abandon any search for regularities. Rather, even in natural sciences, most of these regularities will not be considered universally valid. In the best scenario, they can be described by simple statistical laws that only explain some parts of nature (Williams 2000: 32), and, indeed, they all do increasingly well in accounting for large parts of meteorology, genetics and cognitive science.

The arguments advanced by Guba and Lincoln against positivism not only were already fully developed in post-positivism, as they partially acknowledge, but were already at the core of social sciences. As Elias reminds us (1978 [1970]), the foundational work of Comte explicitly states that social sciences need to be equally inductive and deductive. The word 'positive' is used in the sense of the acquisition of knowledge via the interdependence (not the independence) of theory and empirical observations. Comte's stress of the equal importance of both elements arises from the rejection of a philosophical tradition that insisted on the precedence of one mental operation over the other. Comte rejected the traditional opposition between Cartesians and empiricists, in terms of speculative theories, which cannot be tested against observed facts, or of unstructured observations, without guiding principles that connect and make sense out of them (Comte 1907 [1830–42], vol. 1: 5, translated in Elias 1978). Guba and Lincoln's rejection of positivism and post-positivism on the basis of their adoption of pure deductive inferential principles is unfounded.

A further fallacy consists in the claim that positivism (and later post-positivism) appeals to the necessity of social sciences 'to emulate their older, "harder" cousins' (i.e. natural sciences), by referring to the naturalistic position of John Stuart Mill (Guba and Lincoln 1994: 106). Again, if we go back to the foundational work of Comte, another important contribution is his insistence on the independence of social sciences from natural ones, which does not mean that social science must reject scientific enquiry, but that it is not possible to explain social organisations by simply aggregating individual physical–chemical, biological or psychological characteristics. What differentiates social from natural sciences, in the view of the founder of sociology, is the rejection of the reductionist principle which claims that the whole (the social) can be inferred from the simple aggregation of the parts (the individuals). If Comte stated the problem, Elias developed it by claiming that 'we need to show how and why the interweaving of interdependent individuals forms a level of integration at which forms of organisation, structures and processes cannot be deduced from the biological and psychological characteristics of the constituent individuals' (Elias 1978: 47).

Social sciences cannot be reduced to natural sciences in terms of simple extensions of chemical, physical, biological and psychological characteristics. They also differ in the ontological categories, because while natural sciences normally deal only with physical properties, social sciences deal with elements related to 'physical characteristics (e.g., sex), social or individual interpretations of these characteristics, subjective or intersubjective mental or social properties' (Williams 2000: 64). Therefore, whilst in natural sciences only one level of theoretical construction occurs, social sciences must deal with two levels of social and theoretical construction, the first constructed by people in their everyday life and the second categorised by social scientists.

This idea that natural and social sciences differ in that the latter deal with pre-interpreted actions and events was already proposed by Weber (1978) and subsequently advanced by Schutz (1954, 1966). Schutz, starting from the work of Weber, specifically distinguishes natural sciences, whose objects do not interpret their word, from social sciences, whose actors attribute meanings to their word, and therefore social scientific method requires developing constructs from actors' constructs. More important, in Schutz's definition, social objects are abstracted in scientific theories via second-order constructs, and abstract theories are constructed intersubjectively (Schutz 1966).

Although the foundations of Schutz's and Weber's work have been appropriated by interpretative sociology—thereby becoming the theoretical roots for constructivism—neither author ever denied the importance of the adoption of formal logic and the abstraction of ideal types. Weber defined sociology as the 'science concerning itself with the interpretative understanding of social action and thereby with a causal explanation of its course and consequences' (Weber 1978: 4). Schutz defined the job of social scientists as characterised by the construction of internally coherent models (the Weberian ideal types), which are not only able to make reality intelligible but also to explain it. Both Schutz and Weber insist that it is useful to describe social reality in our everyday life. But when we move to the level of scientific knowledge, we must also be able to abstract the formal relations between its foundational elements in coherent theories that can explain social phenomena. These theories then need to be validated with empirical observations to produce scientific knowledge.

The problems of inferential statistics and some possible solutions

The acknowledgement of fallacies within the qualitative attack on quantitative methods is helpful for rejecting the thesis of incompatibility. However, it does not negate the historical significance of the qualitative reaction against a peculiar version of positivism that was adopted by sociological schools in America and dominated the discipline from the 1930s to at least the 1960s. It is this specific version that forced a reduction of the study of social sciences to the 'quantification tied to the formulation of sociological problems in terms of the hypothetic–deductive model [that] enabled causal explanations of empirical phenomena' (Fielding 2005).

This domination can be dated to William Ogburn's appointment in Chicago in 1927, where he was called to establish the scientific study of sociology based on statistics. Ogburn laid out the rules of what Bryant (1985: 137) defined as 'instrumental positivism', which is the version associated today with the term 'positivism tout court', and the one that attracts the strongest critics (Bernard 2000). During his presidential address to the American Sociological Society, Ogburn claimed that for sociology to be a science it needed to 'crush out the emotions ... and to taboo ethics and values [to eventually turn] all sociologists into statisticians' (Ogburn 1930: 6–10).

Since then, and especially in the 1950s, the discipline became progressively colonised by structural functionalism theory developed by Parsons at Harvard and then by Merton at Columbia. Wellman describes those days in the following terms: '[At Harvard], network thinking was flourishing there under Harrison White and Charles Tilly, and categorical thinking was ossifying into title boxes labelled A, G, I and L' (Wellman 1993: 425). Columbia was also where Lazarsfield did his work on quantitative methods, which caused what Berger calls the 'methodological fetishism' of the dominance of quantitative methods over content (Berger 2002). This also implied the progressive marginalisation of the tradition of qualitative inquiry, a major focus of the Chicago department of sociology in the 1920s, better known as the Chicago School (Bernard 1930). Ogburn took Chicago in a different direction, far from the tradition for which it is famed today (Plummer 1997).

Again, the problem embedded in using a broad term like 'quantitative methods' needs to be untangled. The dominant strategy of enquiry and analysis of social phenomena that dominated American social sciences from Osburn's appointment to the affirmation of structural functionalism was tailored around a specific methodological approach, based on inferential statistics. Inferential statistics differs from descriptive statistics, as the latter simply describes features of the data, whereas the former is used to make inferences from data to more general conditions. It is against this specific historical dominance that we have to read the reaction of qualitative approaches, but it was only by shifting the discussion from specific methodological approaches to the rhetorical construction of underlying philosophical oppositions that qualitative researchers were able to undermine the dominance of quantitative methods (Morgan 2007).

Ultimately, as Rossi illustrates (1994), the battle between the two fields can be better understood as a battle for powerful positions on boards that access grants and publications. But the radicalisation of the debate that constructivists built around the incompatibilities of ontological and epistemological foundations had serious consequences for the methodology of social research, generalising the limits of inferential statistics to the whole approach of mathematical formalisation. Several streams of research now acknowledge those limits and are working on overcoming them, and network science is at the forefront of them, as we will see in the next chapter.

One of the main limits of inferential statistics, which is responsible for attracting most of the critics, is the orthodox view of causal inference (i.e., discovering a causal explanation) [that] depends upon the location of a generalization, which will characteristically take a probabilistic form whereby, given a set of constraints or initial conditions, the probability of C (cause) increases the probability of E (event).

(Abell 2008: 562)

The strength of scientific theories, as we have seen in the previous section, is normally measured according to the capacity of formulating falsifiable predictions around the explanation of certain phenomena. If no evidence is found against the theory through independent tests of its falsifiability, then the theory gains strength, assuming that it is not in contrast with pre-existing theories and that the theory itself can adapt to further evidence and experimental results. A valuable way to accept a theory, for example, is to test it independently with different methods and use it to predict different but related phenomena. If results of a theory can explain and predict not only the phenomena it tries to describe but also related phenomena, and if a theory is not falsified by results of methodologically different tests, then the theory gains credibility, although it never reaches the status of truth, as 'scientific probability statements are only provisionally, but never definitively, refutable by the set of observations which test them' (Braithwaite 1968: x).

The problem is that in social science precise measurements, generalisations and predictability are extremely difficult to achieve. As Abell shows (2008), inferential statistics have not performed particularly well in explaining social phenomena: the percentage of variance explained in social phenomena did not increase from 1960 to 2007 in articles published in the *American Journal of Sociology* and the *American Sociological Review*. Such percentage rarely surpassed 60 per cent, and more frequently settled between 30 per cent and 50 per cent (Abell 2008: 563). Champions of inferential statistics may justify the lack of accumulated evidence by imputing it to the stochastic (unpredictable) nature of social phenomena, which can be confined to measurable errors, or to the role of hidden variables (Abell 2008: 563–4), but this does not diminish the limits of their analysis.

Critical realists, as we shall see, criticise inferential statistics by claiming that inference based on 'numerically measurable probability distributions' (Downward *et al.* 2010: 19) is only possible in closed systems, whilst the social system is an open one and therefore lacks the specific characteristics that are the precondition of inference in closed systems (Dow 2010). Another reason is that objects in social sciences need complex measurements because they cannot be reduced to a simple aggregation of physiological and psychological characteristics but imply the account of the interwoven nature of social interaction. This interwoven nature violates the main assumption of inferential statistics, which requires the independence of observations in terms of measurement, resulting in the non-correlation of standard errors. This specific problem has not been raised within the tradition of qualitative analysis and its critics of the dominance by quantitative social science, but has emerged specifically in social network studies.

I will take this up in the next chapter, but first I want to review some of the attempts to bridge the perceived differences between the claimed foundations of quantitative and qualitative paradigms. I limit the discussion to two philosophical perspectives: pragmatism and critical realism, whose positions have produced specific methodological strategies for social enquiries.

Pragmatism

According to the *Stanford Encyclopedia of Philosophy* (2010), pragmatism is an American empiricist philosophy that reacts to Cartesianism and rationalism. In doing so, it shares many features with the original scientific project of sociology as a discipline (Comte 1907 [1830–42]). Its most important contributors in terms of the social science debate (Charles Sanders Peirce, William James, John Dewey and George Herbert Mead) share the idea that reality has an ontological dimension outside the human mind, but we cannot have true knowledge of what is real in objective terms (the truth) as our perceptions of reality are always mediated by sensations. Sensations are the interface between reality outside our perceptions and our thoughts, which are ultimately the only objects immediately present to us. Against Descartes, they claim that certainty cannot lie in individual consciousness but rests on our embodied activities. We engage with social reality through our activities, and these mediate our perceptions. Thus, theoretical concepts do not possess any a priori ontological consistency, but are fallibilistic artefacts that should be judged only by how well they achieve their purposes in measuring and formalising the empirical realm. None of them can be an absolute transcript of reality: a scientific theory is simply an instrument designed to facilitate action or increase understanding (James 1907: 33).

With one focus on the external nature of reality and the possibility of reaching an agreement in its description and another on the possibility of perceiving reality only through experiential sensations that inform thoughts and are directed by falsifiable theories, pragmatism is a valid attempt to make a bridge between positivism (and post-positivism) and constructivism. Furthermore, pragmatism advances the importance of adopting the inferential practice of abduction (Peirce 1931–58, vol. 5), also known as the inference to the best explanation. Abduction is a logical principle opposite from deduction and therefore similar to induction, but it differs from the latter in that it implies implicit or explicit explanatory considerations. To go back to the lung cancer example, by saying that 80 per cent of people with symptoms have lung cancer and that an individual presents these symptoms, we can abductively infer that it is likely that the individual has lung cancer. We are not declaring this is the truth but we are proposing an explanatory inference for the available data, which is the characteristic that, as we have previously seen in the work of Weber and Schutz, distinguishes the simple understanding of everyday life from the scientific knowledge of its mechanism.

Critical realism

A second interesting proposal for the resolution of the paradigm war can be traced to the epistemological position of critical realism, which again revolves around the differences between description, explanation and prediction, and the logical inference used to reach explanatory mechanisms. Critical realism, a British philosophical stream of thought that emerged in the 1970s, is another attempt to reconcile the naturalistic perspective with the constructivist acknowledgement that knowledge is a social construct. Its main principles are laid out in the two foundational works of Bhaskar: *A Realist Theory of Science*, first published in 1975 (Bhaskar 1978), on the realist scientific approach in general, and *The Possibility of Naturalism*, first published in 1979 (Bhaskar 1998), on the nature of social sciences.

According to Bhaskar (1978), reality is stratified into three domains: the actual domain refers to events and patterns that link them; the empirical domain refers to people's perceptions and observations of events; and the real domain is structured by underlying mechanisms that generate events. These mechanisms are intransitive objects in the sense that they exist independently from people's knowledge of them (Lawson 1997) and are not immediately observable, but they can be observed via transitive objects as tools available to researchers in terms of antecedent theories and methods. Knowledge of intransitive objects can be achieved via the logical inference of retroduction, by which researchers account for new phenomena through analogies with phenomena with which they are already familiar (Baert 2005; Lawson 1997).

As an example, we can consider the case of a glass that breaks if hit by a rock: we can repetitively observe the phenomenon (the actual domain) and we can describe it as the rock causing the break (the empirical domain). However, the causal explanation relies on the underlying mechanism that is related to the molecular structure of the glass, which is modified when hit by a hard object. We cannot observe the molecular structure of the glass directly, but we can infer the intransitive causal mechanism by which its modification causes the break by comparing other situations in which the glass breaks, for example when a liquid contained in the glass is subjected to hot or cold temperature. In these cases, the glass is not actually hit by anything, but it is the modification of the volume of air inside the liquid that puts a pressure (comparable to the pressure of a rock) on the molecular structure of the glass and causes it to break. The shift of attention from events (the claimed object of research of so-called positivism) and from people's perceptions and observations (the claimed object of research of constructivism) to intransitive mechanisms thus implies a modification of the definition of causality.

The traditional and common-sense idea of causality attributed to the so-called positivist and post-positivist paradigms implies that whenever event x occurs, event y occurs or is likely to occur (Baert 2005: 92), and that once a regularity is observed it can be generalised to similar events. Instead, a causal explanation for critical realism does not imply the ability to predict an outcome but only to propose an account for how the observed regularities were produced (Baert 2005: 92).

More important, critical realists point out that perfect regularities are rare, both in natural and in social systems (Kemp and Holmwood 2010), mainly because they can only happen in closed systems, whereas natural and social systems are commonly open. Closed systems are situations in which all the intervening mechanisms are known, isolated and kept under control in their effects over outcomes. This is the case, for example, of scientific experiments where regularities are not observed as in spontaneously produced situations, but are artificially reproduced and therefore can be isolated from the noise produced by other intervening mechanisms (Ron 2010).

In open systems, various generative mechanisms interfere with each other (Bhaskar 1978: 118–26), causing asynchronies between the different domains, as, for example, when people's perceptions do not fully match events (because they are influenced by competing mechanisms), or events do not match the expected outcomes of mechanisms (again because of the intervention of other underlying mechanisms). These asynchronies are one reason we have to reject the symmetry between explanation and prediction (Baert 2005: 94): even when we can explain the underlying process of a mechanism we will still not be able to predict the outcomes because of the interactive effects of intervening mechanisms that cannot be kept fully under control (Bhaskar 1978: 125–6, 136–7).

The consequences of critical realism are in the first instance the acceptance that neither social nor natural sciences actually work under the aim of discovering universal laws (a property that was advanced in Popper's falsification principle). However, agents in social reality deal with indeterminacy by developing institutions, which 'evolve and develop along with agents' own mental models to produce states of closure [...] This can be termed "quasi closure" and provides and reflects stable conditions upon which agents base their behaviours' (Downward *et al.* 2010: 17). In quasi-closure systems, event regularities can be observed as 'demi-regularities' (Downward *et al.* 2010: 18; Lawson 1997), partial and spontaneous patterns that are 'typical of open systems' (Baert 2005: 96). This implies that the relationship between mechanisms and effects is not universal but only temporary and contingent: it 'indicates the occasional, but less than universal, actualization of a mechanism or tendency, over a definite region of time-space' (Lawson 1997: 204).

Pawson (2006: 22) has thus proposed a systematisation of the basic components of realist causal explanations. He states that mechanisms ($M_{1...n}$) produce an outcome (O) within a specific context (C), where the context consists of a particular combination of mechanisms contingent on time and space. Such contextual combination of mechanisms may vary in a different context. As Ragin explains, social changes are normally caused by the intersection of concurrent pre-conditions, where 'in the absence of any of the essential ingredients, the phenomenon—or the change—does not emerge' (Ragin 1987: 25).

In the example Ragin gives, the formation of ethnic parties (O) may be caused by the concurrencies of several conditions, like ethnic inequalities, government centralisation, and domination of regional economies by multinational firms. But the concurrency of factors like ethnic equalities, decentralised governments, and increased migrations could cause the same outcome (interpreted as different contextual intersections of factors). Therefore, we can infer two opposite underlying and intransitive mechanisms, the lure of separatism (M_1) and the infringement of ethnic turf (M_2), which explains the same output in social change (Ragin 1987: 25) and can only be observed through the specific combination of contextual elements.

Methodological implications of pragmatism and critical realism

The two philosophical perspectives presented here have both had noticeable influences over the adoption of a pluralist methodology. Pragmatism has been elected as the epistemological foundation of mixed methods, whereas critical realism has not only led to a broad debate on methodological pluralism (Olsen 2010, vol. 2), but has also produced important advances in systematic qualitative analysis. Although both are extremely important in social science, particularly for the debate around mixing social network analysis with qualitative methods, the two perspectives are profoundly different from each other, both in their approach to ontological and epistemological matters and in their methodological consequences.

The mixed method literature has often claimed pragmatism to be its paradigmatic foundation. However, reviewing mixed method studies makes it clear that the embrace of pragmatism has not been intended as a deep engagement with the theoretical assumption of pragmatic philosophy. Instead, it was meant to be a progressive marginalisation of ontological and epistemological issues that would favour a practical approach to empirical enquiry. This is possibly the main reason why, in investigating the state of the art of mixed methods research, Bryman (2006, 2007, 2008) found that a true integration is only rarely achieved. In particular, the author found that the declared rationale in mixed methods studies is normally mismatched from the practice (Bryman 2008) and that researchers have to face several barriers in the use of multiple methods, especially in the analysis and interpretation of results (Bryman 2007). Bryman also noticed a general lack of agreement on the criteria that should be used to evaluate the quality of qualitative, quantitative and mixed method studies (Bryman 2006; Bryman *et al.* 2008).

The confusion and disagreement about how to conduct mixed methods research has generated, on the one hand, manifold perspectives by researchers across philosophical, methodological and practical issues (Creswell and Tashakkori 2007). On the other hand, it has reduced the mixed method approach to a set of sometimes sophisticated technicalities (Cordaz 2011), with a lack of engagement about underlying philosophical issues (by confounding pragmatism with practical convenience) and a consequent loss of paradigmatic stance. Mixed methods originally emerged from the practice of triangulation and the use of convergence of results from different methods to increase the validity of interpretations (Campbell and Fiske 1959). Since its first formulation, triangulation has been conceptually refined by extending it to the combination of different data sources, different investigators, different theories, and different intra-methodological tools, like multiple qualitative or quantitative methods (Denzin 1978).

Research designs can be sequential or parallel, can have one component (qualitative or quantitative) dominating the other, or, in the case of mixed models, can introduce different methods at each stage of the enquiry (Tashakkori and Teddlie

1998). The combination of these possibilities has monopolised the debate about mixed methods, where discussion is often reduced to endless lists of technicalities and criteria for data collection, analysis, validation and justifications (Dellinger and Leech 2007; Johnson *et al.* 2007; Onwuegbuzie and Leech 2007), whereas the concepts that guide research are not ontological definitions of reality but simply workable lines of actions (Morgan 2007).

Conversely, critical realism has deeply engaged with ontological and epistemological matters, taking into account coherent methodological implications that are not reduced to simple technicalities. The focus on the importance of discovering contingent conditions under which underlying mechanisms are activated implies the acceptance of both extensive and intensive enquiries. Qualitative methods and their attention to contextual and intersubjective perceptions of mechanism scripts is the necessary counterpart of extensive analysis of social regularities, which are considered as empirical traces of intransitive mechanisms.

As we have seen, for critical realists demi-regularities can be produced by different and contingent combinations of intervening mechanisms. Although mechanisms are intransitive, as they cannot be directly observed, qualitative approaches are useful to explore the traces they leave in the scripts that people use to describe actual events. Narrative accounts are claimed to provide an understanding of the subjective perceptions of causal mechanisms, directing the process of research toward plausible explanations: because social reality is pre-interpreted by social actors, theories of social phenomena are necessarily concept-dependent (Bhaskar 1998 [1979]).

Therefore, qualitative methods are advocated in the process of constructing and validating theories, where valid explanations of intransitive mechanisms are reached through conceptual abstraction of determinant elements and their actual combination (Sayer 1992, 2000). This does not mean, as in the interpretative paradigm, that social reality is constructed through subjective discourse and that there are as many realities as people experiencing situations. What it does mean is that actors can give accounts of the demi-regularities that characterise events, although they may not be fully aware of what is happening around them or may misinterpret situations, rendering irrelevant the distinction between correct (parts of) accounts and misguided ones (Kemp and Holmwood 2010).

Through observation of conjoined events, quantitative methods can thus help in the search for regularities that appear in spontaneously generated situations. It is worth repeating that these regularities are only temporally and spatially contingent and do not account for universal causal mechanisms. Also, there can be more than a single combination of events that can produce an output. This is a call for methodological triangulation: quantitative methods can reveal patterns of general sets of co-occurrences, whilst interpretative methods can be used to explore why those specific co-occurrences take place in a contingent moment (Downward and Mearman 2010; McEvoy and Richards 2010).

Although critical realism advocates the use of quantitative methods, it is still highly critical of the dominance of inferential statistics in social research. In particular, it rejects the adoption of regression analysis as a way to discover a contingent causal mechanism by inferring it from a sample to an entire population. Regression methods are welcomed as powerful tools in the search for underlying mechanisms, provided that the analysis of independent variables is not completely determined by theoretical deductions but rather is justified as a way to 'play' with data and uncover underlying patterns.

Ron (2010) confutes the core assumption of regression models by observing that, in line with a critical realism epistemological stance, it is not possible to fit a single explanatory and predictive model for a given dependent variable that can be generalised to the corresponding class of phenomena to which this variable belongs. This is because, as we have seen, an outcome can be produced by several combinations of generative mechanisms, therefore multiple models may be able to describe the dependent outcome: the only way to corroborate and falsify competing models is to collect more empirical observations.

Along this line, critical realists have thus suggested that case studies, more than statistically representative samples, may be more apt for testing theories, which have been often falsified by a single 'black swan' observation (Flyvbjerg 2010). An empirical case in which a proposed theory does not apply calls for reconsideration of the theory itself, and comparison of several case studies can produce reliable results in terms of the possible combinations of intervening mechanisms.

Overcoming the limits of categorical analysis

The philosophical speculations of critical realism have produced some convincing methodological advances that overcome the sterile polarisation of quantitative and qualitative tools. The attention to the conceptual work of abstraction has provoked some critics to question the effectiveness of critical realism for conducting empirical research because 'critical realism develops a huge superstructure of ontological and epistemological insights' (Wad 2001: 12) but fails in elaborating methodological innovations that overcome the traditional distinction between quantitative and qualitative methods. Ron responds by pointing out that critical realism is a 'philosophical framework for understanding social science as practiced by social scientists. ... the power of critical realism is not in inventing new methods for social science but in making sense of the existing methods' (Ron 2010: 284).

Even if it didn't produce any new method, critical realism has stimulated the birth of a set of interesting combinations of already existing qualitative and quantitative methods known as configurational comparative methods (CCM). These methods share many commonalities with social network analysis: both oppose the tradition of categorical analysis in social science; both reject inferential statistics as the dominant way to gain knowledge of social reality; and both avoid the reduction of properties of complex systems to their constitutive micro elements (Hodgson 2000). However, comparative methods are still embedded in a traditional conceptualisation and operationalisation of the fundamental units of analysis. As we will see in the next chapter, social network analysis steps aside from the previous traditions of social science studies, reformulating the constituent elements of theoretical speculation and empirical analysis in relational terms.

Against variable analysis

Because of the commonalities, the approaches of CCM and social network analysis have converged on several occasions, for example in the symposium organised by Charles Ragin and Howard Becker in 1989 at Northwestern University, where a selected group of scholars discussed the nature of the fundamental units of analysis in social sciences. The symposium, which resulted in a collective publication (Ragin and Becker 1992), tackled the problem of competing methods by shifting the attention to the epistemological question of what the object of social science studies is. According to Ragin (1992: 3), it is precisely the different conceptions of the term 'case' in social sciences that are at the centre of the enduring battle between qualitative and quantitative analysis; more specifically, it is the distorted and corrupted operationalisation of a case as a methodological construct. Cases versus units of analysis has become the core dichotomy between qualitative (case studies) and quantitative (analysis of aggregate units) approaches, neglecting the fact that every social science study, no matter how large the sample and quantified the measurements, is a case study in itself.

What really distinguishes quantitative from qualitative approaches, in Ragin's view (1987, 1992) is that the first is variable oriented and the second is case oriented. This distinction brings us straight to the heart of the problem. Quantitative research examines many cases (the units of analysis), but does so by focusing attention on variables. Quantitative approaches normally define the relevant variables by matching them to theoretical concepts (Ragin 1992: 5, although Williams 2000: 61 highlights how a great deal of social research is not about theory testing, e.g. large-scale surveys or censuses) and proceed to collect and analyse data on these variables, leaving aside how these variables fit together in individual cases.

Qualitative research, instead, focuses on cases, defined in terms of spatial and temporal boundaries. But what it really does is compare those cases that are assumed to be 'similar enough and separate enough to permit treating them as comparable instances of the same general phenomenon' (Ragin 1992: 1). Importantly, Ragin reminds us (1987: 36) that the logic of case studies, intended in opposition to variables approaches, was first developed by John Stuart Mill in his formalisation of canons for inductive enquiry (Mill 1967 [1843]); this is the same Mill who was accused by Guba and Lincoln (1994: 106) of fostering the dominance of quantification in social sciences. This is another indication of the rhetorical construction of Guba and Lincoln's argument, which forces under the definition of quantitative studies some fundamental scientific approaches that cannot be equated to the dominance of inferential statistics.

In the collection of essays that follow Ragin's introduction to the book, it becomes clear that both variable- and case-oriented research have serious limitations for the study of social phenomena. The first loses the detailed description of intransitive mechanisms and scripts adopted by individuals and transfers causal inference to the relationship between variables; the second often misses the possibility of generalisation by lacking a clear explanation of what needs to be generalised (Abbott 1992).

In a lucid analysis of some quantitative studies (Bridges and Nelson 1989; Halaby and Weakliem 1989; Pavalko 1989), Abbott (1992), by describing social processes in terms of correlations among variables, shows that the rhetorical style of the arguments of these studies excludes references to individual agency. However, when data do not match theoretical explanations, the focus goes back to hypothetical individual causal scripts, bringing back the role of agency in the complex architecture of variables' links. Abbott explains this phenomena by referring to the fallacy of statistical analysis pointed out by Blau and Duncan (1967: 167), where they admit that regression coefficients that supposedly measure the effects of causes have to assume that the causal model underlying these effects must be the same for each case (individual unit) of analysis.

When data mismatch, authors must go back to the individual case to try to infer the pattern of causality that does not align with the prescribed narrative. Abbot, in line with critical realism, advances the position that quantitative methods (based on statistical inference) are limited in that they must adopt a single causal narrative to be tested against the data, whilst social phenomena always entail multiple narratives. This does not drive the author to reject quantitative analysis *tout court*, and even less to reject any possible causal explanation. On the contrary, Abbot advances possibilities for generalising narratives across multiple cases: what the social sciences should do is create common terminologies for micro and macro phenomena, not by reducing the richness of (micro) qualitative studies to a set of (macro) variables, but by

> encoding their conclusions as predicting certain kind of plots for stylistic or scientific changes across cases ... a very valuable set of concepts for generic links would deal with issues of micro/macro relations *tout court*. I shall call these entity processes.
>
> (Abbott 1992: 77)

Abbot considers this central issue as one of the main problems that needs to be addressed by the social sciences in order to overcome sterile debates about methods and ground itself on solid scientific bases. But Abbot is also aware of other simplifying assumptions embedded in statistical inference, namely the reduction of variability of significance to unique and distinguishable meanings (without considering complexities and nuances that require hermeneutic approaches) and the assumption that cases (as in observations) must be independent from each other. As Abbot points out, the latter is addressed by network theory (Abbot 1992: 73). I would add that the former is not only dealt with in qualitative networks, but is similarly addressed by CCM, an umbrella that subsumes a set of techniques specifically designed to 'allow systematic cross-case comparison, whilst at the same time giving justice to within case complexity' (Rihoux and Ragin 2009: xviii).

Configurational comparative methods

Configurational comparative methods (CCM) aim at the comparative analysis of a series of cases described in terms of the substantive elements that shape them; it is configurational because in order to allow this comparison, it transforms cases into configurations, 'a combination of factors that produces a given outcome of interest' (Rihoux and Ragin 2009: xix). The methods were first proposed by Ragin (1987) to address the problem of detecting causal mechanisms in a set of cases without assuming these mechanisms to be identical across different cases. The approach relies on thick qualitative descriptions and systematic comparison by formalising the combinations of elements that characterise each specific configuration. The methods are laid out in a series of publications (Ragin 1987, 1994, 2008; Rihoux and Ragin 2009) and have been applied successfully in dozens of studies (see www.compasss.org for bibliography, working papers and guides to software). Three elements of the CCM approach stand out.

1. The term CCM refers mainly to qualitative comparative analysis (QCA), a set of techniques that include crispy sets, multi values, fuzzy sets, and the procedure that compares similar or different outcomes together with the similarity or differences of the variables concurring to produce these outputs (MSDO/MDSO; see Berg-Schlosser and De Meur, 2009: 23). QCA is a purely mixed method approach, as it allows hermeneutic analysis of qualitative data; categorisation of the data into crispy (0/1), multiple (0; 1; 2; 3 ...) or fuzzy (ordered or continuous) sets; aggregation of cases into subgroups following Boolean combinations;[2] and the making of general statements about necessary or sufficient conditions (combinations of elements) to infer cause in observed outcomes. In doing so, it aims to discover the underlying mechanisms that are able to explain these configurations: it does so not by relying on variables covariance, but by maintaining the centrality of individual cases and the peculiar combinations that characterise each of them.

    Because of its rejection of variable analysis and its attention to underlying multiple mechanisms that might produce several (not unique) observable outcomes, QCA can be considered as the most suitable technique to conduct studies under the perspective of critical realism, as has been acknowledged in several places (Olsen 2010; Saleh 2009). With critical realism, it also shares the logical practice of retroduction: the patterns of contextualised mechanisms are not deduced from abstract theories and formalised hypotheses, nor are they identified by the inductive logic of the methods of agreement and differences (Mill 1967 [1843]). The possibility of multiple causations renders these sets of methods purely retroductive, as they aim to answer questions related to the reasons why a specific pattern of configuration is observed by comparing it to all the other possible combinations of patterns.

2. Because of its application of formal methods to categorise narratives, QCA is well suited for analysis in middle-range studies, which can be based on a continuum between a small number and a large number of cases (small *n*

and large *N*). As Berg-Schlosser and colleagues pointed out (Berg-Schlosser *et al.* 2009), QCA was first developed to confront the problems of comparative analysis, the main one being that research at a macro level (e.g. national comparison) very often has to deal with a limited number of cases (e.g. 27 EU countries) but a large number of variables. Such a situation violates a major assumption of inferential statistics, where ordinary least squares need five cases per independent variable in the analysis, and maximum likelihood needs at least ten cases per independent variable.

For its combination of in-depth analysis of cases, and systematic comparison of configurations, QCA is best applicable to those studies with an intermediate number of cases (Berg-Schlosser *et al.* 2009: 4) that lies in between the very small (one or two cases studies) and the very large (more than 100 cases). These are also less covered in social sciences: as Ragin points out (2006), if we plot the average number of cases in social sciences studies, the result is a U-shaped curve, with many small-*n* studies and many large-*N* studies, but few in the intermediate range. With its combination of systematic comparison and thick descriptions, QCA offers the possibility of covering this gap.

3. Finally, QCA addresses another major and common problem in statistical analysis, namely the treatment of outliers. When statistical analysis fits a model that explains (or even simply describes) data, it does so by looking at the best fit, represented by the line that best summarises the variance of cases, by minimising the deviations of standard errors. Although powerful at one level, this method only allows finding a single line representing that unique narrative criticised by Abbott (1992). More importantly, it often results in the dropping of outliers, which are individual cases so distant, in terms of standard error, from the fitted line, that they impact what would otherwise be a simple best fit. The problem is that outliers can be truly interesting in terms of causal mechanisms (if their peculiarity is not imputable to some errors in data collection or codification) because they often exemplify different configurations and can indicate the presence of further causal mechanisms.

Conclusions

With its systematic approach to data analysis, QCA is a promising method for conducting qualitative studies. It also presents interesting similarities with social network analysis in its commitment to the systematic observation of empirical phenomena (Freeman 2004) and rejection of categorical and variable analysis. In particular, social network analysis makes explicit the critique not so much of statistical analysis per se but of the historical schools that have monopolised sociological analysis with survey data and opinion pools.

From an epistemological point of view, QCA and social network analysis both take seriously the problem of definition of cases of analysis, although they solve it in different ways. They also both refer to the logic of retroduction in their attempt to generalise not so much contextualised results of single research projects but the underlying configurations and mechanisms that can be translated from one context to the other. Methodologically speaking, they propose different alternatives to variable-centred analysis, which also implies different use of mixed methods. Finally, they both dedicate specific attention to the problem of temporal, spatial and relational dependencies of cases, offering viable solutions (especially from social network analysis) to some of the limits of inferential statistics.

Although QCA challenges the statistical concept of unit of analysis as a carrier of information about variables, it still focuses on independent cases, failing to address the most problematic assumption of variable analysis. To be able to use statistical inferential methods, we have to assume that the cases (or units of analysis) we observe are independent. What we fail to acknowledge, however, is that cases are never independent, because no matter who the agents are we are looking at, they are constantly embedded in interactions. It is exactly this interwoven nature of social phenomena that denies the possibility of reducing sociological analysis to the simple aggregation of individual parts, whether psychological, biological, chemical or physical. And it is this interwoven nature, acknowledged since the formulation of sociology as a discipline, which denies to a certain extent the possibility of adopting inferential statistics. By observing individuals (or any kind of unit of analysis) independently from each other we deprive ourselves of the possibility of accounting for such interdependency. But if we move the focus from agents to relationships, then the dependency becomes observable and knowable: this is exactly one of the advantages offered by a social network approach, extensively discussed in the next chapter.

Notes

1 In the first edition of the book, Kuhn actually used the term in 22 different ways, as noted by Masterman (1970). Kuhn himself replied in a postscript to the second edition of the book (1970) by listing three exceptions: paradigms as epistemological stances, as shared beliefs among members of a speciality areas, and as model examples of research.

2 Boolean combinations are a set of algebraic operations that can be performed on binary variables, the most common being 'conjunction' (and) 'disjunction' (or) or 'negation' (not).

3 The constitutive bricks of qualitative networks

Actors, relations, networks

In the previous chapter, I introduced the longstanding debate about the qualitative and quantitative traditions of enquiry in social science and the fallacy of considering the two approaches as ontologically and epistemologically incompatible. I illustrated the emerging traditions of mixed methods and configurational comparative methods (CCM), grounded, respectively, in pragmatism and critical realism. In this chapter, I compare the definition of intransitive mechanisms, as proposed by critical realism, to two other theoretical frameworks, namely analytical and relational sociology, that likewise propose their own versions of explanatory mechanisms, specifically operationalised in both cases in relational and network terms.

Despite the various traditions of scholars who have adopted the network approach, network scientists share several common ontological, epistemological and methodological assumptions (Borgatti *et al.* 2009; Brandes *et al.* 2013; Kadushin 2012). In some cases, these assumptions are open to debate, but overall they distinguish network science, and its methodological tool of social network analysis, from other theoretical and methodological approaches. After laying this out, I will critically discuss the sociological frameworks of analytical sociology and relational sociology, comparing their definition of the elements that constitute the units of analysis in network sciences, in particular their conceptualisations of mechanisms that regulate social processes. The goal is not to eliminate one or the other in favour of a better approach but to highlight the theoretical elements that are complementary and that can be merged in a coherent framework.

I will use this framework to justify the adoption of mixed method strategies in the study of social networks: by reformulating the foundational elements of sociological enquiry, it will become clear why a mixed approach to the study of social reality can be extremely useful in the various phases of the research process. Instead of discounting analytical tools for their supposed ontological and epistemological incompatibility, the strengths of social network analysis and qualitative methods are discussed and fruitfully combined, and some examples from the now long and established tradition of qualitative network analysis will be offered as illustration. In subsequent chapters, this mixed method research design will inform the presentation and analysis of the empirical examples on how to mix social network analysis with various forms of qualitative data, including interviews, ethnographic observations and qualitative archival data.

Some assessments of the foundational elements of network science

Social network analysis has always been highly interdisciplinary—adopted and developed in various fields. Historical accounts trace the origins of network ideas back to the work of foundational scholars like Comte, Simmel and Durkheim (Borgatti *et al.* 2009; Crossley 2011; Freeman 2004). But references to the role of interconnections as irreducible elements of social life can be found in the work of a vast range of thinkers like Marx, Tönnies, Spencer and Weber (Freeman 2004). Traces of relational ideas are so largely disseminated in social sciences that more or less all classical and contemporary sociologists, even if not adopting a social network approach, have been shifting back and forth between a relational point of view and other approaches (Emirbayer 1997).

However, the development of social network analysis as a distinctive empirical framework can be traced to the development of sociometry in psychology (with the work of Jacob Moreno), the study of social networks in natural settings (developed primarily by scholars trained at the Manchester School of Social Anthropology), and the combination of empirical results with mathematical modelling and graph theory that was the central effort of sociology at Harvard (for a recent review of the historical developments of the discipline, see Prell 2011). In particular, the role of mathematics and especially of graph theory has always been fundamental for social network concepts and measures, both in terms of advancement in mathematical formalisation and in the development of algorithms for the analysis of network data.

The lack of a linear and neat development of the field has produced various attempts to locate streams and schools of social network thinkers. Knox *et al.* (2006), for example, identify three distinct generations of scholars: the first challenging the methodological individualism of rational choice theory by focusing on actors' local embeddedness in egonetworks (e.g. Granovetter, 1973); the second developing a fully structural account of social order, based on relations between positions rather than actors (e.g. Lorrain and White 1971; White 2008 [1992]; White *et al.* 1976); and the third reintroducing the importance of cultural and discursive foundations of social network analysis (emerging from social movement scholars like Ansell 1997; Bearman 1995; Gould 1995; Mische 2003).

Although these attempts to organise the developments of social network analysis are inevitably partial, they offer some systematisation of the eclectic approaches that have emerged in the field. The observation of local structures from focal actors—better known as the egonetwork approach—and the fully structural approach that abstracts and formalises concrete relationships in blocks of equivalent positions (Lorrain and White 1971; White *et al.* 1976) is useful for indicating some parallel developments of the discipline, which can count on long and robust traditions of both egonetwork and whole network studies.

I do not fully agree with the identification of a recent emergence of a cultural approach to social networks, which calls for a wider use of qualitative methods. In my view, shared by Kirke (2010), qualitative methods have always been used in network research, although with various roles and functions. As briefly discussed in the introduction, the adoption of qualitative methods has somehow been hidden by the focus on substantive themes, especially in articles that belong to disciplines different from sociology, where there is less emphasis on highlighting the use of qualitative methods (see, for example, Bodin and Tengö 2012; Lazega *et al.* 2008; Zachary 1977).

Along with the efforts to classify schools and streams of social network analysis, there have been some recent influential attempts to define the theoretical, epistemological and methodological foundations of the field that identify some key elements of network research commonly shared by its practitioners. The first of these attempts is the article by Borgatti and colleagues (2009) in *Science*. After reviewing the historical developments of the discipline, the authors claim that social network theory is based on a systematic conceptualisation of ties: they distinguish between social relations, continuous processes of iterative interactions that stabilise in durable and recognisable relationships (like kinship, friendship, working colleagues and the like) and interactions, discrete events that can be counted over a period of time. In their view, actors' attributes (categorical classifications like sex, age, spatial location and social affiliations) are conditions or states that increase the probability of forming other kinds of ties (Borgatti *et al.* 2009).

Tangible and intangible things flow across ties, and it is by looking at the structural features of the patterns of flows that social network analysis searches for explanations of network mechanisms. These mechanisms include things like homophily, which explains the higher probability of interaction between similar people, or influence, which explains individuals' adaptations to the choices and opinions of others. Such mechanisms are considered responsible for both tie formation and networks' outcomes.

In the first issue of *Network Sciences*, the journal's editors define network science as 'the study of the collection, management, analysis, interpretation and presentation of relational data' (Brandes *et al.* 2013: 2), which can represent any system that exhibits some form of interdependency. Network science is the study of network models, which consist of the network representation of phenomena. In turn, this representation consists of abstracting an empirical phenomenon into a network concept. To do this, a phenomenon needs first to be conceptualised into its constitutive elements: representation is obtained by mapping the structure of relation between these elements via an isomorphism (Brandes *et al.* 2013: 4), whilst interpretation reverses the process and links the abstraction back to the empirical phenomenon.

Network models, as abstract representations of empirical phenomena, are specified by network theories that explicate how to abstract phenomena into networks: for example, what constitutes an individual entity or a relationship, or how to conceptualise the strength of a tie. Because of their definition of constitutive elements of network models, network theories are epistemological theories in the sense that they indicate how to acquire knowledge of network structures. But network models are also specified by network theories that observe structural mechanisms and features, as in properties of network structures. This is why Brandes and colleagues claim that 'there are theories about network representations and network theories about phenomena' (Brandes *et al.* 2013: 5).

This definition of models and mechanisms closely resembles the one proposed by critical realism and discussed in the previous chapter. Models' isomorphism can be (isomorphically) equated to the concept of analogy that is at the core of the logic of retroduction. Both aim to observe structural features in different contexts, to understand the commonalities that can be transferred, and in some cases generalised, across empirical domains. The possibilities of transfers and generalisations are specified by looking at the contingent characteristics of contexts that delimit a complete transposition of mechanisms. Models thus are isomorphic of empirical phenomena and can be analogically extended across cases and contexts.

Brandes and colleagues' work (2013) is essential reading about the bedrock principles of network science, not just for the toolbox of methods but for the ontological substance of network theory. The first ontological element of any social structure is individuals, intended as units of analysis that exhibit some peculiar characteristics, where such characteristics may be represented as classic variables (age, sex, ethnicity). Whilst in statistical analysis variables are assumed to be independent, in network science the structure of these individual dependencies is visible and of central interest: they are the conditions that increase the likelihood of interactions that Borgatti and colleagues refer to (2009).

The second ontological substance of any social structure is the intermediary level of dyads, which represent the individuals connected with each other. Attributes of dyads cannot be reduced to the ones of individuals: wives are only wives when matched with husbands, and there can only be slaves with masters, teachers with pupils, buyers with sellers. More important, features of the dyads emerge out of individuals' interactions, and, conversely, shape the characteristics of the agents involved. Finally, dyads cannot be considered as independent entities because they overlap, creating macro patterning of network structure. The simplest such structure is the triad, 'the beginning of a society that is independent of the ties between a dyad' (Kadushin 2012: 22), where a third actor is added to a pair and increases dramatically the complexity of relationships, as extensively described by Simmel (1976b [1903]).

Dyads and triads combine in variously cohesive groups (cliques, cores, factions, etc.) of informal and formal nature (small and primary groups or organisations). Groups may overlap, and these partially overlapping and relatively loose networks are called social circles (Kadushin 1966, 1976, 2012; Simmel 1955 [1922]). Networks, then, are systems with ontological substance in themselves because inferences at the individual or dyadic level cannot be simply averaged out to derive inferences at the network level. As Brandes and colleagues point out, 'the network system is more than a simple aggregation of its constituent elements: it is patterned, not summed' (Brandes *et al.* 2013: 5).

In the next section, I illustrate the properties of these irreducible elements of structure—actors, relationships and networks—by critically comparing two theoretical frameworks that have contributed to the assessment of network science, namely analytical and relational sociology. Although similar in some of the claims around the nature and content of social research, these approaches are grounded in different sociological traditions: analytical sociology emerges mainly from methodological individualism and shares some features with rational choice theory, whilst relational sociology has its roots in symbolic interactionism and is heavily influenced by the work of Harrison White (2008 [1992]).

For analytical sociology, I will mainly refer to Hedström (2005). For relational sociology, I refer to White (2008 [1992]) and Azarian (2003). I also refer to Emirbayer (1997), to Emirbayer and Goodwin (1994), to Emirbayer and Mische (1998) and to Crossley (2011). Although these works do not cover all critical discussion and applications of the two theoretical frameworks, they illustrate similarities and differences in the conceptualisation of agency, relations and networks. Of these, the conceptualisation of actor and agency is the theoretical locus where analytical and relational sociology are farthest apart.

Actors and identities: analytical and relational perspectives

Generally speaking, analytical sociology (and network science in general) attributes ontological substance to actors due to their agentic nature and the relatively stable sets of dispositions that emerge from iterative interactions, settling in recognisable identities and typifications. Relational sociology instead, although agreeing with the definition of identities as relatively stabilised sets of dispositions, holds that such dispositions are only activated in interactions and therefore do not exist outside social relations. In this section, I attempt to unpack these differences.

In analytical sociology, actors are considered rational agents who purposively engage in agency driven by some kind of interests. Interests represent the intentional aspect of action, explained 'by reference to the future state it is intended to bring about' (Hedström 2005: 36): as such, interests differentiate actions from unintentional behaviours (like snoring or tripping over a stone). Hedström (2005: 38) dissects the concept of action through the DBO theory: Desires that guide it (what actors wish or want), Beliefs (propositions about the world held to be true by actors), and Opportunities (the set of action alternatives that exists independently of the actors' beliefs and desires). Desires, beliefs and opportunities not only cause action, but also make it explicable to and reasonable for other people.

Hedström considers this psychological conceptualisation of actors and agency as a valid alternative to rational choice theory, which, in his view, is limited to the assumption that actors choose optimal courses of actions with respect to their preferences and desires. This rational choice assumption presupposes perfectly informed actors, who instead rarely hold all the necessary information and therefore tend to act reasonably rather than rationally. That is, to be perfectly rational, they should act on the assumption that their beliefs are optimal, whereas actors normally hold only partial information and less than optimal beliefs because both information and beliefs emerge, as Hedström highlights, from interactions with other actors (2005: 61). This important detail is what distinguishes analytical sociology from the tradition of game theory, in which rational choice approaches are mostly grounded. While Hedström focuses on the interactive and communicative nature of agentic efforts, game theory is able to prove that individuals act strategically only by disallowing any type of communications between participants, which may facilitate the emergence of cooperative behaviour (Crossley 2011).

Needless to say, neither rational choice theory nor analytical sociology are so precisely defined and applied in empirical research as in Hedström's presentation. Rational choice theory has developed many variations where actors' rationality, far from being optimal, is bounded by the information actors have access to, the cognitive limitations of their minds, and the finite amount of time they have to make a decision (Simon 1957). 'Thick' and 'thin' versions of the theory have been proposed (Opp 1999), where actors are fully or only partially informed; they are moved by both egoistic and altruistic preferences or only by the former; and they are bound by any kind of opportunity or only by tangible ones.

These different versions of the theory have shaped various attempts to calibrate the methodological instrument of agent-based modelling, which Hedström himself (2005) indicates as the most useful analytical tool to detect social mechanisms within the empirical realm. Agent-based models are computational simulations that model the outcome of actors' interactions over a specific period of time by comparing observed data with randomised results. The model needs specified rules on the purposes of action (why actors decide to interact or not) and on the opportunities of interaction (whom they can interact with). The patterns of the combination of these micro processes of interactions produce macro outcomes, which are emerging and unintentional products that cannot be controlled by any individual actor.

This type of modelling has been applied to many different topics in sociology, from the study of youth unemployment (Hedström 2005) to the analysis of social inequalities (Manzo 2009) as well as to problems in epidemiology, organisational science, logistics, consumer research, ecology and population dynamics.[1] As a method, this type of modelling is highly adaptable because the explanatory mechanisms that it tries to reveal can be specified using a wide range of parameters. However, in the specific theorisation of analytical mechanisms and their application to youth unemployment discussed by Hedström (2005), some limits emerge, which are outlined below.

The first limit is that in analytical sociology, more specifically in rational choice theories, the agentic efforts of actors are described only in terms of the envisaged outcome of their actions: people attempt to optimise their outcomes, which they believe will emerge if they choose a specific course of action. Hedström briefly mentions the possibility that actions may be driven by past events, as in learning theories, but these are seen as a 'specific types of DBO theory that are applicable when actors use information about the past to decide what to do in the future' (Hedström 2005: 41).

The second limit is that actions' purposiveness is reduced to psychological states that can be attributed to individuals and therefore lie outside the area of sociological investigation. Other empirical applications have modified this under-lying model, but most of the attempts have used variations of rational choice theories, in which the explanatory individual elements are represented by inner preferences and desires as if they were irreducible properties of individuals, with-out empirically investigating their interactive and relational nature.

The third limit is that whilst opportunities are accounted for in terms of pos-sibilities and constraints offered by the interactive processes, Hedström does not calibrate his simulation using real network data (i.e. concretely observed patterns of interactions between individuals). He simply uses a proxy for interaction based on spatial propinquity, whereas people living close by have a higher probability of interaction. Although the assumption is not entirely unfounded (Mok *et al.* 2007), it lacks the structural precision of proper network data, where not only individual contacts are counted but the cohesion of the local structure, measured via the mapping of all the possible interactions between these contacts, is also taken into account. However, this limit has been overcome by subsequent empirical studies in which the full structure of social interactions has been used to calibrate simulation models. Bearman *et al.* (2004), for example, asked a set of adolescents to identify their sexual and romantic partners from a roster of other students attending their school. Then the researchers compared the structural characteristics of the observed network to random networks that simulated the possible distribution of ties.

Relational sociology is a different flavour; it proposes an alternative concep-tualisation of agency and actors that addresses the first two aforementioned limits of analytical sociology. Agency is defined by Emirbayer and Mische (1998: 963) as

> a temporally embedded process of social engagement, informed by the past (in its habitual aspect), but also oriented toward the future (as a capacity to imagine alternative possibilities) and toward the present (as a capacity to contextualise past habits and future projects within the contingencies of the moment).

Building on the foundations of pragmatism (in particular Dewey, Mead and Schutz), the authors reject the notion of actions caused by rationally anticipated consequences in favour of an agentic process that gives space to more interpret-ative and creative processes of selection between possible choices of action. Actors exercise a 'deliberative attitude' that consists of the capacity to 'get hold of conditions of the future conducts as they are found in the organised responses we have formed, and so construct our past in the anticipation of that future' (Mead 1932: 76).

Whilst Emirbayer and Mische (1998) stress the necessity of accounting for the temporal flow that embeds actors in overlapping and nested events, in the original 'Manifesto for a relational sociology' Emirbayer (1997) shifts the focus to the interactive nature of agency, addressing the second of the limits of analytical sociology. He rejects a notion of actors as entities characterised by essential psychological properties in favour of a redefinition of the substance of actors in pure relational terms, where the 'terms and units involved in transactions derive their meaning, significance and identity from the changing functional roles they play within that transaction' (Emirbayer 1997: 287). This means that actors do not possess any substantive attribute that belongs to them, like internalised desires and beliefs, but that attributes are defined only when actors relate to other actors, and they become meaningful only in interactions.

The interactive nature of psychological states is fully explored in the work of Crossley (2011), who grounds his observations again on the work of Mead (1934). In symbolic interactionism, consciousness is an emergent property that arises out of interaction of the human organism and its physical environment. The surrounding environment exists independently from our consciousness of it, but the perception of the self is only achieved when the body interacts with the external world. Psychological concepts are not pre-given and unsocialised states of minds, but emerge from practical and embodied inter-activities. In Crossley's example, being angry or jealous is necessarily a way of interacting with others, not an inner state (Crossley 2011: 79).

The relational nature of sensations and emotional statuses is not a recent discovery, but it has been widely discussed in philosophy and social psychology (Collins 1981; Husserl 1960; James 1976). In this tradition, sensations derive from the interaction between the subject and her or his surrounding environment (the physical worlds inhabited by other organisms). Similarly, the consciousness of the self is not an unsocialised state but is produced in an internal dialogue in which individuals reflect about their own experiences and the experience of themselves.

Mead (1934) distinguishes between I, the agentic substance of the actor, and ME, the image that the I forms of itself: this image is composed of the imaginative projections of the ME in future situations, which are grounded on the historical reconstruction of what ME did in the past. Whilst the I acts in the present, it can never catch itself in the process of acting, but only retrospectively through a process of self-reflection, which reconstructs historical patterns of actions in narrative terms, as plots where the ME is a character and the I reconciles its various roles together in a more-or-less coherent sense of self.

The management of the various images of ME is considered by Mead as the essential character of the mind, it constitutes its psychological nature and it is necessary because individuals are social beings, living in a physical and social world. However, the effort of managing a coherent identity, of constructing a meta-narrative that holds together different and sometimes contrasting roles in interactions, seems to have become a major issue in modern times, as individuals find themselves embedded in an increasing number of social circles where they are supposed to engage in a diverse range of activities with a large number of people.

This is a very old leitmotif that has accompanied the development of sociology as a discipline, from the distinction between mechanic and organic solidarity (Durkheim 1964a [1893]), where the division of labour requires individuals to differentiate their working tasks and transform them from interchangeable to complementary, to Simmel's description of the urban life (1976a [1903]), where individuals are embedded in differentiated social circles that require adaptable roles and a more intellectual (as opposed to affective and intimate) style of interaction. In modern sociology, the concept of social circles has been reprieved by Kadushin (1976, 2012), who makes them one of the core foundational elements of network structures.

But the same idea of social circles that are increasingly differentiated in the passage from traditional to modern societies has also given space to the theory of individualisation. According to this thesis, in contemporary times individuals are left alone in defining the normative aspects of their life, as traditional values of pre-urban and pre-industrial societies have lost their role in dictating the allowed content of interactions (Bauman 2003; Beck and Beck-Gernsheim 1995; Giddens 1992). The effects of the lack of rigid cultural prescriptions, which were supposed to regulate expectations and obligations in traditional societies, are also recognised as the fundamental causes of multiplex and contrasting identities in the work of White (2008 [1992]).

White embraces the idea of a contemporary society where individuals, far from being embedded in stable and rigidly defined relationships, are located at the unique intersections of various social circles that require different, and sometimes conflicting, forms of commitment (White 1973). However, instead of drawing pessimistic conclusions about the lack of moral commitment that characterises the superficial and anomic nature of contemporary relationships (Bauman 2003), White does not consider the unique embeddedness of the actor as a condition of isolation. Rather than being overwhelmed by an unmanageable amount of possible and conflicting choices, thus suspending the very act of choosing and engaging in significant relationships (Bauman 2003), contemporary individuals need to increase the amount of control they exercise over the concurrent definitions of various situations in which they interact with other actors, who themselves try to impose their definitions. Azarian nicely summarises White's perspective by highlighting that

> the expectations and obligations that modern social relationships imply do not seldom put significant constrains on the interconnected ends; no matter how flexible and negotiable these constrains may be, they never fail to make themselves felt through various types of rewards and punishments.
>
> (Azarian 2003: 60)

The efforts that actors expend when facing the requirements of their intersecting positions within the structure of interactions constitute their unique identity, intended as the various styles of action that individuals develop to handle the chaos of contingencies. Actors tend to develop typified modes of interactions that constitute a relatively stable, stylised frame of reference on what to do whilst switching between various interactive contexts. By being relatively stable, these interactive frameworks also become recognisable and identify the behavioural style of individual actors. They are also highly adaptable and never fully determined because they are constantly subjected to the unpredictable interplay of contingent and heterogeneous constraints. In particular, identities as repertoires of control efforts emerge more vividly when facing frictions and errors across different settings. In such situations, actors narratively reconstruct, ex-post facto, a coherent sense of identity that keeps together contradictive elements (White 2008 [1992]: 10–11).

Ultimately, then, the important contribution of relational sociology to the conceptualisation of agency (highly indebted to the ideas of Mead and symbolic interactionism) is the stress on the narrative nature of identity, which unfolds temporally in the nested nature of social events and spatially in its unique topological position between intersecting social circles. In other words, whilst analytical sociology still envisages individual actors that exist and are represented as atomistic observations of rationally purposive agentic subjects, relational sociology conceptualises actors as the product of interactions and relationships, which constitute the irreducible elements of social life. Because behaving rationally entails behaving in ways that make sense to others, relational sociology concludes that even being rational is a relational concept (Crossley 2011).

Relationships: stories, conventions and resources

Interactions and relationships comprise the second foundational element of the social theories of network science. The interactive channels that link actors together and embed them in networks are probably the most specific feature of network approaches, although they have been conceptualised and operationalised in many different ways. At the core of this conceptualisation there is the fundamental distinction between gesture, which consists of mostly unconscious reactions to the social and physical environments, and significant symbol, which is a gesture with conventional meanings and uses that produces communication between a sender and a receiver (Crossley 2011; Mead 1934). Despite being mostly unconscious, gestures can influence the reactions of both actors who perform them and the ones who attend to them and may eventually produce unintended communication.

Goffman dedicates a large part of his work to the study of the 'art of impression management', by which actors try to control intentional and unintentional signals they perform in everyday life (Goffman 1959). In his view, both unintentional gesture and intentional interactions should be matters of sociological studies. This contrasts with the position of analytical sociology, according to which social research should be limited to the study of intentional actions, purposive agentic events to which actors attribute explainable desires and beliefs (Hedström 2005). Also, at the opposite spectrum of purposive actions, there is, for Hedström, not so much unconsciously communicative gestures but the automated reactions to stimuli defined as behaviours (Hedström 2005: 38).

Another definition of relation, which similarly excludes unintended gestures, is the one proposed by Borgatti and colleagues (2009). Here, the distinction is between interactions as discrete events that span a relatively short period of time (like the exchange of material or non-material resources such as money or advice) and relationships that stabilise in continuous, recognisable and sometimes institutionalised forms, like friendship or kinship. At the core of this definition is the irreducibility of the properties of the dyads to the ones of individuals (Brandes *et al.* 2013).

Regardless of how stable and durable ties are, they always display emergent properties that characterise both of the actors they link together. For example, an infectious disease links those who transmit it and those who receive it; a contract binds two commercial partners in complementary terms; two natural brothers share the same mother. Actors in dyads are not independent; their characteristics are defined by the very fact that they interact, and establish relationships, with each other. Moreover, dyads can be represented in four essential states: null, where there is no current relation between two actors; directed, where an actor A relates to B, or vice versa; and mutual, where both actors are reciprocally related. Network science engages with the description and explanation of the conditions that favour the emergence and sustainment of a relation, identified by Kadushin (2012) in the effects of propinquity and homophily. According to these principles, actors are more likely to be related to each other if, other conditions being equal, they are geographically close and have characteristics that match in a proportion greater than expected in the population or the network of which they are a part (Kadushin 2012: 18).

The fundamental importance of social relations is recognised both in analytical and relational sociology, although they are operationalised in different ways. Analytical sociology, at least in Hedström's account (2005), leaves the definition of relationships relatively vague, by simply indicating the importance of taking into account the role of interactions as a tool to open the black box of variable correlations. The only way we can explain social regularities that we observe at the macro level of variable correlations is to reduce them to the micro interactive processes that produce them. Polarisation of political debates, for example, cannot be explained by simply looking at individual independent opinions, but become much clearer if interpersonal influence over attitudes is taken into account (Baldassarri and Bearman 2007). Variations in local unemployment levels are better understood if explained by endogenous processes of individual interactions (Hedström 2005). Inequalities in educational attainments are explained by the educational transitions of people individuals are related to (Manzo 2013). In these examples, the link between macro processes of social change and individual choices is provided by the structure of interaction, which produces emergent properties that are not reducible to the simple aggregation of personal opinions, job searches and educational choices.

Although central to the theorisation of explanatory mechanisms, in many studies of analytical sociology that make use of agent-based modelling, social ties are not empirically measured. Instead, as in the examples above and in line with the common conditions that favour the emergence of social relations (Kadushin 2012), they are deduced from homophilous profiles, respectively operationalised as similarities in political opinions, spatial proximity and common educational backgrounds. Using a proxy dimension, the authors of these studies (Baldassari and Bearman 2007; Hedström 2005; Manzo 2009) reasonably assume that the probability of interaction between people with similar political opinions, similar unemployment status, and similar educational background is higher than what is expected by chance, therefore constituting a robust measurement of social ties.

However, although the assumption in Baldassarri and Bearman (2007) is that people mostly interact with people with similar political opinions, the authors allow for the possibility of out-of-chore interactions, random contact with people with different opinions that are crucial in explaining the emergence of political polarisations over take-off issues. In a similar vein, Bearman *et al.*'s study (2004) of adolescents' sexuality makes use of an empirically observed social network, without assuming as a proxy that interaction simply emerges out of homophily and proximity.

Empirical studies in the analytical sociology tradition, especially those that use agent-based models, are extremely useful for investigating the emerging outcomes of micro processes of interactions by simulating the mechanisms of influence and transmission that, once patterned in complex network structures, shape the dynamics of social changes at a macro level. They assume, however, that the underlying mechanisms are already known: by simulating dynamic processes of tie formation and dissolution, they abstract from the hurly-burly of everyday interactions the high variance of the fabric of ties that represent the emergent properties of concrete relationships. But in so doing, they tend to simplify the relational mechanisms that govern interactions and assume that people discussing politics, job opportunities or educational choices influence each other and eventually align into social homogeneity (even within the polarisation of homogeneous groups holding opposite political opinions). They presuppose simple and single mechanisms, without opening the black box of the concrete dynamics of interactions that may equally resolve in agreement and adaptation to each other's opinions, or in conflicts and radicalisation of positions. As White indicates (2008 [1992]), such simulative models need to be confirmed against real data as a necessary step in the formulation of network theories (Brandes *et al.* 2013).

Despite the need to reduce the complexity of concrete relationships to formal and abstract representations, analytical sociology does not deny the complex meshing of nuances of the empirical world, even if they necessarily have to cast them out from their analysis. This is testified by the foundational work of Harrison White, an important bridge between analytical and relational sociology.

White is extremely attentive about not reducing relationships to ossified channels of material transmission (Azarian 2003). He defines relationships as a 'prism for meaning as much as pipes for connectivity' (White 2008 [1992]: 20), borrowing the definition from Podolny (2001). They are iterative interactions in which actors (identities) struggle for control over the definition of the situation, up to a point in which these interactions settle down into some stories that mark the substance of a tie: in White's words, 'a story is a tie placed in context' (White 2008 [1992]: 20).

This definition implies that relationships should be distinguished from occasional interactions as the first consist of 'repeated communication between some pair [that] can get recognised as a continuing relation when its frequency rises above chance expectancy in that context' (White 2008 [1992]: 21). In other words, relationships are continuous properties of dyads that entail a temporality, a collection of past encounters and negotiations for control that guide the present interaction and envisage future engagements. The very essence of a relationship is given by the story that defines it, that can be expressed by verbal and non-verbal communication, and that is constantly produced and reproduced in narrative terms by the actors involved in it. As these narratives accumulate, they fall into patterns that constitute conventions and rules of thumb and that can be transferred across relational contexts (both spatially, as in different sets of relationships, and temporally, as in subsequent interactions).

Although stories can settle in recognisable and taken-for-granted patterns of interactions, they are never completely determined by conventions and rules of thumb. The concrete act of interacting always presupposes a certain amount of control effort by the actors involved, efforts whose outcome, being irreducible to individual desires and beliefs, is often unpredictable (Crossley 2011; Tilly 2002; White 2008 [1992]). It is not only relationships that can be transformed in ways that are unforeseeable from the position of the individual actor; because of their transformations, they also modify the identity of the actors involved, who derive their sense of self from interactions with others. In some extreme relational views, individuals do not possess any substantive ontological essence, but are simply terms of relations (Emirbayer 1997): relations are the primitives of social theories, as actors cannot be independent from the relationships they are embedded in.

Although I agree that individuals possess characteristics by virtue of being relational agents, I do not believe that they lack any ontological substance. As social organisms, actors are able to accumulate iteratively behavioural dispositions and identity traits that make them recognisable to other actors. The fact that they cannot be analytically separated from the social life in which they are embedded does not mean that they do not exist outside relations. By collapsing individuals into interactions and relationships, there is a risk of reaching the opposite extreme of a spectrum, where on one end actors are strategic individuals who act as if there were no one else around them (simply driven by categorical aspects that completely define them), whilst on the other end actors disappear as simple terms of relationships. At this end of the spectrum, actors are reduced to carriers of shared meanings, whose identities are constantly reshaped to the point that each interaction is unique, unpredictable and incomparable to others.

Instead, interactions show some recurrent patterns: these are produced by the typified styles of actions that actors tend to reproduce in their biographical trajectories and that constitute their identity. A central task for social sciences is thus to theoretically classify and methodologically operationalise the nature and content of such typified sets of identities and relations. The iterative content of many interactions comes into play here, as stories and conventions settle into taken-for-granted narratives that actors use to order their relational life and to switch across relational settings. Even if it is impossible to perfectly represent the complex and multifaceted dynamic nature of empirical ties, we can still provide abstract and general descriptions that can help in categorising them (White 2008 [1992]: 20).

Building on Emirbayer and Mische's work (1998), Crossley defines social relations as 'lived trajectories of iterated interactions ... To say that two actors are related is to say that they have a history of past and an expectation of future interactions and that this shapes their current interaction' (Crossley 2011: 28). Social relations have a temporal dimension that unfolds from the past and projects into the future and that partially determines (but not completely, as interactions are in essence unpredictable) the present content of them as well as what is expected and allowed in relationships. By recording and measuring the recurrent elements of constitutive dimensions, we can approximate the amount of determination within a social relation that will vary across relational domains as well as situational settings.

Relationships' constitutive dimensions are identified by Crossley as symbolic, affective, strategic, convention–innovation, and exchange–power. These dimensions proportionally combine in more or less any kind of relationship, which can be more or less emotionally involving (therefore more or less dominated by the affective dimension), more or less conventional, more or less strategic, and more or less balanced or unbalanced in terms of power (Emirbayer 1997). In other words, no relationship can be fully defined by using a singular dimension. Any type of interaction presupposes some form of symbolic communication and conventions, because to understand each other, actors must read each other actions, typify them, negotiate a shared definition of the situation, and internalise one another's role (Mead 1934; Schutz 1972).

Interactions also require an agreement at least on some minimum terms of conventional signs, which can be as simple as the etiquette of dialogue turns or as complex as ceremonial rituals of highly institutionalised cultural practices. They always involve some type of emotional reaction, from bland ones to the most intense, and the emotional style of interaction must be appropriate for the situation. Finally, any kind of interaction presupposes some form of exchange, being as various as the pleasure of each other's company or the money transfer in illegal activities. The multiple dimensions that characterise interactions, when iterated in subsequent encounters, eventually stabilise in recognisable patterns of relationships, which define not only the individual and dyadic expectations in relation to specific relationships, but also the traits that are accepted in a specific culture and that make them recognisable within such a cultural context. For example, it might be commonly acceptable to express affection toward a partner or a friend, whilst it would be considered rather odd to do the same with a business partner.

Depending on the type of dimension that dominates a relationship, a direction of interaction can also be detected: although any kind of interaction presupposes some form of reciprocity, its nature may vary across relational settings. Some forms of interactions and relationships (e.g. talking on the phone, being married, or working together) necessitate a reciprocal and simultaneous engagement of the actors involved, whereas other forms (e.g. giving orders, lending money and selling goods) may be more unidirectional. Again, the nature of reciprocity and direction-ality is contingent on the concrete relational context: in reciprocal relationships, the power and exchange dynamics between partners may not be perfectly bal-anced; conversely, directed relations may presuppose some form of return, even if in different currencies (exchanging goods for money) or in delayed times (return-ing borrowed money). Ultimately, as Mauss explained (1954), even gifts are never 'free', as they always bond actors in some forms of delayed reciprocity.

Finally, relationships are defined by the frequency of interactions, which sta-bilise them in definable and recognisable relational patterns: to emerge as iden-tifiable and eventually as institutionalised relational configurations, relationships need to be settled over a minimum number of interactions in which actors can overcome mismatches and agree on a shared story that defines the content of the tie (White 2008 [1992]). What constitute the minimum number is highly depend-ent on the context of interaction, the peculiar combination of dimension involved, and the specificity of the cultural environment. In Western cultures, we can expect a marriage to need more encounters than a business agreement, whilst that might not be the case in other cultures.

The detailed and complex account of interactions and relationships that White and relational sociologists propose highlights some foundational terms of discus-sion. Any network study should clearly define the type of ties that are theoretically important and that will be measured: unintentional (as in gesture) or intentional (as in conscious interactions and relationships); discrete events (as intentional interactions whose goal is to exchange something, no matter if material or imma-terial) or continuous states (as settled relationships with recognisable features); and directed, undirected or reciprocal ties, and the conditions for reciprocation (type of currency, temporal framework).

Furthermore, the type of tie, and its detailed content, should be defined with reference to the research questions being asked. If we want to study the diffusion of disease, for example, information on the number of sexual partners may be sufficient. If we want to study the influence in political opinions, we may want to know the frequency and content of political discussion. In other words, despite the complex meshing of multiple dimensions that constitute each interaction and relation, an empirical measurement should analytically distinguish between the constitutive dimensions, their intensity and their variable combinatory statuses.

In the next chapter, for example, the analysis of friendship networks is informed by the conceptualisation of ties based on the distinction between ideal, negotiated and situational elements. Ideal elements constitute the collective shared meanings normally associated with the term 'friend' in a specific cultural context. They are embraced by individuals in this context, but also critically evaluated against, and partially adapted to, concrete relationships. Such ideal elements, which define the composition of various dimensions in friendship ties, also inform the shared norms and rules that regulate them and that are tacitly applied in interactions. When these norms are contradicted and challenged in the concrete situational level, they can be renegotiated within the relationship, and the outcome of the negotiation process can partially modify ideals, rules and the concrete interactions in which friendship unfolds. Although contextual to the case study under analysis, the heuristic model that describes the relational dynamics of friendship ties can be understood as a general theoretical framework of social relations in line with the constitutive elements that have been sketched so far.

Social networks, disciplines and social worlds

Dyads, as social relations, are not independent entities, but overlap creating a pattern of network structure. These networks are systems with ontological substance themselves, because inferences at the individual or dyadic level cannot be simply averaged to derive inferences at the network level (Brandes *et al.* 2013). They therefore constitute the third foundational brick of network science. The first indication of the emergent properties of social networks as social systems that are not reducible to the individuals can be traced in the work of Durkheim (1964b [1895]) and its similarities with the theory of emergence. This theory was active in the nineteenth century and discussed the irreducibility of wholes to the sum of their parts (Renouvier 1859) and of higher levels of analysis to lower ones (Boutroux (1916 [1874]).

Similarly, Comte (1907 [1830–42]) insisted on the non-reducibility of sociology to aggregate psychological and physiological phenomena. The main element of the theory of emergence thus consists of the observation that the properties of a system often cannot be predicted by a complete description of its component units. Canonical examples of emergence include traffic jams, colonies of social insects and bird flocks, where the resulting aggregate behaviour of cars, insects and birds is not planned or centrally determined (Sawyer 2002). In social systems, this means that social processes originate from the 'internal constitution of the social group' (Durkheim 1964b: 113), where this internal constitution is defined as social milieu, an emergent system characterised by the size, or number of its social units, and the degree of concentration or density, as the number of individuals with social relations (Durkheim 1964b: 114).

Subsequently, Simmel (1976b [1903]) started to formally describe the properties of overlapping ties and networks. One important element of his discussion is the distinction between dyads and triads. Simmel noticed that in a dyad the resistance of the relation between the two actors entirely depends on the actions of each member, as both of them could decide to leave and terminate the dyadic relation. In triads, even if one member leaves, a connected group of two individuals still remains, rendering the triadic configuration independent from individuals with unique social characteristics that are not reducible to actors' willingness.

Simmel also noticed an interesting structural difference between traditional and rural societies and modern and urban ones. In the latter, there is not only an increase in population size, but also a consequential differentiation of multiple, sparse and partially overlapping social circles (Simmel 1921, 1976a [1903]). The idea was transmitted, in various versions, to the work of Harrison White (2008

[1992]), who describes the social landscape as a vast and dense texture of multi-layered networks.

The tangled nature of social relations, where individuals are connected in overlapping and therefore non-independent dyads, implies that what occurs in one relation may spill over into others, provoking unintended effects that are out of individual (or dyadic) control. Individuals lie at the interlacing points of these overlapping networks, as they are simultaneously embedded in various relational contexts. The unique crossroads in which they are located provide the structural opportunities and constraints that may facilitate or hamper individual action. At the same time, the historical trajectories (as in the collection of past interactions) that conduce actors to occupy specific topological locations also provide them with exclusive knowledge that they can use to orient themselves and organise the social reality around them. The recognition that social networks are emergent properties of interweaving social relations, and that these properties are of different ontological nature to that of individuals, implies that the goal of network analysis is to demonstrate how much more of the variation in behaviour can be accounted for by adding structural (i.e. network) features to individuals' profiles.

Although each individual occupies a unique topological position in the landscape of social relations, these positions may resemble each other as they are connected within similar local structures. White and colleagues define the properties of similarities of relational positions in terms of structural equivalence (Lorrain and White 1971; White *et al.* 1976). They advance the hypothesis that, by virtue of occupying structurally equivalent positions, actors also develop similar behavioural profiles as they relate to similar people and in similar structures.

The most important element in the definition of structural equivalence is that two actors do not need to be directly connected with each other to be analogous: reciprocal influence comes from the flow of communication that circulates through the short paths connecting them and that go through the actors they have in common. The goal of blockmodelling techniques, which are based on structural equivalence, is to reduce the complexity of overlapping networks by distilling the web of actual ties into patterns of a higher level of abstraction, without having to rely on categorical information. Although tempting, the idea that actors display similar behavioural profiles due to their comparable positions in the relational structure has not been fully explored and confirmed by empirical results. This is probably because the definition of structural equivalence, with its assumption of actors being linked to the exact same sets of nodes, is not easily traceable in the empirical world as the variance in the local structure of connections is too high, therefore equivalent positions are very rare (Faust 1988).

In attempts to relax the strictness of structural equivalence, scholars have developed similar but less constraining definitions of equivalence between network positions, like the concept of regular equivalence (Everett and Borgatti 1994; Sailer 1978; White and Reitz 1983). Here, the difference is that while in structural equivalence two actors have to be related to an exact set of actors, in the regular version they relate to a similar set of actors, where similarity is defined in structural terms. It is crucial that the equivalent actors have the same types of relations with equivalent others. Thus, regular equivalence is extremely useful in analysing social roles as it reduces the complexity and variability of concrete relationships to blocks of positions similar to each other. However, the greatest strength of structural equivalence lies in the fact that actors present similar profiles because by being connected to the same set of other actors they can be influenced by similar factors that circulate across these common ties. In regular equivalence, there might not be any connecting path between two actors, who are similar simply because they are linked to others located in similar positions.

Despite the structural similarities, the content of these positions may be completely different, partly because relations are not only spatially disposed, but are also temporally constituted. This means that: (1) even if actors occupy equivalent topological intersections, the trajectory of past interactions that led them there may not be equivalent; and (2) the outcome of current interactions and its projection in the future, being unpredictable and unforeseeable for the individual actors, may lead them into different directions. Despite occupying equivalent positions, actors do not have to fully share the same priority schemes and behavioural styles: it is more likely that in blocks of actors in similar positions, common interactive styles will emerge that guide actors as shared conventions. By looking at the activities and interactions of people they are connected to, individuals compare and assess the appropriateness of their own behaviours (Crossley 2011; White 2008 [1992]): in these terms, the local neighbourhood of an individual, intended as the people he or she is connected to, can be understood as a reference group, a set of people to whom actors can directly compared themselves.

The conceptualisation of the local neighbourhood in terms of reference groups, who exercise some forms of social control in the definition of acceptable and unacceptable behaviours, implies that actors cannot be treated as independent from each other. This introduces, in network science, the important element of dependencies. By virtue of being locally related, reference groups tend to develop shared cultural frameworks that orient the understanding of social reality and order it. These schemas, as regular patterns of cultural conventions, emerge out of social structures and, at the same time, make them meaningful for the actors involved. Analytically, they are not independent from the relational structure that produces them and it is reproduced by them. This means that people are not only structurally but also culturally dependent on each other. The acknowledgement of dependencies between actors and within relationships is the most distinct characteristic of network science, where constitutive elements cannot be simply added up but have to be represented as systemic patterns (Brandes *et al.* 2013).

In statistical terms, this is known as the problem of autocorrelation, or, more specifically, as Galton's problem (Naroll 1961, 1965; Schaefer 1974), and it represents the most radical challenge to the foundational assumptions of statistical inference. The shared cultural traits that emerge in local neighbourhoods violate the assumption of independence of randomly sampled units, and this means that 'neither the actual number of independent cases nor the effects of interdependencies on trait correlations is generally known for any cross-cultural sample' (Dow *et al.* 1984: 755). Therefore, we also do not know how dependency, when not mapped as in network studies, influences results obtained with classic statistical models.[2]

Autocorrelation was first formulated as a problem for time-series data, where it was evident that events at a given point were likely to be dependent on events at previous points: it was then extended to spatial autocorrelation and generalised in network autocorrelation models (Dow *et al.* 1983, 1984; White *et al.* 1981), and several statistical solutions have since been proposed (Bartles and Ketellapper 1979; Doreian 1980; Ord 1975; for reviews, see Dow *et al.* 1983 and Leenders 2002). Along with the treatment of spatial autocorrelation, network science has also deeply engaged with the problem of temporal correlation, especially in the statistical modelling of network dynamics. A good review of these sophisticated and advanced models can be found in Snijders *et al.* (2010).

Networks are not just spatially and temporally correlated in patterned textures of dependencies; they are also hierarchically nested in multilevel systems of higher and lower order. Multilevel analysis (Snijders and Bosker 2012) is a branch of statistics that specifically deals with the lack of independence in hierarchically nested data. In its original form, it presupposes data obtained from multi-stage sampling, where individuals, far from being randomly selected, have a higher probability of being part of a sampled population because they belong to some pre-sampled units. For example, a sample of schools may be selected as primary units, and pupils sampled within the selected schools. In these cases, the dependency of observations within clusters is of focal interest, because it reflects the fact that clusters differ in certain respects.

From multilevel analysis, multilevel analysis of networks and multilevel network analysis have recently emerged. The former deals with networks embedded in clusters, where the structure of social relations is only detected at one level, and nodes at this level are affiliated to higher ordered clusters: the network structure of interactions between pupils in classrooms is conditioned on the various schools from which classrooms are sampled. The latter (multilevel network analysis) deals more specifically with social networks that are nested within each other: pupils interact in classrooms, classrooms belong to schools, and schools are networked together in their common use of infrastructure, for example, or in the exchange of temporary teachers. In such cases, dependencies are found not only at the micro level of individual interactions, but also at the macro level of organisational relationships: the two levels are linked together via affiliations, as in common group membership (Wang *et al.* 2013).

By nesting networks of higher- and lower-ordered nodes and by adopting a multilevel approach, social network analysis offers a viable solution to the problem of bridging between micro and macro levels (Bellotti 2012; Lazega *et al.* 2008; Wang *et al.* 2013). This is because the structural approach to multilevel networks introduces an important distinction in the conceptualisation of those levels. In analytical sociology, for example, the micro level is constituted by individual attributes: these can be classic variables like gender and age and agentic factors like beliefs, desires and opportunities. The macro level consists of aggregate phenomena—for example, the rate of unemployment in a specific country, or the diffusion of innovative production techniques in a specific market.

The micro processes of interactions between individuals, with their unintended and emergent effects, are modelled as endogenous causes that produce effects over the dynamics of macro phenomena. Macro social phenomena do not simply emerge from the co-variations of individual choices that linearly add up over time; they are inherently embedded in the complex texture of networks interactions. In analytical sociology, then, the macro level is represented by the unintended outcome of micro processes of individual actions.

In contrast, in network science, micro and macro levels are more like magnifying lenses that allow researchers to scale up and down in the observation of empirical phenomena. The micro level of analysis cannot simply be the one that accounts for properties of individuals, but it consists in the local and overlapping structures of social networks centred around focal actors, or egonetworks, where information not only considers these focal actors but also the local cohesion of people they are directly related to. Focal and local structures overlap, being centred on individuals who lie at the intersection of social circles; by iteratively overlapping, they settle in more or less stable, recognisable, and sometimes even institutionalised larger network structures (Kadushin 2012). They may become what Coleman (1975, 1990) calls corporate actors: clusters of human actors who combined assume a collective identity and acquire the mandate to speak for whoever they represent.

By being representative of specific structural configurations, corporate actors can interact and form relationships themselves, and their activities cannot be reduced to the human actors that staff them (Crossley 2011). Their networks constitute the macro level of interactions, whose outcomes are of a different scale from the outcomes of small and local interactive structures. Thus, although the endogenous effects of local interactions pattern together and eventually modify the aggregate structure of macro phenomena, as in the case of employment levels, the actions of macro actors, like government and multinational corporations, may impact the same phenomenon on a different scale, as one single act has repercussions on a large set of local interactions and its effects trickle down to the local level of micro interactions. Nation states, governments, trade unions, business corporations, schools, hospitals, firms, gangs, terrorist groups, and so on can all be considered as more or less institutionalised macro actors with their own networks of social relations. Those relations condition the possibility of interactions and relationships for the individual actors who belong to them and affect the macro processes of social dynamics. The patterned outcome of social networks, then, emerges from micro and macro interactions, and can be of various scales, from local and delimitated minor events (the rise of pollution in a city), to extensive and global phenomena (the environmental issues of the planet).

Furthermore, the analytical conceptualisation of levels does not have to be restricted to individual actors as opposed to collective actors. According to the scope of the research, we can variously adjust the focus of our magnifying lens.

For example, the micro level can be some local groups (of which we recognise their internal interactional structure but bracket its observation out for analytical purposes). These groups may be embedded in a higher relational structure, as in the case of local offices of multinational firms or territorial units of international social movements.

Regardless of the granularity of the observations, the meso level comprises the relations of individuals to macro actors, relations that nest them in hierarchical and overlapping social structures. This means that when we observe networks of individuals and networks of groups, and we know the individuals' affiliations to groups, we can adopt a dual approach (Breiger 1974), where interdependencies of individuals and collectivities are taken into account. Fararo and Doreian (1984) extend Breiger's formalism to tripartite networks, where, for example, people are embedded in groups and groups in organisations: they then generalise the conceptual basis and the matrix formalisms of bipartite graphs to tripartite networks and produce a set of matrix equations and operations that can be applied in the study of empirical networks. The observation of interdependences does not have to be limited to two or three levels; it can be extended to multiple levels and account for the nested interdependencies in ordered groups.

The interconnected nature of the social world poses some important methodological challenges in the study of social networks. If individual and corporate actors are respectively embedded in their micro and macro nested and overlapping social circles, how do we determine the boundaries of these networks? The problem has been widely discussed: Laumann *et al.* (1983), for example, distinguish between a realist approach, based on the subjective perception of actors who belong to a network, from a nominalist approach, based on the standpoint of the observer.

Within the realist approach, one technique for setting the boundaries of networks consists of contacting some people who act as entry points, eliciting the names of others who are believed to belong to the network, and carrying on with snowball interviews until no new names are elicited. At this point, the natural boundaries of the network are assumed to be reached (Erickson 1978; Goodman 1949, 1961). This technique leaves the definition of network affiliation in the hands of the people who belong to it, without imposing artificial, research-constructed boundaries. This technique has several disadvantages. Snowball interviews are time consuming; people may not want to share their alters' contacts; and, most important, many naturally occurring groups of actors may not have well-defined boundaries. However, these realistic techniques have been used successfully in ethnographic research (Johnson 1990; Johnson *et al.* 1989), together with observational data that similarly avoid the imposition of a predetermined list of a network's participants.

In contrast, nominalist approaches start with a membership roster for sets of actors who are somehow bounded. Pupils in classrooms, workers in offices, scientists in experiments, and others comprise defined networks that can be observed. This categorical approach works well for small collectivities, but it has also been applied to larger groups (Wasserman and Faust 1994: 33). This approach purposefully imposes artificial boundaries to overlapping networks: pupils in classrooms may ask for advice from their peers on how to study for an exam, but they may also rely on external ties (an older sibling, a neighbour, a teacher) that are not included in the original roster of the classroom. Given that networks overlap, boundaries are always, to a certain extent, artificial, because social relations may well spill out of them.

A case apart is represented by egonetwork studies in which personal network data are collected about a sample of focal actors. In these studies, individual cases are selected with traditional sampling methods (like statistical or theoretical samples). Information is collected regarding the actors' local neighbourhood (the people they are directly collected from, some attribute specifications, and sometimes the ties that link them together). Here the boundaries are either artificially set, by limiting the number of people that can be mentioned, or may depend on the question that is asked to solicit ties. Thus, asking whom a person discusses important matters with will elicit different networks, in terms of size and composition, than asking with whom she or he does business. In such studies, the units of analysis are the independent egonetworks themselves. Because the local structures in these networks are assumed to be independent from each other, egonetwork studies lie in between traditional network analysis (as in the structural analysis of one or more networks) and traditional categorical analysis (based on the sampling or selection of independently observed cases).

With a probability sample, data regarding the attributes of the respondents can be generalised to the larger population. But because egocentric network analysis is labour intensive for both the researcher and the respondent, studies in this genre are usually based on purposive samples. In any event, what cannot be generalised are the properties of dyads' overlap, meaning the properties of alter–alter ties because they are structurally dependent on one another: variation in one of the dyads affects the other dyads (Bellotti 2010). Regardless of the method for collecting data and sampling the fundamental units of analysis, the problem of boundaries still remains. The limits of artificially and theoretically bounded networks have been addressed especially in the relational sociology debate. White (2008 [1992]), for example, proposes the notion of disciplines as structural configurations that emerge out of blocks of equivalent actors who have developed a collective identity.

Within a discipline, because of the internal interactions, actors share priorities and criteria for the acceptance of newcomers, have stable and recognised modes of action, and establish local expressions of social control. Disciplines, in White's words, exhibit 'valuation orderings' (White 2008 [1992]: 63), which are comprehensive and hierarchical schemes of comparison and classification that emerge from the struggle for control. But being grounded on the principle of structural equivalence, White's definition of such macro units of social order presents the same limits that I discussed before.

Instead of relying on pure structural equivalence, Crossley (2009, 2010, 2011) proposes to use the idea of social worlds, an interactionist concept developed primarily from the work of Becker and extended by other interactionists (Becker 1982; Hall 1987; Shibutani 1955; Strauss 1973). In Crossley's view, networks form around social worlds centred on specific shared and overlapping interests, conventions and resources (Crossley 2011). Social worlds are networks of interactions demarcated by participants' mutual involvement in a specific set of activities: in these worlds, interactions are not random but patterned, and the actors involved recognise each other as members. The boundaries of these worlds are thus located where the patterns of interactions, specifically oriented toward the accomplishment of some kind of shared interests and regulated by collective conventions, decay. This does not mean, however, that actors do not interact outside a social world.

Networks extend well beyond any bounded group, granting the possibility for different social worlds to overlap. However, each social world delimits the networks of interactions that are purposive for its development, maintenance and reproduction. When I dance tango, I interact with people who share the same interest (they like tango), possess the required competences and resources (they know how to dance tango, they wear tango shoes), share the same conventions (they follow the norms and etiquettes that regulate the dance floor), and frequent specific places (they go to clubs and venues where tango music is played). When I go to sociological conferences, my tango skills are of no use, and I interact with people in different places, with different interests, skills and shared conventions. I might find a couple of colleagues who are similarly interested in tango; likewise, I might meet other sociologists at tango events.

In such situations, the two social worlds in which I am embedded intersect, but the cultural frameworks that define them do not mesh: interests, conventions, resources and opportunities of one world remain separated from the ones of the other world. In some other cases, though, social worlds may eventually mesh, by virtue of their overlapping networks: music styles may contaminate each other (like the fusion between tango music and electronic music, which produced the emergent style of neo-tango), sports may influence some hybrid evolution (surfing and parachuting mesh in kite-surfing, snowboarding and water-skiing in wakeboarding), idioms may merge in new languages (like the diffusion of Spanglish in some areas in the United States).

There are some interesting resemblances between the notion of social worlds and the sociological framework of the theory of practices (Warde 2005), which presupposes, although without conceptualising them in network terms, overlapping social circles of practices' carriers. These individuals share the foundational elements of practices, as in materials, competences and meanings, and, by the very act of performing, are responsible for the emergence, stabilisation, evolution, decadence and hybridisation of practices (Bellotti and Mora 2014; Shove *et al.* 2012). The concept of social world has the advantage of maintaining its relational essence, as boundaries are set where interaction decays, but also of focusing on the cultural resources that circulate across these entities. Such cultural figurations, and the mechanisms that devise their circulation, are the topic of the next section.

Mechanisms and cultural figurations

In the previous sections, I defined the characteristics of the foundational elements of network science. Actors, social relations and networks are the bricks of social structure, whose ontological properties are irreducible to each other. Social relations are irreducible to individual characteristics because the meaning of any specific relation is an emergent property of the temporal dynamics of actors' interactions; individuals are the terms of relations, whose identity is developed and perceived only in relation to other identities, but they tend to stabilise over time, rendering actors' activities partially predictable; and social networks are the emergent and sometimes stabilised properties of the intersected patterns of social relations. Although these elements can be analytically distinct, they are always interlocked in the real world, thus they are never empirically isolated from each other. This does not mean that they cannot be theoretically distinguished: the theoretical abstraction of the relations between these elements from the contingencies of the empirical world is how structural mechanisms can be observed and explained.

Once a network mechanism is isomorphically described, it can be linked back to the empirical phenomenon, where its formalisation can be checked against real data (Brandes *et al.* 2013). Such scientific procedure highly resembles the analytical strategy of analogical retroduction proposed by critical realism and discussed in the previous chapter. As previously mentioned, Bhaskar (1978) advances the hypothesis that empirical events are caused by underlying mechanisms that may not be fully accessible to people observing them because their perception is confused by asymmetries provoked by the concurrence of several overlapping mechanisms.

The interactive effects of simultaneous generative mechanisms cannot be controlled by individual actors; therefore, the event outcomes will be the emergent and undetermined properties of the contingencies of specific interlocking mechanisms in a definite context of time and space. They exist independently from individuals and exercise causal power over the possibilities of individual actions. Given their emergent and concurrent nature, underlying mechanisms, like the networks models theorised in Brandes *et al.* (2013), cannot be directly generalised across domains but they can be retroductively compared across cases.

It is worth noting that the ontological nature of intransitive mechanisms is the main point of departure of critical realism from analytical sociology. This is because Hedström (2005) is highly critical about the idea of mechanisms that are not directly accessible via empirical observations but that exercise causal power over individual actions. The problem with this critique is that analytical sociology, deeply embedded in methodological individualism, cannot accept a theory in which individuals may hold partial and distorted information (the empirical domain); as in methodological individualism they are, ultimately, the only possible source of observations.

So what are the differences between the mechanisms theorised by critical realism and the mechanisms of network science? In critical realism and its main methodological strategy of CCM, mechanisms are detected via crispy, multiple or fuzzy logic combinations of macro aspects in individual cases, ignoring the importance of spatial and temporal dependences between actors, either individual or corporate. Once a specific configuration of mechanisms is activated, it exercises an exogenous power over individuals, who may not be fully conscious of being determined as such, as they are confounded by the emergent effects of concurrent mechanisms. Furthermore, because mechanisms are contingent on specific contexts, the same combination, in a different spatial and temporal frame, may produce different outcomes: even if we can explain mechanisms' outcomes, these cannot be predicted.

In network science, mechanisms are defined as the processual conditions of interactions between actors: they are not simple combination of macro aspects in contingent cases and contexts. They are produced, reproduced, modified and abandoned in the spatial and temporal patterns of interactions: they emerge out of the dependency structure of interrelated actors and they exercise an endogenous power in shaping the conditions of such interactions.

Mechanisms exist independently from people's knowledge of them, as the localised topological position of individuals only provides them with a limited view of the general structural constraints that go beyond their local environment (Johnson and Orbach 2002). In this, they are similar to the intransitive mechanisms of critical realism, as people's perceptions and accounts of the structural implications of their position are distorted by the perspective available from the concrete intersections in which they lie. Despite their contingencies, and similarly to critical realism mechanisms, structural mechanisms can stabilise in 'demi-regularities' (Downward *et al.* 2010: 18; Lawson 1997): the iterative agreements over shared stories and the stabilisation of control efforts produce cultural figurations that order the otherwise chaotic patterns of multiple interactions.

Cultural formations, as in collections of languages, moral codes, conventions, shared meanings, norms and generalised trust (Crossley 2011), are the by-products of social networks. Likewise, social networks cannot have ontological substance without cultural formations: the interactions that constitute the very essence of networks always require symbolic communication between actors. Meanings are established in relations, relations are purposively tied because they are meaningful, and the interlocking structure of relations, which are spatially and temporally patterned, allows the possibility for meanings to circulate, establish, solidify and eventually end up again under the power dynamics of control efforts which can modify or abandon them.

Culture is produced in and frames actors' interactions: it can be analytically distinguished from structure, but the two are ontologically embedded together, as they cannot exist without each other. The important acknowledgement that social networks and cultural textures are co-produced and co-dependent is one of the claims that Brint (1992) and Emirbayer and Goodwin (1994) have used to criticise the disproportionate unbalance of some network studies on the side of structural configurations. In their view, some applications of social network analysis have marginalised the study of cultural elements in order to prioritise the relations among sets of positions (Brint 1992); more importantly, they have left behind any reference to the historical dynamics that act upon structural configurations (Emirbayer and Goodwin 1994).

Brint (1992), in his review of White and colleagues' programmatic statements of structural sociology (White *et al.* 1976), accuses the authors of rejecting categorical variables, which are useful to represent typifications of behavioural expectations. Furthermore, he claims that structural configurations do not emerge out of a cultural vacuum; cultural elements should be studied independently from social structures, and subsequently interrelated to structural formations. Brint (1992) not only seems to disregard the complex theorisation of the relations between culture and structure advanced by White (whose first edition of *Identity and Control* was published in 1992), but whilst trying to rebalance a supposed marginalisation of culture in social network studies, Brint ends up reifying cultural formations as explanatory causes of structural configurations, as the former could emerge in a structural vacuum. Similarly, Emirbayer and Goodwin (1994) accuse social network studies of neglecting the potential causal role of beliefs, values and normative commitments and propose observing the influential effects of embodied ideas, discursive frameworks, and cognitive maps over the dynamic structure of social networks, as if they could have been developed independently from them.

To a certain extent, the criticisms advanced by early developers of relational sociology can be used to highlight some of the limits of the conceptualisation of mechanisms in analytical sociology. Hedström (2005: 25) defines mechanisms as consisting of

> entities (with their properties) and the activities that these entities engage in, either by themselves or in concert with other entities. These activities bring about change, and the type of change brought about depends upon the properties of the entities and the way in which they are linked to one other. A social mechanism, as here defined, describes a constellation of entities and activities that are organised such that they regularly bring about a particular type of outcome.

Although Gambetta (1998) recognises that several mechanisms may act simultaneously and should therefore all be considered to make sense of a specific social phenomenon, the conceptualisation of mechanisms in analytical sociology seems to be relatively deterministic and appears to effectively marginalise the importance of their spatial and temporal contextualisation, which make both structural and cultural outcomes only partially regular and quite often unpredictable. This is made explicit by Hedström, who claims that despite the recognition that the empirical world is driven by random and stochastic processes, 'theories and explanations are better formulated as if the world were deterministic' (Hedström 2005: 31), simply because we should 'evoke randomness as an explanation only when all plausible alternatives have been proven unsatisfactory' (Hedström 2005: 31).

But aside from some extreme cases of structural modelling in analytical sociology, network science in general does not exclude cultural elements from model formalisations. Conversely, as I hope I have shown so far and will empirically illustrate in the next chapters, cultural elements are to be considered as the other side of the coin of structural configurations, essential elements that are constitutive of social reality.

Qualitative networks: on the importance of qualitative data

As should be clear by now, network models are contingent formalisations of structural mechanisms, highly dependent on the spatio-temporal context in which they work. In any network study, the object of research is a concrete web of interaction, a specific network. This network can vary in size and can comprise different kinds of relationships, but each network represents a case study in itself. Even in the study of network dynamics, 'the empirical data consist of two, but preferably more, repeated observations of a social network on a given set of actors' (Snijders *et al.* 2010: 45). This is the case for whole network studies as well as for egonetwork studies. In the latter, each network, no matter how large, complex, multilayered and longitudinal is a case for study, or a unit of analysis when more than one egonetwork is collected. In whole network studies, on the other hand, individuals who belong to a specific network and the relations that tie them together are the unit of analysis of that network.

Whole networks can vary in size, from very small-*n* (few people, like a classroom), to very large *N* (e.g. the entire UK cattle population; see Robinson *et al.* 2007), with networks of virtually any possible size in between. In egonetwork studies, each actor-centred structure constitutes a unit of analysis, where ego, alters and the characteristics of ego–alter ties can be compared across cases. Comparative case studies where several whole networks are compared do exist, but the direct comparison is complicated by limits to what kind of properties can be directly compared. A classic example is the measure of density: if the network represents concrete face-to-face relationships between individuals, the larger the network, the more difficult it is for people to interact with everyone and the more likely it is that the density will be low.

However, there have been some interesting studies about the direct comparison of networks. Entwisle *et al.* (2007), for example, account for variability in network structures of multiple villages in Nang Rong, Thailand, and show how such network structures co-vary with context in meaningful ways; Skvoretz and Faust (2002) compare 80 networks across different kind of relationships and different species (humans, non-human primates, non-human mammals) to test the hypothesis that the structure of a set of relational ties over a population is more strongly determined by type of relation than it is by the type of species from which the population is drawn.

These examples show that network research is more similar to the disciplines that work with a small and middle range of number of cases, like palaeontology, archaeology, geology, ethology, biology, anthropology and linguistics. All of these disciplines rely on a relatively small number of observations, and cases are selected for the production of idiographic theory. This resembles the theoretical sampling strategy proposed by Glaser and Strauss (1967) in the development of grounded theory.

According to this theory, in dealing with a limited number of cases when we observe a local condition of causal relations, any generalisation is a working hypothesis, which has to be transferred into another context with similar conditions. Any attempt at generalisation relies on the degree of congruence across cases, following the logic of retroduction that uses isomorphism and analogies, as proposed by critical realism. In this research scenario, the mechanisms that connect cause and effect are illuminated in intensive qualitative studies of variance across cases.

Similarly, the strategy of analytic induction, laid out by Znaniecki (1934), starts with a few cases, derives working hypotheses, tests them across the available cases, and revises them if they fail to be confirmed by even one case. The revised set of working hypotheses is then tested against new cases, and the process ends only when the hypothesis are not refuted and new cases do not add any more variance. The inferential potential of working with a limited number of cases, where the logic of analytical induction or retroduction is applied is not provided by statistical inference, which simply assesses the existence of two or more linked characteristics in some wider population from a sampled population.

Mitchell (1983) cites an example from Lykken (1970), in which people with eating disorders tend to see a frog in Roschach ink-blots. The correlation is statistically significant, but the interpretation of the causal link, where eating disorders are related to 'an unconscious belief in the cloacal theory of birth' (Lykken 1970: 267) is, if not arbitrary, at least unverified. Scientific inference instead aims to assess 'the process by which the analyst draws conclusions about the essential linkage between two or more characteristics in terms of some systematic explanatory schema—some set of theoretical propositions' (Mitchell 1983: 200).

The limits of the logic of statistical inference, highlighted by Mitchell, are recognised by many network scientists as these limits come mainly from the rejection of the assumption of independence of observations that characterises network science, the same critique shared by qualitative researchers. The use of social network analysis is intended as a 'non-quantitative mathematical way of rigorously stating the implications entailed in a set of relationships' (Mitchell 1969: 1). By taking distance from the specific quantitative traditions of inferential statistics, social network analysis can be equally mixed with sophisticated statistical techniques that discharge the assumption of independency of observations and with qualitative methods that provide the thick descriptions of the cultural peculiarities of structural environments.

In the next sections, I review a selection of network studies that have adopted three different qualitative techniques, namely qualitative interviews, ethnographic observations and archival data. Far from being an exhaustive review, the goal is to introduce and frame the three empirical examples that, in the following chapters, illustrate some possible applications of the mixed method design. In particular, the adoption of a mixed method research strategy is particularly apt to represent the narrative texture of interactive processes and the thick content of cultural configurations that emerge out of and shape social worlds.

Social networks and qualitative interviews

One of the most common methods of qualitative research is face-to-face interviews, which have long accompanied data collection. Wellman, for example, conducted semi-structured interviews with a sub-sample of the first East York study's respondents (Wellman 1990), investigating general life events and changes as well as household composition and daily life, and producing detailed descriptions of close relationships. Since then, numerous studies have combined various forms of name generators with qualitative accounts. Bidart and Lavenu (2005) use panel interviews conducted with the same sample of people every three years, to investigate the evolution of their personal networks and the events marking their entry into adult life. Hollstein (forthcoming) combines fuzzy set analysis of qualitative material and network data to investigate youth transition from school to work.

Bernardi *et al.* (2007) use interviews to investigate the social mechanisms at work and the variation in the composition of the networks of informal relationships in relation to fertility behaviour. Their research strategy mixed a semi-structured interview with a name generator and a brief socio-demographic questionnaire. The researchers then interviewed three members of each ego's social network: one of ego's parents, ego's current partner, and a close friend, when available. Although the analysis focused on dyads of close friends, the researchers collected a large amount of qualitative material, which they regard as 'best suited not only to explore the meaning of parenthood but also to identify the relationships salient for contributing to the construction of this meaning and for their translation into intentions and behaviour related to family formation' (Bernardi *et al.* 2007: 24).

A wide variety of research designs have been adopted, from multi-staged sequential design, where qualitative interviews precede network analysis (Neaigus *et al.* 1994) or where the network structure is used to select informants for subsequent qualitative interviews (Johnson 1990; Martinez *et al.* 2003); to parallel designs, where network visualisations are embedded in interview tools (Bellotti 2008a, 2008b; Hogan *et al.* 2007; Lubbers *et al.* 2010). In some cases, authors have adopted the version of in-depth interviews (Broadbent 2003; Gluesing *et al.* forthcoming; Menjivar 2000; Smith 2005; Wong and Salaff 1998); in others, interviews are focused on specific themes (Bellotti 2008a, 2008b; Bernardi *et al.* 2007; Lonkila and Salmi 2005; Scheibelhofer 2008).

In general, qualitative interviews are useful for investigating the relational nature of actors' identities and the content of their interactions with specific sets of alters. Given the narrative texture of the unfolding process of identity formation, interviews seem to be by far the most suitable approach, in which actors reflexively discuss their perception of self-identity, the nature of their interactions and relationships with significant others, and the meaning and dynamics of their egocentred local structures.

When, like in the case of Bernardi *et al.* (2007), interviews are also conducted with some of the relevant others, the social network extends beyond the first zone of the analysis, and the narratives can show the interactive process by which actors negotiate a shared definition of the relationship that ties them together. Structural mechanisms of reciprocity and balance can be better observed, as the narratives report the reflexive accounts of both actors involved in a relationship, exploring retrospectively the dynamics of actors' control efforts to resolve mismatching views and produce a shared definition of the situation.

When data are collected not only for dyads, but for entire egonetworks, it is also possible to observe triads and group dynamics. If all the alters are not available for interviews, the researchers end up with what Heath and colleagues call the 'shadow network' (Heath *et al.* 2009): far from being a random process of selection, the actual portion of the second zone egonetwork that becomes available to researchers is limited either by egos' willingness to give access to it, or by alters' refusal to get involved in the research. In the example of Heath and colleagues, the empirical boundaries that were drawn by the accessibility to alters were highly significant and reflected some interesting relational dynamics of the social networks.

Although interviews have been widely used in egonetwork studies, it is much more complicated to combine them with rosters in whole network research. As the example of Heath and colleagues demonstrates (2009), it is fairly difficult to reach every member of a network, even in the case of small configurations like egonetworks. This is even more demanding in whole network studies: Kirke (2010) reminds us that in some notable examples of studies where social network analysis and qualitative methods were combined (Curtis *et al.* 1995; Pearson and Michell 2000; Wellman *et al.* 1988), qualitative information was collected only on a fraction of the sample covered by the research. Even in Ryan (2013), where qualitative interviews were collected for all the participants of a social network representing relationships within a classroom, the analysis of the narratives only focused on some individuals, selected for their either highly central or highly peripheral position within the network. This poses some challenges about how to combine the findings of the two methods as we cannot assume that qualitative interviews conducted with a small portion of a network are generalisable to the rest of the participants.

As noted earlier in this chapter, each position in a network structure is irreducible to the others, even when they are characterised by structural or regular equivalence. The subjective accounts of individuals are framed from the local perspective of their topological position; thus, unless data are collected for each network participant and matched with their exact structural position, a whole account of subjective perspectives cannot be provided (Kirke 2010). In such circumstances, the best that can be done is to interview a sub-sample of individuals according to the structural peculiarity of their position (e.g. by selecting the most central actors, some of the isolates, people belonging to cohesive subgroups, or brokers who lie at the intersections of these cohesive subgroups).

Social networks and ethnographic observations

Qualitative interviews are not new in social network research and are useful for exploring the relational dynamics in local structures, but ethnographic observations have an even longer tradition and are optimal to explore the overlapping nature of social circles. Ethnographic observations were the main tool for data collection in the studies of the tradition of the Manchester school. As Mitchell recalls:

> in many ways ... the most reliable and adequate information is most likely to be obtained through direct observation. The observer over a period of time is able to make his own assessment of the interaction of an individual with others around him and to record its characteristics.
>
> (Mitchell 1969: 31)

Epstein used direct observations to study the spread of gossip (Epstein 1969a, 1969b); Kapferer used them to map interactions between a group of African mine employees (Kapferer 1969: 184). Wheeldon (1969) studied a black community in Southern Africa, focusing attention on six leaders who were frequently named by other members of the community, whilst Boswell (1969) observed the mobilisation of personal networks during periods of crisis in the African city of Lusaka (in present-day Zambia).

The Manchester School, although having a central role in popularising the use of ethnographic methods, was neither the first nor the only one to use qualitative data in the study of social networks. A notable antecedent is the famous study of an Italian neighbourhood in Boston by Whyte (1943).

Whyte started by shadowing Doc, a man living in the area. Shadowing consists of following a single individual over an extensive period of time to record the whole range of activities and social relations the person gets involved in (McDonald 2005). Doc was the leader of a group of corner boys, but also liaised with the club of college boys and their leader Chick. Corner boys came from families of Italian immigrants, often had limited or no formal educational training and worked at unskilled jobs. In contrast, college boys were people of Italian origins who were able to enrol in the US education system and were better integrated and acquainted with the host culture. As such, they aspired to better jobs and political careers and were keen on distancing themselves from the lower-class corner boys.

By recording Doc's daily interactions over an extended period of time, Whyte was able to map Doc's personal network and subsequently extend the observations to the overlapping social circles within the neighbourhood, eventually mapping a large part of the whole network within the area. By the end of his observations, Whyte had collected enough data to show how some anomic phenomena, like the local criminal organisation, were not the emergent effects of the lack of organisational structure, intended as the absence of internalisation of dominant values and norms of the host country from the side of immigrant communities. On the contrary, the social structure of the neighbourhood was internally highly organised, with various groups connected by the brokering relationships between their leaders. Groups identified with and coalesced around their leaders; leaders connected them with other groups (like in the case of the overlapping relationships between the corner boys and the college boys, which were highly structured in hierarchical positions); and local racketeers and politicians had to rely on the support of groups' leaders to conduct their own affairs (Whyte 1943).

Similarly, Mische (2008), in her analysis of youth movements in Brazil, adopted the technique of shadowing some key actors, following them in their daily activities and reconstructing their lives and political trajectories. These actors were used as cases to exemplify some interesting positions in the wider network of youth affiliation to political groups. Over a long period of time, Mische recorded their interactions and relationships with a wide number of people: teachers, parents, church leaders, party organisers and various activists who were part of a larger network of more-or-less organised social movements. She eventually enlarged the observations to include the various settings activists were involved with and the numerous people who belonged to them. Mische's study

> examined the intersection of multiple networks—students, religious, NGO, antidiscrimination, professional, and business, as well as partisan—in a changing field. [She wanted to study] not just the structure of relations, but also the way individuals and groups made sense of these networks and responded to the opportunities and dilemmas that they posed.
>
> (Mische 2008: 9)

Participant observations, combined with in-depth interviews and formal analysis of affiliations and careers, are far more efficient in mapping social networks without imposing artificial boundaries because despite the limits imposed on data collection by the substantive focus of the research, shadowing and ethnographic work involve following actors across the activities and social settings in which they interact. By doing this, it is easier to observe the overlapping nature of these settings, where the patterns of social interactions extend beyond the local structure of individual networks.

Finally, direct observations have been extremely useful in assessing the validity and reliability of data collected via structured and unstructured interviews. In a series of experiments, Bernard and colleagues (1984)[3] tested the accuracy of people recalling their contacts, compared to measurements by diaries, direct observation and electronic monitoring. They conclude that, overall, people can recall or predict less than half their communications, either measured in terms of the number of contacts or their frequency. The figure is not improved if people keep records of their behaviour, if they have been previously alerted to the data collection, or if they are aware of being watched.

People are more accurate in their recall of recent events in terms of who they talked to in the previous 24 hours compared to the week before (Bernard *et al.*

1984: 499). However, when name generators are mixed with in-depth interviews and the data collection relates to established relationships rather than interactions and communication events, people seem to do a pretty good job in describing their local structure (Bellotti 2008b), although we need more evidence of these types of biases.

Social networks and archival data

Finally, archives are a valuable source of network data, and the use of such data is gaining increasing importance with the development of electronic resources and software for data mining. For most archival resources, the researcher has no influence in the production of the data. However, given that archival data are produced in natural settings, they provide unique information on the cultural configurations of social worlds. Because they represent recorded and fixed information on some kind of social phenomena, they are likely to be the final outcome of some longstanding interactive struggles for control over finally settled definitions of situations. They constitute the tip of the iceberg that hides the multi-layered and dynamic nature of interactive agreement, whose outcome was considered definitive enough by whoever compiled the archive to be reported as it is. Also, by virtue of being included in the archive, information must have been considered relevant enough to be retained.

The collection of documents that constitute an archival source is likely to represent the cultural conventions of a specific social world, whose boundaries, in case of ancient material, are settled at the point when information is not further available. Within the available material, analysts must select only what they consider relevant for the aim of their research, filtering out non-relevant information. This process of selection inevitably entails a constant and active decision as to what should be included and what should be discarded as useful/useless data from the archival text.

The study of interlocking directorates is a good example of network research based on archival sources.[4] This research is done by creating affiliation matrices for persons who sit on boards of directors of corporations. The emergent interlocked structure of overlapping boards is useful to observe, for example, the practices of collusion, the strategies for monitoring firms' debts and investments, the establishment of firms' reputation and of individuals' careers, and the formation of cartels that can exercise control over large areas of international markets (Mizruchi 1996).

The formation of cohesive groups of elites also facilitates and is facilitated by the emergence of a shared cultural environment that aims at the maintenance of rigidly monitored group boundaries. Padgett and Ansell (1993) used archival sources to investigate the structure of relationships among oligarchic families in Florence during the Renaissance. The authors examined historical accounts as well as primary data like tax assessments, marriage agreements and censuses to establish neighbourhood co-residence. Marriage agreements between families are embedded in the wider structure of daily political organisation that defined the historical context of possibilities and constraints in which these agreements were made. They represent the overall cultural environment that, together with the structural configurations of network ties, favoured the emergent dominance of the Medici family.

Similarly, the work of Crossley (2008, 2009) on the development of the punk scene in London and Manchester has made large use of historical material, including histories of the music movement in Manchester and London, biographies and autobiographies of key people, and online archives. As in the previous cases, the data show how the structure of relationships facilitates the emergence and establishment of the punk scene in England through channels of interactions, the circulation of information and resources, and the development of conventions that constitute the very nature of the punk movement.

The studies described so far are of whole networks. Less common are actor-centred studies based on archival data. One example is the work of Edward and Crossley on the egonetwork of Helen Kirkpatrick Watts, a suffragette who was one of the founding members of the Nottingham Women's Social and Political Union and, due to her militant activism, was imprisoned twice in 1909 (Edwards and Crossley 2009). The authors draw on 23 letters (dated 1900–14) written by Helen or her family about her activism and on eight of Helen's written speeches (dated 1909), which are deposited at the Nottingham Archive Office.

The authors analysed the material in three stages. The first stage concentrates on the quantitative records of who wrote letters to whom, when, and with what frequency, combined with qualitative analysis of the content of the letters (Edwards and Crossley 2009: 43). This stage produces network data on connections between Helen and her correspondents. The second stage analyses the connections between people named in the letters by looking at the relationships that are described in the letters, adding the alter–alter ties to the egonetwork produced in the first stage. In the third stage, the network structure is implemented and cross-checked with information obtained from local and national newspapers on fellow prisoners and co-attendees of events (Edwards and Crossley 2009: 49).

In all the stages, qualitative analysis on the nature and content of relationships between the people who surround Helen during her involvement in the suffragette movement and the radicalisation of activities accompanies the recording of the simple presence and absence of these ties. Similar to the previously mentioned whole network studies, the thick description of Helen's networks in the suffragette movement illustrates not only the structural opportunities and constraints she faced in her involvement in the movement, but also the richness of the cultural environment that was produced and led to the collective fights for women's right to vote.

Conclusions

In this chapter, I outlined the elements of network science. In line with the literature (Borgatti *et al.* 2009; Brandes *et al.* 2013), I identified these core elements in actors, social relations and overlapping networks, whose boundaries are located within social worlds. Social worlds are delimited where the structural effects and the cultural configurations cease to be effective over the life of actors embedded in them and where the interactive processes of communications between these actors do not produce and modify the shape and content of the same social worlds. I illustrated how the dynamic and processual mechanisms at the basis of these social worlds can benefit from the use of both formal social network analysis tools and qualitative methods. The former are useful for abstracting the structural characteristics on overlapping interactions in formal configurations that can be compared across cases. The latter are useful for investigating the contextual aspects of these structures and their cultural content.

In the next three chapters, I discuss three empirical examples where social network analysis has been variously mixed with qualitative methods.

The first example mixes egonetworks with qualitative interviews in investigating friendship ties for a small sample of single youths. The two methods are used simultaneously in data collection via name generators, name interpreters and in-depth interviews. They are equivalent in the analysis (Tashakkori and Teddlie 1998), which is done by combining categorical information, social network formalised structures and the content of the interviews. The example shows the relational nature of actors embedded in relationships, where both individual identities and interactions are defined within the local structure of friendship networks.

The second example investigates the relational world of two youth street groups, where the focus is on the intersecting and overlapping networks in which the street groups are embedded. The dominant method for both the collection and the analysis of the data is ethnographic observation, and the quantitative formalisation of overlapping networks is derived from the qualitative data.

The third example explores the shape and content of the social world of a field of science in Italian academia. Here, a large network of collaborations on research projects is derived from archival data. Qualitative data on the content of the projects (analysed using content analysis) allow us to observe the strategies for chasing research funding that scientists adopt when setting up research collaborations. In this last case, the two methods are both used for data collection and analysis, but the research design is sequential, with quantitative information collected and analysed first and qualitative data added to illustrate the meaning of structural configurations.

The combined perspective of formal network analysis with qualitative material will show the importance of contextualising structural mechanisms in their idiographic environment: in particular, as noted in Crossley's studies (2010, 2011), similar underlying mechanisms, like homophily, cohesive subgroups, and brokerage roles, are likely to be found in various social networks, but their role for the processual dynamics of the whole cultural and structural configurations is dependent on the context in which they operate and on the awareness of actors involved.

Notes

1 The list of application is obviously not exhaustive in any way and only offers a couple of examples. For a review of applications, see Matthews *et al.* (2007) and Gilbert (2008).

2 This is not the place to discuss the technical implications of the effects of autocorrelation over statistical inferences. Dow *et al.* (1984) is a good starting point for basic understanding of the problem.

3 The whole set of experiments is reported in a series of articles on informant accuracy: Bernard and Killworth (1977); Bernard *et al.* (1979/80, 1982); Killworth and Bernard (1976, 1979/80). Results of the experiments are summarised in Bernard *et al.* (1981, 1984).

4 This is not the venue to review the vast literature on interlocking directorates. A good starting point is the review article by Mizruchi (1996) and the book by Scott (1997).

4 Talking ties

Micro processes of local structures in friendship networks

This first example of combining social network analysis with qualitative methods is a study of friendship networks which uses egonetworks from a non-representative sample of 23 heterosexual singles (12 men and 11 women), 25–35 years of age, living in Milan. The study used a classic name generator, in which individuals are asked to name their friends, specify some of their friends' attributes, and indicate the existence of relationships between these named friends. This information was formalised in independent network structures centred on each interviewee, and the resulting graphs, visualised with Netdraw (Borgatti 2002), were used as inputs for in-depth interviews on the content, meaning, history and dynamics of friendship. Because of their function of collecting information on the subjective perception of social phenomena, qualitative interviews are a good way to gain an insider view of the interactional processes that generate network structures (Edwards 2010).

This chapter explores the nature of these local structures by looking at the bricks that constitute them. These bricks are represented by actors engaged in relationships, where repeated interactions build up into patterns that, conversely, shape the social environment in which interactions takes places. Actors, relationships and network structures, in line with the theoretical framework sketched in the previous chapter, are not considered as categorical elements, like attributes attached to individuals. Who actors are, how they perceive and define their friends, the nature and content of their relationships, and the opportunities and constraints offered by local networks are defined and contextualised in interactions: they are relational by nature, as they are negotiated within the relations that link actors together and bundle them into networks. The combination of social network analysis and qualitative methods allows observing and measuring at the same time the formal structures of networks and the content and dynamics of these structures.

At the level of individuals, social network analysis formalises the process by which people select the friends they want to relate to and illustrates how the selection process is influenced by attributes that egos and alters have in common. This process is informed by the mechanism of homophily. But the categorical analysis of individual attributes is also matched with the qualitative accounts of the history of relationships and of alters' descriptions. There it is possible to observe how the mechanism of homophily operates within the context of concrete relationships and how similarities and differences cannot be predefined in classificatory categories but are constructed within the unfolding process of building these relationships.

Moving beyond the individual actors, the analysis then focuses on the nature and content of dyadic relationships, the social norms that regulate them, and how these norms are again negotiated in interactions. Although social network analysis allows us to formalise some aspects of dyads, like reciprocity, multiplexity and the embeddedness of relations within the overall structure of personal networks, qualitative material provides narrative texture to the measured ties. The subjective descriptions of the relationships' dynamics illustrate the mechanisms that define and regulate the norms of reciprocity and balance: the qualitative material describes the interactional work that people do when they relate to others, how they negotiate reciprocal relationships, and how they balance the possible lack of reciprocity across the whole personal network.

Finally, the analysis combines the theoretical elements that emerge from the analytical descriptions of actors and dyads and observes them within the local structure in which they are embedded. Friendship networks are thus categorised and classified in a potential taxonomy that overviews and explains their specific shapes and the possibilities and constraints that these shapes may offer to individuals.

The chapter is organised as follows. The next section reviews the sociological literature on the nature of friendship; based on this literature, a theoretical and operational heuristic model of the interactive processes that inform friendship is proposed, and this model guides the subsequent analysis of empirical data. Narrative accounts are used as first-order constructs that constitute the empirical realm of the analysis: they are then systematically classified following the theoretical elements sketched in the previous chapter, to build second-order constructs. Second-order constructs are intended as analytical categories that allow access to the actual level of friendship processes. They do so by abstracting from concrete events, as they are narrated by interviewees, the common elements that characterise these events. These elements are then aggregated in descriptive categories.

By looking at the distribution and combination of these categories (both the common and the rare ones), I am able to identify the recurrence of theoretical elements that can, to a certain extent, explain friendship processes and reveal underlying structural mechanisms that regulate the relational dynamics of friendship. These elements are thus combined in the model and organise the analysis of qualitative material. Once the analytical strategy is in place, I describe the data collection techniques that have been adopted and the sample that has been selected for the empirical case study. I then move to the analysis of the individual and relational attributes that characterise the homophilous mechanisms of selection, the dyadic nature of exchange and reciprocity, the structural dynamics of balance, and the possible taxonomies of friendship networks.

Defining and operationalising friendship

Along with the numerous social network studies of formal mechanisms in the development of friendship ties and their function as channels of influence (see, for example, Hallinan 1978/79; Johnson 1986; Knecht *et al.* 2010; Lewis *et al.* 2011; Burk *et al.* 2007; Van de Bunt *et al.* 1999), sociology has also produced some important theoretical and empirical contributions (Allan 1979; Bidart 1991, 1997; Bidart and Lavenu 2005; Fischer 1982a, 1982b; Heath 2004; Heath and Cleaver 2003; Roseneil and Budgeon 2004; Spencer and Pahl 2006; Wellman 1979, 1990).

In some cases, the focus has been on observing how friendship is variously conceptualised and performed across social categories. Previous research, for example, illuminated differences in how males and females establish friendship, with males preferring relationships based on shared activities and females privileging discussion of emotional and private matters (Wright 1982). Such gender differences were confirmed in several studies (Gouldner 1987; McRobbie 2000; Mesa 2003; O'Connor 1992, 1998; Werking 1997). Other studies have found differences in the size of friendship networks, with working-class people's networks being smaller than middle-class ones (Adams and Allan 1998; Allan 1979).

Some contributions have combined social network analysis and qualitative interviews, addressing the critique by Smart (2007: 7) that calling friendship a 'network' 'robs the concept of relationships of much of its emotional content and certainly does not invoke the special importance of connectedness, biography, and memory in how people relate to one other'. In fact, the whole tradition of mixed methods in social network analysis is vitally concerned with the multifaceted and interactional constructed meanings, biographies and memories embedded in relationships. Furthermore, it has enriched these 'stories' with the observation of structural embeddedness that can provide opportunities and constraints for relational life (Bellotti 2008a, 2008b; Bernardi *et al.* 2007; Bidart and Lavenu 2005; Edwards and Crossley 2009; Fischer 1982b; Hollstein forthcoming; Wellman 1990).

This research tradition, from the late 1970s, has come to conclusions similar to the ones reached by Smart (2007) and by the qualitative tradition regarding the ubiquity and variety of meaningful and significant relationships that overcome the limits of legal and ascribed bonds (Wellman 1979). Also, the combination of network data and qualitative accounts has stimulated a useful discussion about the validity and reliability of data collection tools (Bernard *et al.* 1984).

The mixed methods approach in social network analysis has made clear the variability of meanings associated with the concept of friendship. Fischer (1982a) found that the term 'friend' does not identify a particular kind of relationship but is used to name all the people who, although considered important, do not belong to other categories such as family, neighbours or colleagues. In 1984, Burt proposed a set of questions to elicit egonetworks in the General Social Survey planned for the following year, which specifically asked for names of 'people with whom you discussed an important personal matter' (Burt 1984: 331). To address the expected variability of the term, Burt also proposed to add a question that asks respondents to specify other ways in which nominated alters are related to them (being a relative, a neighbour, a co-worker, a friend, and the like).

Another way to reduce the indeterminacy of the term 'friend' is to ask people to name individuals they go to for certain kind of resources: who they ask for advice, who they discuss important matter with, who they ask for money or for small favours, and so on. They are subsequently asked a similar question that specifies the type of relationship that characterises these connections (e.g. if the named people lending money are relatives or friends). The main limitation of this method is that it only elicits names of people who are known for possessing specific skills or for providing some sort of support.

Although results from previous studies indicate that friendship is a good source of emotional support, material support, companionship and information (Spencer and Pahl 2006; Wellman 1990), the approach that relies on resource exchange excludes relationships where the direction of the support is inversed (from ego to alter), or any person who might be related to the interviewee but who provides no support. Furthermore, it may fail to turn up critical friendships, where relationships can become demanding and exploitative and that stiffen into patterns of interactions that make them difficult to change according to people's needs (Davies and Heaphy 2011; Smart *et al.* 2012). Quantification of the type of support provided by friendship may not describe fully the nature and extent of reciprocity, and when alter–alter ties are not collected, we do not observe the local structures in which friendship relations are embedded and whose configurations may vary in terms of size, density, structural holes and components.

The various types of friendship networks may have an impact on the overall balance of reciprocity and exchange that people can count on, and that balance may vary over time. By balance, I mean two distinct but related phenomena. Balance is intended as a relational situation within a dyadic tie where the level of reciprocity is satisfactory for ego, regardless of the equality of the exchange. It is also intended as a triadic and network configuration, where conflicts within a dyad spill over to other dyads and require a structural readjustment. The social mechanisms that describe and explain the dynamics of modifying and balancing ties across networks have emerged in the preliminary analysis of the qualitative material and may be formalised in a heuristic model (Figure 4.1).

The model can then be used to further analyse the interviews, in a proper grounded theory approach (Glaser and Strauss 1967): the first-order constructs, detected in the narrative accounts of the interviewees, inform the second-order constructs (Schutz 1966) that constitute the analytical categories of the research. In talking about friendship, the interviewees refer to an ideal dimension (the ideal level) that describes what friendship should look like and that is informed by collective definitions of the term. Such definitions constitute the stereotypical and collectively shared concept of friendship and include expectations about the potential availability of friends in providing support, their honesty, the lack of instrumental ends and exploitations, and the ease of interaction.

These definitions have stabilised over time as cultural configurations that emerged from longitudinal and overlapping multiple relations of friendship. Such ideal definitions and expectations are operationalised, over time, within concrete relationships, as rules about what in a relationship is permissible and desirable in terms of relevancy and how reciprocity works in terms of equivalence (Paine 1969: 509). Those rules are wholly contextual in friendship, meaning that they

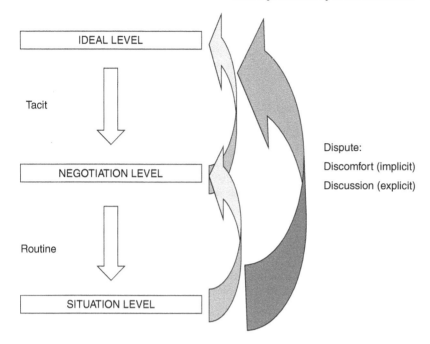

Figure 4.1 Dynamic mechanisms of friendship ties

are commonly negotiated in interactions (negotiation level) and represent the out-come of iterative struggles for control by friendship partners who have reached agreement on norms that specify friendship ties. These norms are mostly tacit: they emerge in interaction, develop over time, and eventually become taken for granted. By their tacit nature, they belong to the contextual definitions of relation-ships and require various degrees of impression management (Goffman 1959).

If situations occur where friends feel uncomfortable, if reciprocity is violated, or if networks result in unbalanced equilibriums (the situational level of concrete episodes as they are narrated in interviews), the ideal level becomes the term of reference by which relationships are evaluated and norms renegotiated, informing new routines, modifying the content of specific friendships, or moving friends across network positions. Thus, although rules are tacitly respected and routines are taken for granted, the alterable nature of friendship renders these dynamics highly unpredictable.

When forced to face serious betrayal or disillusion in concrete circumstances, people intervene in concrete situations (the situational level), for example, by changing the overall concept of friendship, discounting some ideal aspects, and cutting them down to size. Alternatively, they may stop a relationship that breaks the negotiated rules and that no longer conforms to the ideal. Those three levels—the ideal, negotiation and situational—influence and modify each other in a pro-cess through which friendship is renewed, reaffirmed, modified or rejected in each

encounter. Their definition is in line with the theorisation of relationships proposed in the previous chapter, where the various combinations of the dimensions
that constitute relational ties were argued to emerge out of the dynamic process
on interaction.

Mixed methodology and purposive sample

I move now to the case study at the heart of this chapter. The name generator was
open ended. Respondents were asked to name their friends, however they defined
that word and without limit to the number of alters. For each alter listed, I asked
about their age and gender, where they live, where they were born, with whom
they live, if they are single or partnered, their educational level, what job they
do, and how long they have known ego. Finally, I asked about the presence of
alter–alter ties, defined as the ego's perception of the existence of a relationship
between two friends independently from the one they have with ego. The result is
an emic version of each ego's personal network and does not necessarily reflect
changes in the evolution of actual ties between pairs of ego's friends.

In a subsequent meeting, the interviewees were shown a visualisation of their
personal network and told: 'Let's talk about these friends; you can start wherever
you like.' I used a funnel approach, beginning with general 'grand tour' questions
and moving to questions about specifics (Spradley 1979). Interviewees could cover
the topics in any order they wished and were not forced to cover all of them. If a
topic did not emerge spontaneously or after an interviewer's probe, it was recorded
as non-relevant for the interviewees. Topics were related to personal experiences,
relationship phases, normative aspects, and ideal definitions of friendship, ranging
from abstract concepts and ideal scenarios to concrete examples.

In this technique, the path of the interview is not shown to the interviewee: it is
memorised by the researcher, who is not allowed to ask direct questions but only
to guide the respondents to the listed topics using neutral inputs. These can take
the form of repeating interviewees' exact words and asking them to explain what
they mean by them, repeating previous sentences where general or abstract topics
were mentioned, and asking for concrete examples of what people refer to. This
technique is meant to minimise the impact of the researcher on the respondent by
getting people on to a topic and then getting out of the way (Bernard and Ryan
2010: 29). In a well-designed and conducted interview, the researcher intervenes
only a few times, without stopping the natural flow of the account, and only to
direct the narrative on a specific topic when it comes to a natural end. Finally,
interviewees were asked to place all the friends on a target of concentric circles
(similar to the one used by Hogan *et al.* 2007; see also Kahn and Antonucci 1980),
where people they felt closer to were placed in the inner circles and others in the
more distant ones.

In combination with in-depth interviews, network visualisations produce interesting and even unexpected results. For example, some interviewees grouped
friends together and defined the criteria that differentiate the groups. Others talked
about one friend at a time and then moved on to a dyadic level, discussing alters'

relationships with other friends. Some respondents named only very few close friends; others extended the network to a wider range of people they frequently interact with, using a more articulated and differentiated definition of friendship (friends they discuss important matters with, friends they share social activities with, friends of friends who they often see, and the like). Others named close friends in the network and more distant ones in the interview, specifying the criteria of inclusion.

These distinctions resemble, to a certain extent, the differentiation between friendship and friendly relationships, as formulated by Van de Bunt and colleagues (1999), the first being of a more intimate and personal nature, more demanding, more voluntary, but also involving more unique relationships than the second ones, which serve social and instrumental purposes like providing companionship or being handy in times of need. Despite their strict categorisation, Van de Bunt *et al.* (1999) admit that there are various degrees of friendship and that the term itself refers to an ambiguous, vague and multidimensional concept. Any attempt at classification should better locate concrete relationships on a continuous scale from close friends to acquaintances (Morgan 2009) and expect these relationships to be allowed to move along the spectrum rather than being encapsulated in categorical classifications.

These data collection methods were applied to a non-representative and purposively selected sample of 23 heterosexual singles (12 males and 11 females) living in Milan, between 25 and 35 years of age. Using theoretical sampling, the cases were not selected to generalise results to a larger population but to represent some of the possible variances in friendship configurations indicated in previous research. Thus, the choice of single youth was justified by the aim to investigate the role of friendship amongst a group that previous research indicates as relying on friends more than on other type of relationships, like family and neighbours, especially compared to their coupled peers or to people of older age (Fischer 1982b; Wellman 1990; Heath and Cleaver 2003; Watters 2003; Rosenail and Budgeon 2004; Spencer and Pahl 2006).

In addition to age and gender, people were selected for educational background (eight people with degrees, eight who left school after secondary education, and seven who left school after compulsory education).[1] This was done to explore possible differences in relationship styles and in the size of personal networks indicated by previous research (Adams and Allan 1998; Allan 1979; Wright 1982). All participants were born in Milan but lived in different areas of the city. People were selected using the snowball method, with different starting contacts. The starters were strangers or acquaintances who I selected via personal contacts (e.g. the owner of a shop close to the bar where I sometimes bought coffee, who was introduced to me by the barman; the working colleague of an acquaintance; the instructor of a friend's girlfriend; and the like). None of the participants were previously known to me nor did they know each other. The threshold to be included in the sample was simply the subjective perception of personal affective status.

All the people who participated in this research considered themselves single: this did not mean that they were not dating occasionally or that they had

Table 4.1 Sample's details

Name	Code	Gender	Educational background	Year of birth	Living with
Alberto	MM32	M	Compulsory studies	1973	Parents
Antonia	FM30	F	Compulsory studies	1975	Parents
Battista	MD28	M	Secondary school	1977	Parents
Caterina	FD33	F	Secondary school	1971	Alone
Daniele	MD34	M	Secondary school	1971	Alone
Giacomo	MM27	M	Compulsory studies	1977	Parents
Giovanna	FL26	F	Degree	1979	Parents
Jolanda	FM28	F	Compulsory studies	1977	Alone
Leonardo	ML27	M	Degree	1978	Parents
Leopoldo	ML31	M	Degree	1974	Friend
Marco	ML35	M	Degree	1969	Parents
Marisa	FM31	F	Compulsory studies	1975	Alone
Maurizio	MD35	M	Secondary school	1971	Alone
Melissa	FD27	F	Secondary school	1978	Sister
Michele	MM34	M	Compulsory studies	1971	Parents
Micol	FD28	F	Secondary school	1977	Parents
Monica	FL34	F	Degree	1970	Alone
Simone	ML28	M	Degree	1977	Parents
Sebastiano	MM28	M	Secondary school	1978	Parents
Silvia	FD35	F	Secondary school	1969	Alone
Tiziano	MD29	M	Secondary school	1976	Parents
Vanessa	FL30	F	Degree	1975	Alone
Veronica	FL28	F	Degree	1977	Parents

Note: The code (second column) indicates gender (M = male / F = female), educational background (M = compulsory studies / D = secondary school / L = degree) and year of birth.

not experienced important relationships in the past. Finally, the sample was differentiated according to living conditions, with 13 people still living with their parents, eight people living alone, and two cohabiting with friends. This was done to explore possible variations in the function of friendship for youth who reached some traditional targets of transition to adulthood, including leaving school, getting a job, and leaving their parents' household. Details of the sample are presented in Table 4.1.

People, relationships, local structures

Data analysis involved descriptive statistics, qualitative accounts and formal network measures and was conducted in three steps.

The first step describes the attributes of named friends. This was done through the compositional analysis of the characteristics of people included in the networks, which are derived both from the name interpreters and from the narrative accounts recoded in numerical terms. I used standard descriptive statistics—cross-tabulations. Although the sampled egos and their friends do not represent any larger population, this kind of analysis is still useful to explore the homophilous tendencies of friendship selection, observed in several studies (for a review, see McPherson *et al.* 2001). Along with the classification of similarities and differences in categorical terms, narratives offer contextual information about the nuances of perceived relationships. Informants' accounts of the histories and dynamics of friendships move beyond categorical attributes—friend, business partner, member of same church, and so on—and uncover people's understanding of similarities and differences in the ties that link them to their alters. In other words, narratives show how identities of actors embedded in relationships are framed by the content of interactions.

The second step of the analysis focuses on the features of dyadic exchanges by looking at the type of resources friendship provides. Again, the content of ties is seen not simply in terms of the quantity and type of capital exchanged but in the relational nature of the interactions, where individuals contextually define what, within each concrete friendship, was expected and allowed to be exchanged and what instead was considered demanding and exploiting. The analysis of the content of exchange allows us to observe the dynamics of reciprocity and balance, adopting the heuristic model described earlier.

By looking at reciprocity and balance, the third step of the analysis involved description of the whole egonetwork structure, where dyadic dynamics impact and are impacted by the structural features of interlocked friendship connections, by moving friends across positions, and by keeping the network connected. In the following sections, the results of these various steps are presented and discussed.

Homophily: compositional analysis of people's attributes

Overall, the 23 interviewees nominated 236 friends. The average age of friends is 29.48 years (st. dev. 4.8), which indicates a substantial age homophily: when there is a large age gap between friends, this is normally addressed in the interview where differences are thematised in terms of unbalanced reciprocity. Younger friends tend to ask for advice from older friends, but the direction of the advice exchange is rarely reciprocated within the same dyad. Friends are also homophilous in the place of residence, with 78 per cent living in Milan, 9 per cent in the regional area, 7 per cent in another Italian region, and 6 per cent abroad. This testifies, on the one hand, to the local nature of friendship networks, which tend to be formed within narrow spatial boundaries, and on the other hand to the maintenance of friendship ties at distance, with 22 per cent of friends not living in the same urban area (Mok *et al.* 2007).

With regard to educational background, in line with previous research (Allan 1979; Di Nicola 2003), respondents who completed secondary school tend to have larger networks than those who left school after compulsory studies, but also larger networks than people with a degree, indicating a non-linear relationship between educational level and size of networks (for the organisation of Italian educational system, see note 1 above). Conversely, the higher the educational level, the fewer non-educated friends are included in networks (Table 4.2).

Table 4.2 Total number of named friends by educational background

Educational background of the interviewee	Educational background of named friends				
	Compulsory school	Secondary school	Degree	Total	Average
Compulsory school (7 cases)	16	27	9	52	7.4
Secondary school (8 cases)	9	72	23	104	13.1
Degree (8 cases)	0	15	65	80	10.6

Table 4.3 Total number of named friends by gender

Gender of the interviewee	Gender of named friends		
	Male	Female	Total
Male			
Abs. Val.	80	37	117
%	68%	32%	100%
Female			
Abs. Val.	48	71	119
%	40%	60%	100%
Total			
Abs. Val.	128	108	236
%	54%	46%	100%

Finally, homophily has been observed to a certain extent also for gender, although networks do show some variance in their composition, with a slightly higher preference towards same-sex friendship for men (see Table 4.3).

These descriptive statistics show the overall homophily of friendship networks, but we can contextualise them with data from the interviews where respondents discuss their friendships in relational terms and where friends who are apparently similar in every respect are nonetheless differentiated according to interactive and dynamic features of the relationship. For example, in some cases friends are considered different from ego because of some different trajectories in life experiences, different points of view, or different behavioural traits:

> Marco and I are not very similar, as he lives in a tiny village, he comes from a very religious family, and he goes to church. Therefore I see him as quite naïve: coming from a big city I am much more materialistic, and I am an atheist.
>
> (Maurizio, MD35)

> Antonietta is a very deep, fantastic person, but she is also very meticulous, and she always wants to control other people's lives. I am very independent, and I struggle with these characteristics. Therefore she is a friend I can go out

Table 4.4 Examples of numerical coding of contexts of meeting

	IC	CO	VI	PA	SC	VZ	AA	RA
'Neri is someone I met at work as he used to be my colleague' (Daniele, MD34) 1		1						
'I met Marialuisa ten years ago in the bank I work. She taught me the job and passed me information. Then we started to see each other out of work, as we share the interest in salsa dance' (Monica, FL34) ...	1	1						
'We met at school, as we were all in the hockey team' (Tiziano, MD29)	1				1			
'I met Giulia at school, and Silvia a little later through Giulia' (Silvia, FD35) ...					1		1	

Note: IC = Common interest; CO = Co-worker; VI = Neighbour; PA = Relative; SC = School; VZ = Holiday; AA = Friends of friends; RA = Romantic relationship.

with for dinner and talk all night about my most intimate problems, but if I go on holiday with her I will kill myself.

(Monica, FL34)

Table 4.4 illustrates the extraction from the narratives of where and how friends met. These data show that categories do not have to be mutually exclusive, as friendship develops in overlapping contexts. Monica (FL34), for example, indicates that she met Marialuisa at work, but that they also shared an interest in salsa dance. Table 4.5 summarises the number of friends that each interviewee met in the various contexts identified in Table 4.4, presenting them both as absolute values and as a percentage of the whole egonetwork aggregated by gender and educational background.

These data show that men tend to meet their friends at school and in the neighbourhood more often than women do, while women prefer establishing relationships during holidays or through other friends. People who left school after compulsory studies tend to meet friends in the neighbourhood, at work or via common interests; people who completed secondary education tend to meet friends through already existing ties; and people with a degree tend to meet friends mainly at school. This descriptive analysis suggests that men tend to be more independent than women in establishing friendships, as the latter rely to a greater extent on existing friends. Also, the formation of friendship in different contexts for people with different educational backgrounds seems to reflect the time spent in specific social contexts, with lower-class youth who started to work earlier in life using neighbourhood and work environments more than people with a degree. Those

Table 4.5 Contexts of meeting named friends by interviewees' gender and educational background

		IC	CO	VI	PA	SC	VZ	AA	RA	Tot
Male (12 cases)	%	15%	9%	14%	1%	25%	11%	20%	5%	100%
	(Abs. Val.)	(20)	(12)	(18)	(1)	(33)	(15)	(27)	(7)	(133)
Female (11 cases)	%	17%	10%	6%	2%	22%	13%	25%	4%	100%
	(Abs. Val.)	(23)	(14)	(8)	(3)	(29)	(18)	(33)	(6)	(134)
Compulsory school (7 cases)	%	21%	13%	28%	2%	10%	7%	16%	3%	100%
	(Abs. Val.)	(13)	(8)	(17)	(1)	(6)	(4)	(10)	(2)	(61)
Secondary school (8 cases)	%	12%	12%	7%	2%	13%	14%	35%	5%	100%
	(Abs. Val.)	(15)	(15)	(8)	(2)	(16)	(17)	(42)	(6)	(121)
Degree (8 cases)	%	18%	4%	1%	1%	47%	14%	9%	6%	100%
	(Abs. Val.)	(15)	(3)	(1)	(1)	(40)	(12)	(8)	(5)	(85)

Note: IC = Common interest; CO = Co-worker; VI = Neighbour; PA = Relative; SC = School; VZ = Holiday; AA = Friends of friends; RA = Romantic relationship. The total number of people in this case (267) is not the same of the total number of named people (236). This is due to the fact that for some friends the meeting happened in overlapping contexts: school friends can also be neighbours or co-workers might share interests. In these cases, relationships are counted for more than one context, for example in both 'school' and 'neighbours'.

with a degree, having spent the longest time in education milieus, unsurprisingly met nearly half of their friends whilst studying.

Again, along with the categorical classification of friends according to the place or occasion on which they met, and the cross-tabulation of this information with other attributes, interviews show the relational nature of these definitions. In fact, regardless of the context of how people met, what distinguishes friendship from other kind of relationships (such as relatives or colleagues) is the free choice of sharing leisure time. This fundamental aspect is what informs the ideal definition of friendship as a freely chosen relationship, whereas the boundaries with other connections are blurred: relatives and colleagues are defined in friendship terms because the interaction is not dictated by ascribed expectations of commitments, but it is intentionally and reciprocally pursued. These are the terms, for example, by which Daniele (MD34) describes his relationship with co-worker Neri:

> I met Neri at work, because he used to be my colleague. I have to say I do not normally appreciate working colleagues because I do not like salesmen in general, thus it is very rare that I get along with them. I first hung around with Neri at working dinners, then we started to go out, and then one thing leads to another, he introduced me to his wife, he disclosed his problems to me, and I always enjoyed his company.
>
> (Daniele, MD34)

Social support: dyadic analysis of provided resources

Using the interviews it is also possible to code the kinds of support friendship offers. These, too, are in line with previous research (Wellman 1979, 1990), with friends providing emotional support (in terms of discussing personal issues), sociability (in terms of shared activities), material support (intended as help with practical tasks), information, and occasional economic help. As we have seen in the previous chapter, these dimensions, in variable combinations, are constitutive of any relationship (Crossley 2011), although every concrete relationship may display some dominant traits, like a specific focus on companionship or material support. For example, Simone, ML28, a 28-year-old university student who lives with his parents, divides his network into three groups, according to the kind of support they provide (Figure 4.2).

The group on the left in Figure 4.2 is composed of male friends, who only provide companionship when they share activities, go out for drinks, and go on holidays. The group on the right is made up of university friends, whom Simone meets up with when preparing for exams, sharing lecture notes, exchanging course books, and the like. The group at the bottom are all females and are the people Simone talks to when he has an intimate problem, as he does not feel comfortable in sharing emotional issues with his male friends. A similar role is covered by Marzia, on the bottom right, his former girlfriend.

Emotional disclosure is the most common type of support in friendship; it does not happen equally across all relationships, as it depends on the level of trust: the

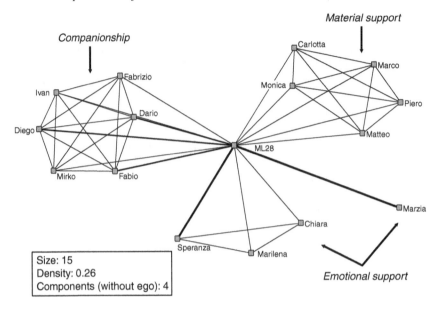

Figure 4.2 Simone's network, ML28

Note: Visualisations of egonetworks are done by keeping ego in the structure. This is because the relationships between ego and alters are valued, where values represent the position of alters in the concentric circles, 4 meaning a tie to a person located in the inner circle, and 1 being a tie to a person in the outer circle. The value is represented by the thickness of the line.

higher the level, the more intimate the friends are considered to be. Often the confidence relates to problems with romantic partners, but it also includes topics like arguments with friends, family matters and issues at work. The support can take the form of listening to individuals' disclosure or simply spending time together:

> Last year I had a difficult relationship with a man and Elena was always there listening to me, giving me very concrete advice. She is able not to deceive someone, but at the same time to say things in the right way, unlike me, I am harsher and more direct with friends, while she is always very sweet.
>
> (Marisa, FM31)

> Stefano went out with a woman for eight years and when she left him he was really down and did not want to do anything. Therefore I was always trying to take him out, to distract him in a way he would not think about her at least for the couple of hours he was out with me.
>
> (Michele, MM34)

Friends are expected to give honest advice and objective views, but are also expected to be understanding and to show affection. They can be entrusted with delicate matters without the risk of being morally judged, but also with the reassurance that intimacy allows friends to speak out in disagreement. The balance between confidentiality and discretion within an interaction becomes evident, according to Simmel (1921), when one person overcomes the intimacy boundaries of the other, who reacts with constraint. Although this dynamic can be found in any kind of relationship, the sensibility of alter towards ego is higher the more personal the relationship is, where ego feels more comfortable in disclosing her- or himself and alter knows ego well enough not to force intimacy boundaries.

> Given the length of the relationship, with Silvia, Elena and Camilla I can face more intimate matters like family problems, my career aspirations, the moments in which I doubt of myself, an ex-partner. They are the ones who can shake me, they can kick my arse when I cannot do it by myself, because sometimes I stagnate in a situation where the habit is more comfortable than a radical change that requires sacrifices and renunciations. When I get stuck in a habitual but dysfunctional situation I need them to get out of it.
>
> (Vanessa, FL30)

Companionship is another form of support largely provided by friends. Whilst it is a characteristic that differentiates friends from other types of relationships, as reciprocal companionship is freely chosen by friends, it is also needed by single people to avoid loneliness. Friends are good companions for going out, going on holidays, doing sports, organising dinners, spending time together at home, or watching movies: they are the source of companionship that helps one avoid spending free time alone.

> There is the Easter dinner, which we renamed the dinner of the abandoned who are left alone when everyone is on holiday.
>
> (Leopoldo, ML31)

> If you are 30 and you go out on your own, you are a loser. If you see a 30-year-old sitting alone in a bar, drinking something, you will think he is a poor soul, with no one to go out with. Because at that age you should have a friend to go out with, while going out on your own sounds quite strange.
>
> (Michele, MM34)

Shared activities, when done with a more or less stable group of friends, also facilitate the emergence of a collective identity. Leopoldo, for example, names a group of long-term friends he plays basketball with, and refers to them as his 'reference friends, the ones I spend my time with. We are the historical core; we have known each other for more than 10 years' (Leopoldo, ML31). Out of the network, but named during the interview, there is a larger circle of less-close friends, who are not involved regularly enough in the shared activities to be part of 'them'. This distinction resembles the definitions of reference groups proposed by White (2008 [1992]) and noted by Crossley (2011). In this case, the reference group of friends develop a shared sense of belonging that draws symbolic boundaries around the

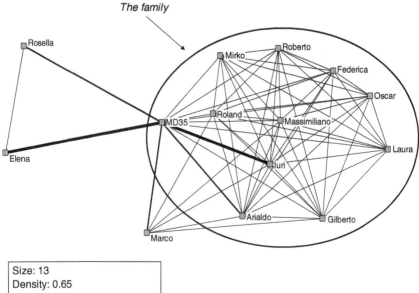

Figure 4.3 Maurizio's network, MD35

network and are mainly, if not exclusively, recognised by the actors who belong to it.

The distinction between emotional support and companionship also introduces interesting elements of gender differences in relationship styles. In some cases, like Marisa (FM31) and Michele (MM34) discussed above, the narrative accounts confirm traditional gender stereotypes, like men's preference for shared activities and women's preference for intimate connections. Other cases do not confirm such stereotypes, like that of Simone (ML28), presented earlier, who seeks emotional support from his female friends (see Figure 4.2), or of Maurizio (MD35), who confides equally in male and female friends (Figure 4.3). Similarly, the narrative accounts give examples of women who prefer the friendship of men for disclosure of intimate and personal matters and others who reject this kind of support from their friendship networks in favour of simple companionship.

Finally, friendship is a source of material support, such as the exchange of gifts, help with studying or work, small economic loans, or exchange of information. The examples provided by the interviewees are all of the small and short-term variety and they are adjusted according to the level of familiarity: the closer the friends are perceived to be, the more the interviewees feel they can rely on them. The combined analysis of qualitative accounts with network structure and concentric circles of alters shows that according to the type of support and the multiplexity of provision, friends might occupy different positions within personal networks, and the relationship with them varies in strength.

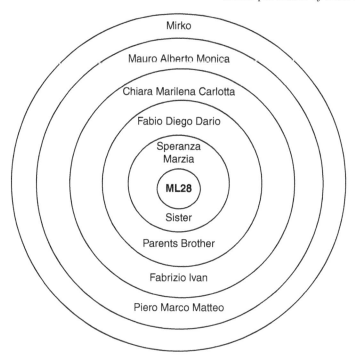

Figure 4.4 Concentric circles of Simone, ML28

In general, friends who provide emotional support or a combination of several kinds of support tend to be placed in the inner circles within the target. For example, in the case of Simone (ML28, Figure 4.2), the women who grant emotional help are placed closer to ego in the concentric circles than the men providing simple companionship or the university friends providing material support, regardless of the length of the relationship, which is longer for the clique of male friends (Figure 4.4).

Reciprocity: from dyads to structure

The combination of structural analysis and qualitative accounts is also useful for disentangling the tacit aspects of reciprocity and balance across networks. Empirical evidence suggests that friendship selection tends to evolve reciprocally, meaning that over time friends are inclined to align their reciprocal definitions of friendship (Van de Bunt *et al.* 1999). In other words, a statistically significant probability shows that if someone chose someone else as a friend, there is a higher chance that the relationship will be reciprocated.

Van de Bunt and colleagues' results are important for understanding the diffusion of a relational mechanism (Van de Bunt *et al.* 1999). Narrative accounts, however, help illuminate how reciprocity works: they tell us, from the perceptions of the interviewees, about the content of the expected obligations implied by reciprocity and about what is actually exchanged in reciprocal relations. What emerges, for example, is that reciprocity in dyads does not have to be explicit or immediate: friends do not keep count of provided support, and sometimes it is accepted that reciprocity might be deferred for future times, or might be exchanged with different currencies. Thus, a friend who is going through difficult times may need intensive emotional or material support without being able to return the favour in the near future; friends can exchange confidence with companionship, for example, by listening to someone's problems whilst doing social activities.

The overall balance can be found not only at different times or in different currencies, but can also be spread across the whole personal network: the interviewees may receive material support from a specific friend and reciprocate with companionship, whilst conversely offering material support to someone else who reciprocates with emotional help. The type of provided support, its continuity, and its quality depend on what friends have to offer and what they need in specific circumstances. The networked nature of friendship support and the deferred or heterogeneous reciprocity that circulate across different ties emerge in the interviews:

> Germana is someone I dedicated a lot of time to when I thought she needed it. Our friendship has always been based in this way, she talks to me and I listen, but I never say anything private to her. I am not the kind of person who looks for friends in order to talk, I am more than happy to listen, but I never feel the need to open up with them.
>
> (Marco, ML35)

> Friendship with Deborah is somehow unbalanced, because she is not happy at the moment. She is not a person I have fun with, but I do care for her, and the care sprang out from the love I have for Jennifer, who is her very close friend. Deborah needed help and Jennifer was not here, but I was. And she reciprocated with so much love that we became very close.
>
> (Giovanna, FL26)

> It is more Massi who looks for me if he needs to spill out some problems. If he needs a chat he will send me a text, but I do not do the same with him. I see him as too young; therefore if I need to talk I prefer to go to Yuri or Marco.
>
> (Maurizio, MD35)

Balance: dynamics of friendship ties and networks

The possibilities of balancing reciprocities across friendship structures do not imply that equilibrium is always reached. Sometimes dyads and network dynamics result in unbalanced situations, which can be sources of frustration and discomfort: in these situations, people can try to modify the nature of dyadic interactions by discussing it with friends. They may also try to break dysfunctional habits and routines or modify the structure of the personal networks by distancing themselves from or getting closer to people, ending relationships, or adding new friends. The adoption of the heuristic model of the dynamic nature of friendship ties, shown in Figure 4.1, is useful to analyse the qualitative accounts that report situations of discomfort and discussion and the ways in which conflicts have been resolved. For example, Marco (ML35) describes his relationship with Stefano, in which the two men tacitly agree not to talk about private issues. When noticing an obvious discomfort in the friend, Marco tries to break the rule, but Stefano reclaims it in its original terms, and the friendship realigns on the previous agreement:

> Ideal Level: Stefano and I are both not very open to dialogue; we do not have a friendship in the sense of talking about personal matters.
> Negotiation Level: We keep each other in high esteem, but there is the tacit agreement of not digging into inappropriate matters.
> Situational Level: There has been a period in which I felt that things between him and his wife were not going that well; therefore it happened a couple of times that I asked him 'Well … so?' At the third one he replied: 'Mind your own business.'
>
> (Marco, ML35)

There are also cases in which disputes imply a modification of the negotiation level, which conversely informs new routines, to realign unbalanced friendships to the ideal level. This is the case in Vanessa (FL30)'s long-term relationship with Donatella, which is weakened after repetitive exploitation. At the ideal level, Vanessa believes that friends should not take advantage of her availability, but she adjusts the ideal in loose terms in relation to Donatella, who has a habit of borrowing things. The continual requests are tolerated by Vanessa because of the length of the relationship, and they are excused as it is a typical trait of Donatella's personality. The ideal feature of friendship, according to which friends should accept each other's faults, plays a role against the ideal balance of reciprocity. However, the unbalanced relationship reaches a threshold when Vanessa realises that Donatella's requests have become arrogant and insistent:

> For example, Donatella will call saying, 'Please I have a date with this guy and if I don't wear that outfit he won't even look at me!' The outfit is the one that I have longed for for ages, I saved money for, I bought it and never wore it because it is too beautiful to be worn, and she wants exactly that one. And I have often given in, I give her an inch, she'll take a mile, at the point in which I could not stand it anymore and I told her to get lost. In theory she is a fantastic person, someone to have fun with, and with fewer flaws she would be part of the core of intimate friends, while now she is out. She is not even out, she is only in through Mariafiore and Chiara.
>
> (Vanessa, FL30)

Here, the breaking of the rule of reciprocity and the subsequent unbalanced situation has caused a reaffirmation of an ideal level of lack of exploitation, and the informed rule of not taking advantage of friends' willingness. By reaffirming

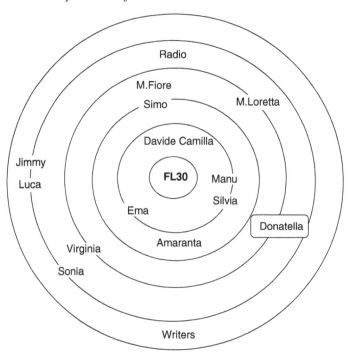

Figure 4.5 Concentric circles of Vanessa, FL30

those levels, Donatella's position within Vanessa's personal network changes as shown in the target of concentric circles where she is located far out, much further than the core of close friends (Figure 4.5).

A similar case that involves the removal of a friend from the network and her repositioning in the outer circle of the target is that of Samantha, an old friend of Antonia's (FM30) who betrayed her, causing a whole reconfiguration of the ideal level of friendship, the informing of a new set of rules, and the entire modification of the network (situational level):

> Ideal Level: Samantha and I used to go out for hours, and then come back home and spend the nights at the phone. It was a very close relationship, but I never considered it obsessive as it was natural for me.
> Negotiation Level: She wanted our relationship to be exclusive, she used to say we should not go out with anyone else, and I paid heed to her. She said she was too jealous of other friends.
> Situation Level: Then she started to hang around in a bar of a guy she knew, and she met other people. They did not like me, so she had to choose between me and them. And she chose them.
>
> (Antonia, FM30)

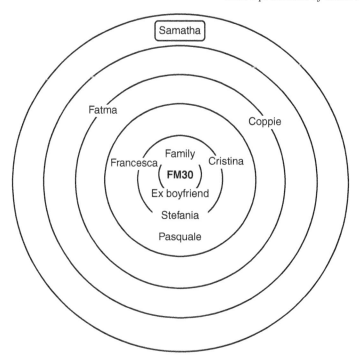

Figure 4.6 Concentric circles of Antonia, FM30

The two girls shared an ideal level of friendship based on exclusivity, which they concretised in the explicit rule of not seeing anyone else. Such high demand, which is not commonly required from a friendship and does not belong to the collective cultural scripts defining this kind of interpersonal relationship, was betrayed by Samantha, who slowly and silently walked away from Antonia without discussing any possible reconfiguration. Antonia could not negotiate a new ideal that informed a new set of rules within the specific relationship with Samantha. She therefore modified the ideal level of what she means about friendship, found new friends who are more attuned to her and with less demanding ideals, and negotiated a new set of rules that implies the whole modification of the personal network:

> Reconfiguration of the Ideal Level: I thought it was a forever friendship; nothing lasts forever, not to mention friendship! No, I don't believe anymore in forever friendship.
> Reconfiguration of the Negotiation Level: Exclusivity is something Stefania [one of the new friends] explained to me. After the disillusion with Samantha I do not want to have any other exclusive relationships, because otherwise I tend to exclude other people in my life.
>
> (Antonia, FM30)

Reconfiguration of the Situational Level: Whilst Samantha was previously Antonia's only friend, Antonia's network has now enlarged to include a clique of three friends, although in the target Samantha still appears in the outer circle (Figure 4.6).

Finally, there are cases in which the effects of unbalanced friendship spill over into other relationships, like in the case of Simone (ML28) discussed above. Simone recently had an argument with Mirko, who was part of the companionship clique. Mirko, like the other men, was an old friend who had been part of the clique for many years. The group had the tacit rule (Negotiation Level) not to flirt with each other's partners. However, Mirko fell in love with a woman who, instead of reciprocating, had feelings for Simone, and Simone decided to go out with her (Situational Level). Mirko and Simone fell apart, but the whole argument ended up dividing the clique of old friends, with the other men taking Simone's side.

> The problem with Mirko was that he accused me of stealing his girlfriend. But everyone told him how stupid it was, as he never dated her. He made this story up, well, that is what I think, but the others think the same. And we couldn't even talk about it, he pretended he was right, therefore the relationship weakened and seeing him was embarrassing. Since that episode, everyone judged him in a different way, as everyone was against him, and they started to criticise him on other aspects of his personality. Things that were hushed up before were now spoken. Therefore he started to distance himself from our group and buddy up much more with the guys in his band. And we now don't talk to him much. We still see him, he is still part of the group as we have many friends in common, but the relationship is not much more of just saying hello.
>
> (Simone, ML28)

In this case, the different interpretation of the friendship rule is not discussed between Mirko and Simone, as Mirko refuses to negotiate (Lack of Reconfiguration of the Negotiation Level). As a result of the dyadic unbalance between them, the entire clique of friends modifies their perception of and their behaviour towards Mirko. He ended up by leaving the group, and the distance is reflected in his position within Simone's target of concentric circles, much further than the other men (Reconfiguration of the Situational Level, see Figure 4.4).

Structural configurations of friendship networks

In the last part of the chapter the previous analyses of attributes, dyadic exchange, and ties and network dynamics are combined with the structural characteristics of egonetworks to produce some possible types. By combining size, density measures, component analysis, and the subjective description contained in the qualitative accounts, it is possible to identify four main network types: the small clique, and its variation of the star; the company, and its variation of the fragmented

Table 4.6 Typologies of friendship networks

Name	Code	Type of structure	Size	Density	N. components
Marisa	FM31	Company	10	1	1
Leonardo	ML27	Company	7	1	1
Jolanda	FM28	Company	6	0.86	1
Caterina	FD33	Company	11	0.85	1
Leopoldo	ML31	Company	12	0.78	1
Giovanna	FL26	Company	20	0.75	1
Micol	FD28	Company	26	0.71	3
Sebastiano	MM28	Company	11	0.69	1
Daniele	MD34	Company	17	0.66	3
Maurizio	MD35	Company	13	0.65	2
Melissa	FD27	Contextual components	6	0.66	1
Michele	MM34	Contextual components	6	0.6	1
Battista	MD28	Contextual components	14	0.56	1
Simone	ML28	Contextual components	15	0.26	4
Veronica	FL28	Contextual components	6	0.26	3
Vanessa	FL30	Core–periphery	19	0.49	1
Silvia	FD35	Core–periphery	15	0.33	1
Giacomo	MM27	Fragmented group	11	1	1
Alberto	MM32	Fragmented group	5	1	1
Antonia	FM30	Small clique	3	1	1
Tiziano	MD29	Small clique	3	1	1
Marco	ML35	Small clique	3	1	1
Monica	FL34	Star	3	0	3

group; the core–periphery; and the contextualised components, where subgroups can be defined according to various criteria.[2] These are not rigid taxonomic types in the sense that a network may straddle two categories or may have evolved from one to another; they are not even exhaustive, as within a larger sample of egonetworks other types may emerge.

More importantly, narrative accounts show how similar structures may have different meanings and functions and how similar functions may be exercised by different configurations. They are, however, useful to categorise people's friendship networks and to identify possibilities and constraints embedded in those structural configurations. These elements are summarised in Table 4.6: basic measures of egonetworks (size, density and number of components) are calculated excluding ego. This is because ego is, by definition, connected to everyone else; therefore its inclusion would bias the measures and it would make it impossible to distinguish separated components. Also, valued ties from ego to alters impact on density measurement, which for valued data is equal to the average value of ties.

The small clique and the star

The main characteristic of the first typology of friendship networks is that the small clique, and its variation the star, includes only three friends, either fully connected (clique), or completely isolated (star). Although different, these structures are merged in a single category because they present similar characteristics: the small number of named friends depends on a very narrow definition of friendship that includes only long-term and close friends highly homophilous in terms of gender. The difference between the two variants lies in the fact that while ego describes the clique as a little group of friends who normally interact together or used to interact in the past, the star is composed of people who know each other but have not developed a relationship independently from ego, who interacts with them separately.

Three people typify the structure of the clique. Antonia (FM30), female, 30 years old, who left school after compulsory studies, works in a factory and lives with her parents. We already met Antonia in the previous section, where the reconfiguration of her friendship with Samantha implied a shift of investment from a single friend towards three women who are all close friends with each other. She describes them as equally close to her and as a valuable source of emotional support, although she complains about the lack of shared interests, which means she does not obtain the companionship she would like from her network:

> I had to calm down: sometimes I would get up in the morning, feeling up for so many things; then I called them and none of them wanted to do anything. So what was I supposed to do, go out on my own? At the beginning I used to get incredibly angry, do you know how many times we argued about it? But they are who they are, they don't like to go out, and we very rarely go clubbing.
>
> (Antonia, FM30)

A similar specialisation in the type of support characterises the clique of Marco (ML35), male, 35 years old, who is studying for a degree in architecture whilst working as a software instructor and living with his parents. As we saw earlier, Marco only requires companionship from his friends, excluding any kind of emotional exchange:

INTERVIEWER: What do the people you named give you?
MARCO: We spend time together ... well don't let me reduce it like that, it seems very superficial. But at the very core, I believe everyone sees friendship in his own personal way. With Stefano, for example, there isn't a friendship in the sense of talking about things, as we both are not very talkative. There is reciprocal respect, and there is the tacit agreement of not talking about private matters.

(Marco, ML35)

The exclusive specialisation of friendship in a specific type of support, although not always intended (as in the case of Antonia), seems one of the main reasons for the narrow size of the network. For Marco, the rejection of any kind of emotional involvement limits inclusion in his network of friends to the point where he feels the need to justify his ideal dimension for the researcher, who is perceived as a 'generalised other' (Mead 1934: 90), someone with a broader and collectively shared idea of friendship. For Antonia, such a small configuration is the outcome of previous disillusions that modified the ideal dimension according to which she defines friendship.

A similarly narrow definition of friendship that seems to derive from past disillusionment is the one utilised by Monica (FL34), female, 34 years old, and graduated with a master's degree. Monica works in a bank and lives alone. Her network typifies the shape of a star, which includes three women who have proved their loyalty and availability over the years. They provide different kinds of support and don't know one another. One is a senior colleague who mentored Monica at work and with whom Monica shares the passion of salsa dance and exotic travel. Another is an old friend who lives in another city and used to be a travel partner. She provides Monica with emotional support but is now less available due to family commitments. The last one is Monica's sister-in-law who provides only emotional support. During the interview, Monica also mentions former female friends who, on past occasions, have revealed themselves as competitive and envious people. Due to those negative past experiences, she now only fully relies on her three current friends, referring to several other people as acquaintances with whom she would go out for a drink but whom she would not directly include in the network, nor in the concentric circles.

Finally, the last person who presents the structure of a clique is Tiziano (MD29), male, 29 years old. He left school after a secondary school diploma, works in a factory, and lives with his parents. He named three male friends he met in primary school who were classmates until the end of secondary school. The four men grew up together and used to spend the whole day hanging out at school and after school. In the past, they were a multiple source of companionship, providing social and material support for each other. Two of them still provide emotional support, companionship and material help (helping to fix the bike, moving furniture, and the like). A third now lives in another city and does not provide support anymore, but he is still considered part of the clique due to the length and the intensity of the relationship. Whilst these are the only people named in the network, several other people are mentioned as acquaintances in the target but not discussed in the interview: the narrow criteria of inclusion seem to depend not so much on past disillusionment, but on Tiziano's discretion and shyness that emerged through the interview.

The company and the fragmented group

The second type of friendship networks is what I call 'the company', intended as a close-knit group of friends, which is also the most common in the sample (nine people). There is also the variance of the fragmented group (indicated by two people in the sample). These configurations are characterised by a larger and broader range of sizes, from five to 26 nodes, and a high density, from 0.65 to one. They are also normally composed of a single component, although sometimes a few minor components of very small size appear outside the main one, indicating friends with an independent and dyadic relationship with ego.

The company is normally a group of a few long-term friends who met in childhood or adolescence and have developed a collective sense of belonging and a shared identity over time. It is distinguished from the fragmented group as the latter lacks this specific collective identity, being simply a group of people who tend to frequently interact for common activities or through ego's mediation. This is the case of Alberto (MM32), male, 32 years old, who left school after compulsory studies, works as a computer technician, and lives with his mother. He named a close-knit group of five friends who only interact together in playing role games. They don't share any other activity so, although they all know each other, they aren't described in the interview as a group with a shared and collective identity.

In contrast, members of a company tend to spend all their free time together, whether in dyads or small subgroups, and to meet up in a set of regular locations (a local park, someone's house, the neighbourhood basketball court, a holiday resort, a bar). By virtue of their shared sense of belonging, the company can sometimes develop a set of rituals and rules by which they evaluate possible emerging conflicts and resolve disputes. The case of Daniele (MD34), male, 34 years old, with a secondary school diploma, who works as a salesman and lives alone, is particularly significant for the illustration of how those tacit, shared rules work.

Daniele's company formed during childhood at a holiday resort not far from Milan: every year the group organises an end-of-summer party, an annual ritual where everybody is invited, marking one's belonging to the company. Once they set a date for the party, the invitations are sent by word of mouth. Recently, several people had arguments with one member, who was accused of being an opportunist: no one in the group felt comfortable about inviting him to the party and when they gathered, they noticed his absence and realised he had been excluded. The tacit rule developed in the company, of not taking advantage of friendship, produced an unspoken, collective behaviour that excluded the friend who purportedly had violated the norm.

The company's high density and shared identity can also imply that people may be included for the simple reason of being highly connected with everyone else, although they are just slightly more than familiar strangers (Milgram 1977). This is the case of Micol (FD28, female, 28 years old, with a secondary school diploma, who owns an ironmonger shop and lives alone) and of Marisa (FM31, female, 31 years old, who left school after compulsory studies, owns a wax shop, and lives alone). They both include in the clique structure of their company people they do not interact with, either because they do not share much in common with them, because they do not particularly like them, or because they don't know them very well. Interestingly, even during the interview, when describing these people in indifferent or negative terms, they refused to pull them out of the network, as the stickiness of the clique is so high (Krackhardt 1998) that it keeps these 'unfriendly' friends in the structure.

Alessandro is the one I know less. Because in the company there are people I normally ignore. I mean, they are always there, but I don't interact with them; not because I don't get along with them, but just because I have no interest in knowing them better. I don't know why, but there are people I do consider friends, even if I am not interested in knowing what they do with their life. I don't do it on purpose, sometimes we exchange few words, but then we don't have anything to say, maybe because we don't have much in common.

(Micol, FD28)

The development of a sense of shared identity and belonging is sometimes represented by the adoption of a collective name. Leopoldo (ML31, male, 31 years old, with a degree, who works in a bank, and lives with a flatmate), simply refers to his company as 'us', opposed to 'them', 'them' being more distant friends who are not named in the network but only during the interview. Maurizio (MD35, male, 35 years old, with a diploma from secondary school, works as a computer technician and lives alone) calls his company 'the family' (see Figure 4.3), indicating how friendship, as an elective family, can become a substitute for ascribed families.

Such a substitutive role has been previously noted and widely discussed in qualitative research (Roseneil and Budgeon 2004; Weeks *et al.* 2001; Weston 1998). In these last two examples, the elective 'families' provide multiple type of support, regardless of the substantive gender homophily: unlike the case of Simone, who relies on his female friends for gaining emotional support, Leopoldo and Maurizio confide equally in men and women, and confidences are spread across the company that collectively takes care of its members' well-being. But similarities with elective families also mean that sometimes friendship 'stories' and networks are so settled and locked in habits and routines that they end up refusing to accept changes and personal developments.

Giovanna (FL26, female, 26 years old, with a university degree, works as an art director in an advertising agency and lives with her parents) is part of a company mainly composed of long-term friends from the Jewish community in Milan: they all went to the same school since childhood, and developed a durable, intense and highly dense network. After finishing secondary school, Giovanna spent two years in Israel: the experience had a strong impact on her personality, on her relationships with some friends, and on the overall network. She became a more confident person, but she found that people back home did not adapt to her new identity very well. The lack of recognition of her grown-up identity prompted her to make new friends outside the Jewish community, but the stickiness of the highly cohesive structure has prevented her from leaving the company altogether. Similar effects of network density in hampering the adoption of new identities and social roles were also observed by Bott (1956) in relation to conjugal roles.

The core–periphery

The third type of friendship networks presents a core of close and intimate friends who provide multiple kind of support, who are all located in the inner circles of the interview target, and who constitute a denser cluster within the network. This dense core is connected to one or more peripheral friends, or sets of friends, who only provide companionship. Two women in the sample present this structural configuration. Vanessa, FL30 (30 years old, with a university degree, works in an embassy during the day and as a DJ at night; see Figure 4.5 for concentric circles), and Silvia, FD35 (35 years old, with a secondary school diploma, works in a small import–export firm). They both live alone and report a highly cohesive core of very close friends, mainly women, who provide emotional support, material support and companionship. The core is linked to groups of other friends, with whom these women share specific activities like going out for drinks, doing sports, going on holidays, attending courses, and the like. The distinction between core and peripheral friends is made explicitly by the interviewees:

> There are the intimate friends, the ones who know me better; and then there are the wider circles of friends, people whom I like to go out for a drink, to go to the cinema, to a festival or a gig, but whom I don't see very often for several reasons. Mainly because I don't have enough time, I already have all these friends, and others I would like to know better, so I tend to organise occasions in which I invite them all. Like Davide's friends, I should put them together in a single node, as when I organise a party they always come together, and they ended up knowing all my other friends.
>
> (Vanessa, FL30)

> Let me start with friends I am closer with, who are Paola, Giulia, Silvia, Michela, because I have known them forever. There is also my sister ... well she is my closest friend really. The others are more recent, and they are more acquaintances than friends. With Paola we got closer this year because we went on holiday together, but she is very reserved so it is difficult for her to disclose confidences. But I see the others only when we go out in the night, we go drinking or clubbing. I cannot consider them real friends; we do not call each other.
>
> (Silvia, FD35)

The main criterion of inclusion in the core is the length of the relationship, which also implies emotional support: such close and intimate friendship demands investment of time and resources, confirming the existence of a maximum number of strong ties individuals can maintain due to the effort required to sustain them (Bernard *et al.* 2001; Dunbar 1992). These strong ties are also referred to in terms of elective families, the robust and stable circle of people who always remain in someone's life even when life situations, like acquiring a new partner, reduce the time able to be spent with friends:

> A new love does not know me as they do. Then there is obviously the excitement of novelty, but there is also the feeling to recover in the safe circle, the one that represents my family. And there is also the delicate moment in

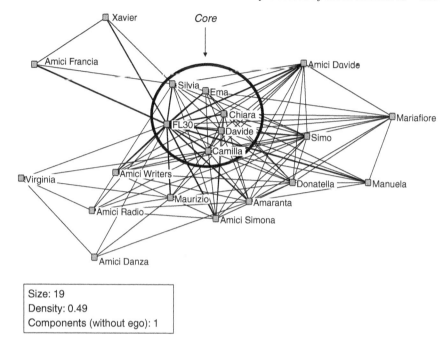

Size: 19
Density: 0.49
Components (without ego): 1

Figure 4.7 Vanessa's network, FL30

which the new lover is introduced to friends. What if they do not like him? I might be madly in love, what do I do? Do friends come first? But also giving priority to the man is a pain in the heart. But then when I had a boyfriend what happened was that I had to leave all those friends, the circle narrowed down to the first base, the core, because they are the friends who count most.

(Vanessa, FL30; see Figure 4.7)

Here again the network of friends is defined with the metaphor of the family, testifying to the central role of friendship in the affective lives of single people (Roseneil and Budgeon 2004; Spencer and Pahl 2006; Watters 2003).

The contextualised components

The last type of friendship networks is that of contextualised components, where people differentiate their relationship in independent subgroups according to various criteria. One of these is the distinction based on the kind of support friends provide, as we have seen in the case of Simone described earlier. Another criterion is the context of interaction, according to which people distinguish friends at work from friends they see in leisure time, or friends they only see on holidays, or friends they only see when they go to the city. Five people indicate this type of structure, although in three cases the components are connected not only by ego but also by one or two bridging friends, who interact with the distinctive groups.

This is the case of Battista (MD28, male, 28 years old, with a secondary school diploma, a salesman who lives with his family) who distinguishes between friends he interacts with during the day in the estate agency where he works and friends he grew up with in the neighbourhood. These are connected by himself and by one colleague who plays football with Battista's neighbours' friends.

A similar distinction is presented in Veronica's network (FL28, female, 28 years old, with a university degree, who works as an accountant in a small firm of her friend's father and lives with her parents). In her case, components distinguish university friends from work colleagues and a neighbour she has known since she was a child. In the case of Melissa (FD27, female, 27 years old, with a secondary school diploma, a primary school teacher who lives with her sister) and Michele (MM34, male, 34 years old, left school after compulsory studies, is unemployed, and lives with his family), components differentiate the group of friends they see exclusively on holiday from the group they see at home.

Conclusion

In the previous chapter, I laid out the foundational bricks of network science: actors, social relations and networks. The case study of friendship presented in this chapter, with its mixture of egonetwork structure and in-depth qualitative interviews, illustrates how these analytical bricks can be observed and disentangled. The combination of the two methods has also revealed itself to be extremely useful in detecting relational mechanisms and in observing how they operate in specific interactional contexts. Homophilous mechanisms of friendship selection, for example, suggest the resistance of social boundaries between classes, ethnicities, age and, to a lesser extent, gender.

By enlarging the perspective from individual actors to dyadic interactions, we see how attributes defining these actors are not fixed and ascribed individual characteristics, but are relational constructs defined in interactions. Moving on to network configurations we have also started to observe a high level of dynamism. Friends evaluate their relationship by relying on subjective and collective ideals that emerged from past interactions and the overlapping texture of friendship ties. These ideals are negotiated in adaptable norms, which, in turn, inform interactions allowing the management of unbalanced situations. In doing so, actors adapt and modify their friendship networks according to shared and settled cultural frameworks. The frameworks are built up with stories that define the nature of each relationship: although each story is specific, the frameworks can be transferred across friendship ties and networks and used to observe similarities and variations in the relational dynamics.

The mixed method approach allows us to overcome the limits of categorical analysis, which, by simply relying on the aggregation of variable data, may miss some important transformations of dyadic ties and networks. Qualitative accounts explore the subjective perceptions of personal network dynamics and the mechanisms that regulate reciprocity and balance, and social network analysis provides the overall structural configuration that regulates individual opportunities and constraints. The combination of the various levels and methodologies of analysis shows the reciprocal effects that both attributes and meanings have over networks, where dyadic interactions shape the forms of structural configurations, and that networks have over dyads, allowing people to be moved across positions or to be substituted with new friends.

Notes

1 The educational system in Italy is organised as follows: primary school is from the age of 6 to 10 (five years); middle school is from the age of 12 to 14 (three years); secondary school is from the age of 15 to 19 (five years). In secondary school, students can choose the type of course, focusing on technical skills (where courses can last for three years instead of five) or on various academic subjects (scientific, humanistic, linguistic, artistic). After the five-year courses, students obtain a diploma and can access university degrees. School is compulsory for everyone up to the first year of secondary school regardless of what course they choose.
2 A preliminary analysis is presented in Bellotti (2008a, 2008b).

5   Ethnography of overlapping networks

Resource exchange in street groups

The second empirical example I use to illustrate how social network analysis can be incorporated in a qualitative study involves two informal street groups of young Italian men, between 15 and 23 years old, living in a peripheral suburb of Milan. The suburb is characterised by several kinds of social deprivation and the members of the street groups are highly engaged in petty criminal activities.[1]

The groups were longitudinally monitored via ethnographic observations, following a research design in line with the method of analytical induction and retroduction discussed in Chapter 2. According to this strategy, one group was initially observed in its daily activities. Ethnographic data were used to locate the boundaries of the group, as they were perceived by its participants. This subject-ive perception was grounded in a long-term and established core of reciprocal, intense relationships, from which the group developed a collective shared identity, cultural norms and conventions.

The ethnographic data collected with the first group were then used to formulate some working hypothesis that I tested against a second group. This was accessed through one of the boys, who belonged to both groups. I shadowed him for a period of time long enough to become acquainted with the second group, until I felt able to conduct participant observation with them. As with the personal networks discussed in the previous chapter, these groups were fundamentally based on friendship. Whilst information in the previous cases was collected as narratives in interviews with independently observed focal actors, in the street ethnography I followed actors in their daily activities over an extended period of time. In doing this, I was able to check the consistency of their reported ties to other members of the groups. By following them, I was also able to observe their meaningful interactions with other people and with members of different, similarly structured groups and to see the points of intersection of overlapping networks. I was then able to look at the identity dynamics and the resource exchanges that were tak-ing place when the groups interacted with other relevant actors (e.g. other street groups, youths and adults).

The first group was observed via 'moderate participant observations' (Spradley 1980: 60) and ethnographic interviews (Spradley 1979). Moderate participant observation entails playing an observation role without actively participating in the activities that observed people do (Spradley 1980: 60). These activities involved, for example, smoking hashish, driving scooters around and doing wheelies, and selling drugs. Informal and unstructured ethnographic interviews were used to ask the boys to clarify what was going on in specific situations or to describe something that happened while I was not there so as to obtain details about shared cultural norms and conventions (Bernard and Ryan 2010).

The second group was observed during six months of participant observations, where I identified and took part in the group's salient activities, either during the day (buying and selling drugs, scouting tours of potential thefts, exchanging stolen goods) or during the night (drinking aperitifs, going out for dinner, going to bars and clubs). During the observations, I also conducted informal ethnographic interviews and organised a focus group with six of the boys. Aside from these primary data, I also had many informal discussions (about data collection, analysis and interpretation) with the coordinator of the local youth centre (who was working with the first group), and I did an in-depth interview with the coordinator of another local youth centre (Youth service coordinator #2) who was not directly involved with any of the groups under observation. The interview with a second coordinator was useful to verify the consistency of the descriptive frameworks that youth services adopt to define street groups and to work with them. Both interviews provided consistent interpretative keys to understand some of the group dynamics and the social background of the boys, especially regarding their relationships with the adult world (family, school, social services and the authorities), which were not always directly observable.

Translating working hypotheses from one group to the other showed the similarities in the internal structure of the groups and in the legal and illegal activities they were involved with. They also showed how both groups were embedded in a complex structure of overlapping networks that constitute a highly organised system for sharing material and symbolic resources. The empirical elements that emerged from the qualitative observations were thus organised in a theoretical framework that explains the underlying mechanisms of social inclusion and exclusion characterising the topological positions of these groups. In particular, by looking at the overlapping structure of the various networks in which they are embedded, it is possible to show how these positions assume opposite meanings when described from the conflicting perspectives of clashing social circles.

The structure of the chapter is as follows. First, I review the gang studies literature and follow with an initial description of the structure and practices of the groups. This review shows how a categorical definition of social structure runs the risk of imposing artificial boundaries that limit our ability to understand the organisation of a gang. By mixing ethnographic data with formalisation in network structures (in simple descriptive terms), the analytical strategy does not limit us to collecting information from a predefined artificial group, but allows us to look at the embedding positions of such groups within their social contexts.

I then introduce Bourdieu's field theory as a useful but limited theoretical approach to the study of street groups. Using a modified version of this framework, especially in its conceptualisation of social capital, I show how social relationships, and their interlaced network structure, constitute the interactive channels through which material and symbolic resources can circulate or are strategically retained. The observed collaborative or conflicting relations are matched with the narratives that actors use to define the value and utility of such resources that can then assume different symbolic meanings depending on the network of relations in which they flow.

Defining groups: categorical attributes and structural boundaries

Disadvantaged and illegally oriented street groups have been classically defined in the literature as 'gangs'. The social phenomenon of gangs dates at least to the early waves of industrial urbanisation (see, for example, the historical accounts of gangs in Manchester by Davies 2008). The work of the Chicago School was the first academic attempt at an empirical classification: William Foote Whyte (1943), for example, challenged the common perception of the social disorganisation of immigrant communities.

In his study of a street corner society in Boston's North End, Whyte showed how the first generations of immigrants in the United States tended to closely replicate the traditions and mores of their cultures of origin. These immigrant cultures were in conflict, by definition, with local authorities and the dominant culture, but they were also clashing with the next generation, whose members were becoming acculturated to the host country. The members of the second generation found themselves positioned between and across the networks of immigrants—with their traditional culture—and those of natives of the host country. Compared to the first-generation immigrants, those who grew up in the United States were more likely to interact with native people in schools and workplaces. This was the case of the 'college boys' in Whyte's study, who, with their overlapping positions, produced a hybrid of both cultures they experienced. These hybrids merged the elements of the traditional and the host culture in conflicting ways. Such conflicts required extensive discussions and negotiation to reach new collective identities capable of resolving the mismatching definitions of the clashing cultures.

Similarly, Thrasher, in his study of Chicago gangs (1963 [1927]), advanced the idea that areas of settlement in the United States were interstitial spaces in which different cultural traditions encounter one another, clash, and eventually trigger the formation of alternative local organisations. In this context, gangs are defined as

> interstitial groups originally formed spontaneously, and then integrated through conflict. They are characterized by the following types of behaviour: meeting face to face, milling, movement through space as a unit, conflict, and planning. The result of this collective behaviour is the development of tradition, unreflective internal structure, esprit de corps, solidarity, morale, group awareness, and attachment to a local territory.
>
> (Thrasher 1963 [1927]: 46)

The definition of gangs proposed by Thrasher contains most of the elements that we need to understand the peculiarity of youth socialisation in deprived urban areas. In particular, the stress on the group's interstitial nature, captured between competing social words and reacting by developing a collective line of conflicting behaviour, indicates the need to observe such social formations in the local territory they develop, at the intersections of these overlapping and conflicting networks.

The high variation of localised phenomena is reflected in the subsequent wide range of definitions that, since the seminal work of the Chicago scholars, have been proposed to describe gangs. Miller (1982), for example, stresses the importance of including identifiable leadership, internal organisation, and engagement in violent and illegal behaviour in the territorial definition of a gang, whereas Hallsworth and Young (2004) indicate durability and recognisability as additional features alongside territoriality and crime. Brotherton (2008) insists on the marginalised experiences of deprived youth, who react by developing a resistant collective identity to challenge dominant values. Several authors have proposed hierarchical typologies of youth groups, from simple informal friendship cliques, to properly organised criminal associations (see, for example, Gordon 2000; Hallsworth and Young 2004; Klein 2001; Pitts 2008). Other scholars focus on the importance of the element of conflict for gang formation and identity (Hagedorn and Macon 1988; Klein 1995; Sanchez-Jankowski 1991; Short 1996; Sullivan 1989), and Short (1996) adds to that the characteristic of gangs as being non-adult supervised.

A more comprehensive attempt to reach an agreement over a common definition has been pursued by the Eurogang programme, which involves several US, UK and European institutions dedicated to the systematisation of conceptual and methodological instruments for the comparative study of youth gangs. The project has produced the following definition: 'a street gang (or troublesome youth group corresponding to a street gang elsewhere) is any durable, street-oriented youth group whose involvement in illegal activity is part of its group identity' (Weerman *et al.* 2009), where again the stress is on illegal activities as constitutive of the perception (both of the youth themselves and of others) of group identity.

Although the various attempts to reach an overarching definition applicable to different onsets of youth gangs have their own merits in terms of systematisation and comparability of cases, Sullivan (2005) warns against the risk of generalising gang studies to any form of youth violence. The author points out that by indiscriminately using the term 'gang' as a group category, we risk reifying the object of research by attaching a formal label to aggregation processes that vary enormously, and that it is 'too much for us to assume some universal essence' (Sullivan 2005: 187).

Sullivan makes two fundamental points in his critique. The first is that we cannot apply the definition of gang to every form of youth violence and crime because there are many manifestations of violence that do not take the form of gang organisation. The second is that by adopting the term 'gang' based on the self-nomination of its members (Esbensen *et al.* 2001; Thornberry *et al.* 2003), we end up studying individual membership, rather than the collective unit of a gang. The author proposes instead a heuristic social network approach, where the definition of social aggregation is based on the quality and durability of relationships between members.

Sullivan (2005: 175) differentiates between action sets, cliques and named gangs that 'distinguish types of association in terms of joint activity, enduring association, publicly acknowledged criteria of membership and identity, and law-violating behaviour'. Action sets are temporary associations around a coordinated set of activities, which disaggregate at the end of those activities and do not produce any enduring shared recognition; cliques are more enduring forms of association, which produce some sense of belonging but are distinguished from named gangs by the lack of shared ritual symbols of group membership and of recognisable leadership.

Sullivan's attempt is notable because it moves in the direction of rejecting categorical affiliation in favour of a relational approach, where forms of belonging are measured according to a map of the networks that shape the forms of aggregation. Cliques, for example, are characterised by the maximal connectedness and reciprocity of ties (Luce and Perry 1949). Although groups may be organised around a clique social structure, an empirical observation of the structure of the group might reveal a different configuration, like a core–periphery structure or contextualised components, similar to the friendship networks I delineated in the previous chapter.

Out of these configurations, subgroups might form specifically and temporarily for sets of coordinated activities, constituting transient action sets. They might adopt some signs of symbolic membership if required by a specific situation (e.g. a fight against another group might involve the adoption of some temporary marks of belonging). Likewise, leadership might temporarily emerge as required and become successively latent.

In the next two sections, I describe the analytical process through which I abstracted, starting from ethnographic observations and interviews, the structural features that characterise the social networks of both the street groups and the relationships that connect them within the wider structure of overlapping networks. The abstraction of network data is constantly matched and supported by the narratives that the boys use to describe these structures as they perceive them from their own particular position, as cultural frameworks that come with specific locations across social worlds. In line with Sullivan's criticisms (2005), I prefer not to adopt the term 'gang', as it never emerged as a definition used and recognised by group members. I use instead 'street group', because the only way in which the boys define their groups collectively is by using the name of the streets (or *piazza*) where they normally meet. This territorial system of classification has consequences for the life of the groups, as I will explain later in the chapter.

The contextualised boundaries of street groups: delineating units of analysis

To assess the social boundaries and the network structures of the two groups analysed here, I collected observations and informal interviews with a group of young men hanging around a little park surrounding a local library in a suburban area of Milan. The boys were all from a second generation of immigrants whose families came from Sicily, especially the city of Palermo. The localised nature of their area of origin was due mainly to chain migrations, by which 'prospective migrants learn of opportunities, are provided with transportation and have initial accommodation and employment arranged by means of primary social relationships with previous migrants' (Macdonald and Macdonald 1964: 82). But together with chain immigrants, the 1960s and 1970s also saw the arrival of Mafia families, who either escaped Sicily or were confined elsewhere by law. Therefore, the group grew up not only in the interstitial space between Sicilian and northern Italian culture, but also in the middle of the conflicts between the local population (both Milanese and immigrants) and the illegal culture of Mafia organisations.

The group outside the local library comprised between seven and 15 young men and some women who were mostly their girlfriends (only one girl was not romantically involved with any of the boys). They were between 15 and 22 years old; at the time of this study, none of them was employed in a stable occupation, which meant they could spend afternoons and evenings in the library park. All of them had a scooter, and one of their favourite leisure activities was to drive around with these scooters making noise and doing wheelies. The group heavily consumed light and hard drugs (marijuana, hashish, cocaine and ecstasy), and one of them (whom I will call Alpha[2]) was in charge of dealing. The drugs were provided by Alpha's father, involved in larger national and international circles of couriers and distributors, whilst the street dealing was informally organised by Alpha, who was either dealing himself or delegating some of the boys who worked on commission.

The income from dealing was not the only reason the boys were keen to be selected by Alpha. In several informal interviews, they mentioned that one of their major life aspirations was to become respected criminal leaders. Learning the skills of dealing and gaining the trust of Alpha, and consequently of his father, was perceived by them as a first step for accessing larger criminal organisations.

From my initial observations, it appeared that the group at the library park had a core clique of six friends (Alpha, Beta, Gamma, Delta, Epsilon, Zeta), related by strong and reciprocal ties. The strength of their ties was given by the amount of time spent together, their interchangeable roles in dealing drugs, and the code of honour of not reporting each other's names if they were under interrogation by the police.

The central clique was surrounded by other boys, who were not fully considered part of the group, and were only occasional attendees in the park. They were weakly linked to the core group, as they were considered superficial friends, not to be trusted in the criminal affairs; and they were weakly linked to each other, constituting a structural periphery. In network terms, a core–periphery structure is defined by a highly connected central set of people (the core) and some peripheral people mostly connected to the core and not to each other (Borgatti and Everett 1999).

I was not able to record all the peripheral people who sporadically interact with the core clique. I only recorded peripheral elements who more frequently interact with the group, or who were involved in salient situations. An example of these peripheral boys was Eta, who started to hang around the group together with a couple of friends. The three boys rarely socialised with the rest of the group and spent time in the adjacent bar rather than in the park. Nevertheless, Eta aspired to be part of the core clique and to take on a dealing shift. Alpha assessed the inclusion of this potential new member by considering how comfortable and trustworthy he might be with dealing and eventually decided to test him. Eta was arrested the first night he was left alone in the park. To avoid charges, Eta saddled Alpha with responsibility, and the police then broke into Alpha's flat with a search warrant. Not finding anything to accuse Alpha and his father with, the episode concluded but Eta and his friends were then banned from frequenting the bar and the library park.

Alpha's father, whom I never met, provided the group with relatively easy access to the drug market and to the adult world of organised crime. A similar role was played by the uncle of Theta, who owned a garage where stolen scooters were taken apart and resold. Theta could be considered as a peripheral element of the library park's group, but I soon discovered he was part of another street group whose meeting point was about a mile from the library. The link to the adult's world through Alpha's father, and the link to other street groups through Theta, suggests a preliminary network structure (Figure 5.1) of the street group embedded in two hierarchical levels: the dominant one including adult figures that provide connections to the criminal world, and a subordinate and horizontal one that includes various equally positioned street groups.

The relationships with adults represent up-reaching ties in a hierarchical structure of vertically nested networks, where the adult world is located in a dominant position embedding and conditioning the activities of the youth world. At the same time, Theta represents the link between horizontally overlapping networks, connecting street groups in similar positions. By shadowing Theta, I went on to test these structural observations of the hierarchical and horizontal dimensions of the network structure on a second street group.

Shadowing connections: the system of 'piazza'

After getting acquainted with the first of the two groups under analysis, I convinced Theta, an 18-year-old young man originally from Sicily, to let me shadow him and to be introduced to another group, located in another park of the same suburban area. Theta identified the two groups by naming them after the parks, a practice also recognised by the two coordinators of the local youth services. This territorial identification is the only observable and durable mark of belonging and distinction between groups. In other situations, when the groups were outside their local territories like in clubs or in other areas of the city, together with the claim of territorial belonging they also adopted some temporary forms of identification (e.g. wearing the same pair of sunglasses or the same coloured clothing).

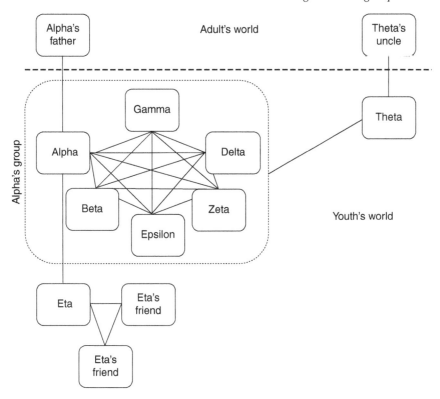

Figure 5.1 The preliminary network structure of Alpha's group
Note: Straight black lines with no arrows indicate reciprocal ties.

Similar to Alpha's group, Theta's group was composed of a number of boys aged between 15 and 23, slightly older than Alpha's group's average age. Whilst Alpha's group was much more neighbourhood based as they all lived in the same blocks of council houses, Theta's friends, although still locals, lived all around the area. Like Alpha's group, everyone owned a scooter. Theta and his best friend Iota were in charge of dealing the same types of drugs (marijuana, hashish, cocaine and ecstasy), and again they were supplied by an older man (aged approximately 35).

Unlike Alpha's case, the man was not related to any of the boys and was introduced to me as Theta's neighbour. Also, unlike Alpha's group, Theta and Iota never delegated anyone else in the dealing: from early afternoon until late night, they made sure there was always at least one of them in the park, as they did not want to rely on anyone else. Sometimes they separated to score drugs, when Theta's neighbour was not available or did not have drugs to sell. In that case, Theta would go around to other groups (during the shadowing, we came into contact with at least two other groups, plus Alpha's) and buy a minimum of drugs to

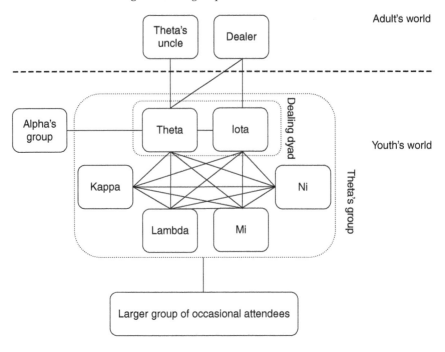

Figure 5.2 The preliminary network structure of Theta's group

cover the market until the next load from his neighbour. Likewise, other groups
sometimes scored from Theta and Iota to supply their business.

During the shadowing, Theta explained to me that selling points are called
piazza (roundabout in Italian), and that once they are assigned to a group no
one else is allowed to deal nearby. The process of assignment is informal, in the
sense that it tends to be decided by simple occupation: the group starts meeting
in the *piazza* from an early age, as in kids' playgrounds. Once the boys grow
up and eventually get involved in the dealing business, they claim the *piazza* as
their exclusive selling place. Other groups, who grew up in other *piazza*, recognise this occupation and tend to respect these informally decided boundaries.
This is why groups define themselves with this territorial identification: over the
years, the *piazza* becomes not only a meeting point, but also a recognised illegal
business owned by the group, and controlled by it. Another indication of the
identification of the *piazza* as a business hub is the distinction between it and a
bar about two miles far from the park, owned by an acquaintance, where Theta's
group often gathered in the early evening for drinks. The bar was considered the
'after work' meeting point, distinguished from the 'working place' represented
by the *piazza*.

Theta's group (Figure 5.2) was structured similarly to Alpha's. Both groups
presented a clear core–periphery structure, with the core being composed of a set
of close friends revolving around the dealing units. While the dealing unit was

dominated by Alpha in the first group, in the second it was formed by the dyad Theta–Iota, surrounded by four boys (Kappa, Lambda, Mi, Ni), who were also the ones who, together with Theta and Iota, participated in the focus group, although Ni left before the end and Mi arrived late. The mark of belonging to the core group was identified by the boys as the close friendship that bonded them together:

THETA: We are very close; for better and for worst we will help each other, obviously only between us ... there are many acquaintances, but only few friends.

INTERVIEWER: What do you mean by 'friends'?

THETA: With friends I mean them. When I was in need I knew I could count on them, I know I can go to Lambda and talk about my own stuff.

KAPPA: You went to Lambda even for money; you have a debt with him! (Everybody laughs)

THETA: Do you know what I mean? If I have a problem, I won't talk to an acquaintance.

KAPPA: You go to Iota.

THETA: I know I can talk to them, I know they won't reply just to make fun out of me, or with some bullshit. Their word, their opinion is important to me. Acquaintances are different; they are people we know for interest, for work, there are many circles of acquaintances.

IOTA: Between us there is the will of seeing each other.

THETA: There are so many shared experiences, we spend every day together, we go clubbing together.

KAPPA: There are groups here in the suburbs where friendship does not even exist, because there are too many interests.

The boys defined their relationship in terms of friendship, from which they expected instrumental interests to be excluded. This definition was useful to distinguish the group of friends from acquaintances who frequented the *piazza* attracted only by the possibilities offered by the illegal business. Around the core there was a much bigger group of those who came and went who showed up on some evenings or over the weekend. It also distinguished their group from other groups, with which they are in contact but only for business purposes, like exchanging drugs or goods.

Theta and Iota's dealing business seemed to be much bigger than Alpha's, with a constant coming and going of people during the evening, especially over the weekend. The clientele was also more differentiated: whilst Alpha was mainly selling to other kids living in the council estates around the library, Theta and Iota served people coming from different areas, of different ages and from different backgrounds, as suggested by their general appearance and the occasional chats I had with them. This could also be due to the location of the park, which was much more central (and close to Milan's internal ring road) than the library park. The rest of the group, not involved in the drug dealing, was engaged in other criminal activities.

Kappa and Lambda briefly worked together for a company setting alarms in private apartments and specialised in robbing apartments, having learnt how to deactivate alarms. Mi was dedicated to stealing and laundering scooters, relying both on Theta's uncle and on a couple of other compliant garages to resell stolen parts. Overall, all the boys seemed to have their own criminal specialisation, although aside from the dealing these could be interchangeable. During the shadowing, I accompanied Theta on several patrol trips, in which he checked cars and scooters parked in the same places for an extended period of time (usually a couple of days) indicating the possible absence of the owners, a detail that could give the boys time to steal and get rid of the vehicle before the thefts were reported to the police. They were also involved in laundering stolen goods, like clothing, accessories and mobile phones. This laundering was recognised by a coordinator of the local youth service:

> None of them would buy a mobile phone or a card: they all buy from laundering circles. Sometimes it's the scooter, or the scooter's external parts: one of them steals the scooter, and sells the external parts to another. In this way they can change the model of the mobile phone or the colour of the scooter every six months. Sometimes it's even the clothes, or the shoes.
>
> (Youth service coordinator #2)

The ability to acquire accessories and keep them up to date with the latest fashion was also a way to obtain status and prestige within the group. This emerged clearly both from the observations and the interviews: the less the boys could claim they paid for status symbols, or the more they had illegally earned money to spend, the more resourceful, successful and cunning they were considered. For example, Theta's neighbour was greatly respected for his higher and more remunerative position in the criminal organisation of the drug market. This emerged clearly one afternoon when he arrived in the park on a big scooter with three shopping bags. All the boys circled around him, asking him to show what he had bought: he showed off two pairs of classic shoes and a pair of trainers, immediately underlining how much he spent for them. The boys went on admiring him and talking about the shoes, whilst Theta, thrilled and excited, tried to capture his neighbour's attention as he was keen to introduce me and show me how great he was. In the words of the youth service's coordinator:

> The status within the group depends on the art of getting by, on showing how good they are ... because the leader is not the one who works, well he might even work, but he is the one who shows better autonomy, practical and dialectic skills, who is better in getting by and obtaining the latest model of a mobile phone, or in selling the previous one for a higher price.
>
> (Youth service coordinator #2)

The preliminary analysis of qualitative material, combined with a simple formalisation of the structure of relationships, was thus useful to compare the structural shapes of the groups, their sense of belonging, their daily and night activities, and their attention to fashionable looks. The working hypothesis that emerged from the observations—that the structure of both groups comprised a set of horizontally and vertically nested social circles—was confirmed.

But the ethnographic material collected for Theta's group also produced new working hypotheses. In particular, I started to focus my observations around a set of situations that I identified as exemplary for some of the relational dynamics of the overlapping networks in which the groups were involved. The selected situations were a night out with the boys, an aperitif in the local bar, and the projection of a movie in the local library. Because these situations were in public spaces, they gave me the opportunity to observe the group's behaviour when they were engaging in activities outside the reassuring, familiar and comfortable environment of the *piazza*. The aim was to understand how the relational dynamics that emerged in settings where the group interacted with other people, and on which it could not exercise any form of control, could be read along the theoretical framework of Bourdieu's social fields (Bourdieu 1992). This framework is useful for abstracting from the specific contexts of the groups' experiences and analysing them in the light of the social reproduction of class disadvantages. More important, the case study was used to compare Bourdieu's field theory with the concept of social worlds that was sketched in the third chapter.

Social fields and social worlds: objective relations, concrete interactions

The ethnographic observations of the groups' network structure were effective tools for identifying who was affiliated with the groups and the specific structural configuration that emerged out of this affiliation. The criteria that regulate the affiliation process and the network shape, once formalised and matched with the narratives used by the members of the first group to describe their aggregation, were then used as analytical instruments to see if they could be observed in the second group, located in a different, although comparable, context.

The 'stories' that people used to distinguish between internal ties, characterised by disinterested friendship and external ties, of instrumental collaboration and competition between groups that manage the system of *piazza*, were found in both of the observed groups, indicating a collectively shared cultural definition of this peculiar type of informal organisation. On the one hand, this means that the mix of qualitative narratives and the social network approach allows abstracting from the empirical realm the essential elements that define cultural and structural features of the groups and comparing them across cases. On the other hand, it avoids the risk of decontextualising these characteristics from the specific environment in which they operate. The narrative content of the relationships links the theoretically abstracted elements back to the interstitial nature of the groups, which flourish in specific social and cultural contexts at the intersection of different cultural frameworks (the immigrant and the host culture) and various overlapping networks (the horizontally and vertically nested structures that link youths and adults).

A comparable theoretical attempt to abstract from the spatial and temporal specificity of a social phenomenon without losing the richness of the content and the peculiarity of configurations and mechanisms is the theory of social fields proposed by Bourdieu (1992) and sometimes applied to the study of gangs (see, for example, Pih *et al.* 2008). In Bourdieu's approach, a social field is a theoretical abstraction that represents a specific configuration of overlapping structural positions. Such positions are defined by the type of resources required to occupy them, where these resources can be economic, cultural or social.

The boundaries of a field are located up to the point at which the actors who belong to it recognise the aspects of these resources, and their variously distributed combinations, as relevant, meaningful and worth fighting for. If actors do not evaluate these fights as relevant, they do not occupy positions in the field. In the case of street groups, indicators of deprivation like school dropout, drug abuse, anomalous families, ethnic exclusion, and the consequent difficulties in finding and maintaining jobs that push youth towards illegal activities (see, for example, the descriptions of 'status zero' youth in Williamson 1997 or 'underclass' youth in Murray 1990) are not seen as categorical elements that alone can explain social exclusion. They are seen as indicators of unfavourable combinations of several kinds of capital that characterise peripheral positions within a social field and that assume such negative meaning in relation to other positions where the composition of capital is more favourable: if there is an underclass, there must be an upper class that functions as a point of reference.

This means that resources are not meaningful per se, but their value depends on the specific perception they assume within a field and are weighted against their overall distribution across the field's positions. The peculiarity of an historical composition might change over time (e.g. different ways of conceptualising cultural deprivation, different ranges for measuring economic poverty and richness), but the formal set of relations by which economic, cultural and social disadvantages are linked to each other tend to remain the same, at least in Bourdieu's theorisation. The structural set of relations between positions can be transferred to the study of other fields in search of 'trans-historical invariants, or sets of relations between structures that persist within a clearly circumscribed but relatively long historical period' (Bourdieu 1992: 78), even if the meaning that each field attributes to the required peculiar combination of resources is unique. Each field presents its own system of classifications, a specific configuration of relative positions, and unique game stakes and rules, but the overall norms by which properties are combined, trajectories are channelled, and positions are related can be generalised across fields.

When applied to the study of gangs (Czymoniewicz-Klippel 2011; Pih *et al.* 2008), Bourdieu's approach is helpful in understanding how the specific combination of capital held by deprived youth not only discriminates against them in finding legal jobs or pursuing educational careers, but also locks them into specific structural dispositions, called *habitus*, that are produced by, and reproduce, social disadvantages. In Bourdieu's conceptualisation, the *habitus* is the system of disposition linked to every specific position in a field. It is the generative principle

of objectively classifiable practices and, at the same time, the system ᶜ
tion of such practices (Bourdieu 1984).

In this way, the *habitus* is a structuring structure because it is in ch
organisation of practices and their perception (therefore, it reflects the iɪ
agents over structure and positions). But it is also a structured structure
is the solidified product of social trajectories. In such a view, there is no ᵖᵣₑᵢₑᵣᵣₑd
way of influence: actors internalise their *habitus* since they were born and use its
dispositions to obtain their position in the field. However, they cannot think of different ways of obtaining what they want (apart from the rare cases in which they
act reflexively, when they happen to be aware of structural constraints and change
their behaviour accordingly) because they are constrained by the set of dispositions that the *habitus* makes available. In Bourdieu's words:

> being the product of history, [*habitus*] is an open system of dispositions that
> is constantly subjected to experiences, and therefore constantly affected by
> them in a way that either reinforces or modifies its structures. ... It is difficult
> to control the first inclination of habitus, but reflexive analysis, which teaches
> that we are the ones who endow the situation with part of the potency it has
> over us, allows us to alter our perception of the situation and thereby our
> reaction to it.
>
> (Bourdieu 1992: 133–6)

Just a few pages earlier, however, the author also specifies that: 'there is a probability, inscribed in the social destiny associated with definite social conditions,
that experiences will confirm *habitus*, because most people are statistically bound
to encounter circumstances that tend to agree with those that originally fashioned
their *habitus*' (Bourdieu 1992: 133).

As a device representing individuals' system of dispositions, *habitus* closely
reminds White's concept of identity (2008 [1992]). However, in Bourdieu's conceptualisation it is not clear how the *habitus* can change. As we have seen, people
tend to reproduce their *habitus*, but they can sometimes hold a general capacity
of reflexivity, by which they can be aware of their structural position and act upon
it. Even with the theoretical device of reflexivity in place, we are still left without
knowing how such reflexive power can be gained, if it is a contextual and temporary condition or an accumulating resource (we are always reflexive or only in
some situations) and if there are people located in positions more favourable than
others for being reflexive.

The main limit of this conceptualisation is that it casts out the role of concrete interactions in the development and modification of *habitus*. Identities are
devices that are constantly reframed and adapted in relationships, although tend-
ing towards a certain degree of stabilisation that makes actors recognisable (for
themselves and others). The *habitus* instead is the abstract production of the structural overlap of objective positions that is interiorised by actors by virtue of occupying these positions and presumably changes when actors move. In Bourdieu's
theoretical system, the strenuous work that actors do in interactions, in attempting

to control the definitions of situations and eventually to align shared meanings, completely disappears.

As Crossley nicely summarises, Bourdieu's fields end up being inherently asocial spaces of atomised individuals that do not interact with each other (Crossley 2011). Despite its limits, Bourdieu's theory of fields has the advantage of identifying the importance of various types of resources, and their circulation, for the specific definition of a field. In this theoretical framework, resources are not measured in absolute categorical terms but assume a peculiar meaning within the unique system of classification of a specific field. In this way, the meaning of resources can change when they are spent within different fields.

In an illegal field, the capacity for dealing drugs or laundering stolen goods may be evaluated as worthy to invest in, whilst the same skills would be useless, if not counterproductive, in a legal field. But the same limit that I highlighted for the conceptualisation of *habitus* also applies here, as the peculiar schemes of classifications of resources have to emerge out of iterative interactions between people belonging to the field, otherwise we cannot explain why defining criteria are established and how they can change over time.

The only reference to the importance of concrete interactions, in Bourdieu's work, is in the idea of social capital. In his view, social capital is an individual asset that can be strategically converted into other forms of capital, namely economic and cultural. It specifically consists of 'the sum of the resources, actual or virtual, that accrues to an individual or group by virtue of possessing a durable network of more or less institutionalised relationships of mutual acquaintance and recognition' (Bourdieu 1992: 119). Combined with economic and cultural capital, it is used by elites to mark symbolic boundaries of class distinction: the importance of having a famous surname with a long-term tradition of success, for example, is recognised by the upper classes as a mark of belonging and a tool for discrimination against whoever does not hold a well-known surname. Affiliation with some elitist associations, like golf clubs or not-for-profit foundations, can be similarly useful.

Implicit in Bourdieu's definition is a conflicting view of society, where different social groups struggle against each other to define boundaries and mark segregations. The idea of network is suggested, in terms of the establishment of durable relationships with influential others, but it is used by Bourdieu in a metaphorical way, as he does not adopt any structural measurement of these relationships, preferring indicators like the notoriety of the name and the affiliation to associations. In another extract, Bourdieu is even more explicit in recognising the importance of networks when he says:

> the volume of the social capital possessed by a given agent thus depends on the size of the network of connections he can effectively mobilize and the volume of the capital (economic, cultural or symbolic) possessed in his own right by each of those to whom he is connected.
>
> (Bourdieu 1986: 249)

However, Bourdieu elsewhere distances himself from social network analysis by criticising its focus on concrete relationships (1992: 114). He accuses social network analysis of neglecting the underlying forces (objective relations) that are the source of concrete relationships (Bottero and Crossley 2011: 101).

In other words, Bourdieu refuses to accept social relations as the structural counterpart of a cultural system. Instead, he insists on the causal mechanism of pure homology, where 'the proximity of conditions, and therefore of dispositions, tends to be translated into durable linkages and groupings' (Bourdieu 1985: 730). Objective relations have causal effects over the development of concrete relationships, as occupying equivalent positions implies a higher chance for actors to interact socially. Although this resembles the theoretical formulation of structural equivalence proposed by White, and presupposes the mechanism of homophily at the basis of the conditions of interactions, the lack of empirical measurement of concrete relationships in Bourdieu's work renders his theoretical assumptions unverified.

The homophilous effects of similar objective relations in producing the emergence of a comparable *habitus* is axiomatically assumed but is never tested against empirical data. This is the same fundamental problem of the empirical operationalisation of many agent-based models designed by analytical sociologists. Here, like there, the assumption of homophilous interaction, without any empirical verification, ends up being ultimately deterministic.

Bourdieu is not the only scholar who is interested in the study of social capital but lacks the empirical observation of it. The foundational work of Coleman and Putnam is also limited in its conceptualisation of social capital in terms of affiliation to primary and secondary groups (Coleman 1990); or to various types of associations that represent bonding and bridging ties (Putnam 2000). As a reaction to these types of studies, social network scholars have focused on the empirical measurement of the two main elements that characterise social capital: connections and resources.

Lin and colleagues, for example, developed sophisticated methods to map the type of relations individuals can activate, and the kind of resources these relations provide (Lin 1999; Lin and Dumin 1986). Like Bourdieu, they stress the importance of father's name and family background, where the higher a person's initial position, whether inherited or achieved, the better the social resources reached through a contact (as shown in previous research; see Lin *et al.* 1981a, 1981b). But, in addition to Bourdieu's theory, they also show that weak ties are important for low-status people, while strong ties are better for high-status people because the latter, being already at the top of the pyramid, cannot establish high upward-reaching ties.

Of a similar flavour is the resource generator, a data collection tool designed by Van der Gaag and Snijders (2003) to measure social capital, its distribution across a population, its productivity, and its goal and context specificity. Similar to the position generator, the resource generator measures the potential access to social resources instead of their effective mobilisation and their distribution across a population. Unlike the position generator, which relies exclusively on the assumed importance of job prestige for the interpretation of results, the resource generator investigates how social capital concretely helps people attain their goals, and which part of it is responsible for which effect (Van der Gaag and Snijders 2003: 3).

These studies aim to overcome the reification of objective relations that, especially in the work of Bourdieu, hinders the possibility of interpreting youth experiences, not only in terms of the cultural reproduction of the inequalities and disadvantages incorporated in the *habitus*, but also as the activation of concrete possibilities embedded in the topological position the occupy by virtue of being located across overlapping social networks. Whilst social hierarchies still play an unquestioned role, how they are reproduced in daily relationships or challenged by other forms of distinction and resistances is left unexplored.

By looking at the structure of these overlapping networks where youth play their symbolic stakes, and at the concrete relationships they engage with their peers, other youth, and the adult world, together with the opportunities and constraints such relationships might offer, we can try to reconstruct the channels of access to different capitals that locate them in relative positions within these different networks. In the following sections, I discuss the types of capital that the street groups accumulate and can count on and the opposite value that capital's composition assumes according to the social network in which they act.

Illegitimate economic capital

In general terms, economic capital consists in the quantity of economic resources an agent can count on: 'it is immediately and directly convertible into money and may be institutionalised in the form of property rights' (Bourdieu 1986: 47). Economic resources can come from work, family inheritances and assets, and they possibly represent the most objective type of resource, universally measured and convertible in exchangeable money. However, its worthiness (how important it is to have money) may be perceived, and therefore displayed, in different ways according to different fields.

In some social networks, for example, economic capital should be possessed, but only displayed in its conversion into forms of high and rare cultural capital (e.g. in exclusive circles of rich people, a flashy and shameless display of money is considered tacky). In other social networks, economic capital may still be considered important, but given its scarce distribution (like in poor communities), display of economic wealth is considered a sign of achievement. Thus, it is not only the mere quantity of money that defines the relative position of an agent in relation to others, but also their familiarity with money, the *habitus* developed by being acquainted with managing economic resources and the knowledge of the conventions that regulate their display in interactions.

The youth that I studied all came from highly deprived families: ideally young people should be in a position where the direction of economic exchange goes from adults to them, but in their situations the direction of exchange was often reversed, with families asking the boys for money instead of providing them with subsistence resources. Investment in going to school was often discouraged because parents needed their children to go to work as soon as possible and to contribute to the family's income. But finding jobs without qualifications is difficult, and these boys often started working with relatives or family friends. They had to rely on the social capital embedded in immigration chains to find work. Within their familiar networks, they were normally offered informal positions, where the offer was typically considered not as a reciprocal contract between an employer and an employee but as a personal favour that friends and relatives extend to the family. In these informal situations, salary was usually below minimum wage since, under the circumstances, there was no need to formalise contracts and provide decent pay.

> Those are extended families from the south, extremely large, with many uncles, aunts, cousins, family friends, thus within them there is always someone with a bar, a café, a garage, and the like. They will informally hire the son for few hours a day, and give him 300€. The boy keeps half of the money, and gives the other half to the family. He is exploited, because the job offer is considered as a personal favour. All the boys go through this apprenticeship and the families are happy just for the fact that they bring back home some money.
>
> (Youth service coordinator #2)

With the informality of the job environment and the lack of formal contracts, the boys never developed a work ethic of punctuality and responsibility. They often felt entitled to show up late without notice and never thought of a job as a personal investment from which they might learn useful skills. In these situations, the boys internalised negative experiences in the regular job market, feeling exploited, without positive recognition, and without any possibility of planning for the future. Compared to poor opportunities in the regular job market, the criminal world offered much better conditions: money, recognition, prestige. The time spent in the *piazza* constituted a good opportunity to earn quick and easy money. Criminal activities granted fast access to economic capital that could be spent in recreational activities and fashionable items. But they also provided the training needed for accessing the job market of organised crime.

What type of cultural capital?

According to Bourdieu, cultural capital is a resource that comes in three forms: in the embodied state, as in the form of long-lasting dispositions of the mind and body; in the objectified state, as in cultural goods (pictures, books, dictionaries, instruments, machines, etc.); and in the institutionalised state, as in educational qualifications (Bourdieu 1986: 47). In these groups, unlike economic capital that could easily be accumulated illegally by virtue of social relations that provided a link to the criminal world, cultural capital could not be simply bought or easily faked.

The boys tended to internalise the culture of familiar models that promoted a discounted vision of the embodied dominant culture. In these immigrants' circles, culture was perceived as a waste of time compared to more profitable investments in occasional jobs or illegal activities. The boys thus received a culture from previous generations that is not aligned with the dominant one, and that, as Bourdieu said, would require 'the labour of deculturation, correction and retaining that is needed to undo the effects of inappropriate learning' (1984: 70–71).

Similarly, legitimate forms of objectified capital, apart from fashion items, were not held in high esteem. The schools struggled to integrate these young men: none of the boys I interviewed managed to complete the compulsory educational path of nine years. They often had to repeat academic years, or ended up attending recovery programmes that allow students over the age of 16 to complete compulsory education in one year. Their scholastic failure derived primarily from their low levels of embodied capital: their lack of familiarity with standard Italian (they were more accustomed to speaking non-standard dialects in their families and neighbourhoods) and a poor cultural background (their parents and relatives often didn't receive any formal education) translated into a disadvantaged starting position, making school more difficult for them and encouraging early drop out.

However, within the groups, the boys did not feel culturally discriminated because they all shared the same difficulties in schools, which mitigated any feeling of inadequacy. The importance of this shared experience emerged clearly during the focus group: when asked about their studies, all the boys minimised the importance of school, although one of them (Mi) shyly admitted attending a secondary school. Suddenly, the interviewer[3] interrupted the collective conversation to focus the attention on Mi, indicating an attribution of importance to his peculiar school experience. As a reaction, the others ganged up against Mi, diminishing the importance of his studies, teasing him about his physical faults, and raising their voices to cover Mi's replies. Mi minimised his experience in school, explaining that he was in a recovery programme for gaining a secondary diploma in one year.

Realising that Mi's scholastic achievement was not that different from that of the other boys, the interviewer dropped the topic and shifted attention back to the rest of the group. This was taken by the boys as a negative judgement of a poor educational experience. Mi was now facing discrimination from a stranger who had, however inadvertently, pushed him into a marginalised position, and Mi suddenly became one of them again. The boys rallied to his side, emphasising Mi's commitment to his job and minimising his poor school results.

As opposed to institutional education that marginalises these youth, the *piazza* gives them the skills in dealing drugs, in laundering stolen goods, and in stealing. Although access to the illegal market is not as easy as it might seem (as in the case of Eta), with the right contacts and a good apprenticeship, career possibilities are faster and more accessible, making it worthwhile to invest in accumulating cultural capital for the illegal world.

The homophily of social capital and channels of distinction

The last form of resource considered by Bourdieu is social capital—the sum of powers and resources that social networks allow us to mobilise. Because of its function as the social infrastructure in which resources circulate, social capital cannot simply be seen, as in Bourdieu's conceptualisation, as an individual resource that can be added up to economic and cultural capital. The very presence or absence, and the direction and sign of relationships, are the conditions under which various forms of capital can be transmitted, as their symbolic evaluation and concrete exchange only happen in interactions and relationships.

In social relations, people define what is worthy to acquire and accumulate and how other forms of capital (economic wealth, cultural conventions) are to be handled. This also means that the same type of resource, when exchanged in different fields, can assume completely opposite meaning and value. Therefore, the objective positions that people occupy by virtue of possessing a resource will be relative to the specific field in which they play. Similar arguments were already developed by Homans (1958, 1961), whose work attempted to link the experimental results of behavioural psychology (Festinger *et al.* 1950) with the empirical observation of real-life small groups (Blau 1955).

Homans was highly interested in sketching the rules that regulate exchange in social relations, although he insisted on adopting the economic framework of maximisation of utility in a cost–reward schema (Homans 1958). This is not the place to discuss the importance and limits of such an approach; rather, what is important is that by observing the sign and direction of capital exchange within the empirical social circles in which street groups are embedded, it is possible to observe the structure of positions occupied by them, which are central in the illegal world, but peripheral in the legal one (Figure 5.3).

To locate the relative position of the groups in the overlapping social circles they are embedded in, I first need to look at the type of relationships they established. The main sources of social capital for those groups were the groups themselves: both relationships within groups and across them, which can be read in terms of strong and weak ties (Granovetter 1973), were essentially similar in terms of economic and cultural resources.

Within the groups, the boys could manage the sense of inadequacy and deprivation they felt when interacting with different kinds of youth, like the middle-class clients who used to buy drugs from them or who were met out in bars and clubs. This is because the high homogeneity that characterises the horizontal social circles that internally connect street groups did prevent internal discrimination. Some of the boys, like Alpha, Theta and Iota, were better located by virtue of their relationships with adults who occupied central positions in the illegal field. Through these relationships, the young men gained facilitated access to increased amounts of economic capital earned via illegal activities.

The control over a *piazza* not only required the establishment of up-reaching, vertical relations to the adult's world, but also the development of a network of

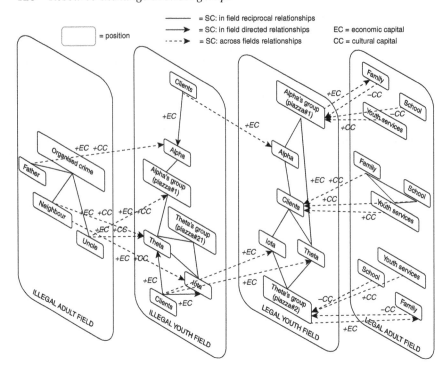

Figure 5.3 In-fields and across-fields network structure and resource transmission

horizontal, collaborative and competitive ties with other groups. In some cases, collaborations were established to supply the dealing business, whilst the system of overlapping groups constituted a wide market for the competitive business of stolen goods. As the coordinator of the youth service explained, there was an established hidden code across these groups, by which the best stuff (the better quality drugs, the latest model mobile phones, shoes, clothes, and the like) was sold internally to a group, whilst lesser-quality goods were distributed to other groups. By occupying brokerage positions across these groups, some boys like Theta were well located, as they could obtain the best deals.

The structure of cohesive groups connected via brokers proved to be a favourable one in the illegal field of criminal activities, as the diffusion of criminal behaviours was generally accepted and rewarded within and across groups, and brokering connections favoured the establishment of collaborative and competitive ties. However, these advantages assume a completely opposite value in the field of legality. As we will see in the next paragraph, when the groups interacted with other youth in the public space, their composition of capitals relegated them to symbolic peripheries. Also, the more illegal social capital they had, the more illegal economic and cultural capital they could gain, so the more visible they were to the police, as they would be the ones who change scooters more often or who have more money than others. Theta, for example, had already been charged for minor crimes, whereas Ni, at the time of the research, was under house arrest.

Finally, their contacts with adults outside the criminal world did not produce valued resources, as these people were often themselves highly peripheral in the symbolic field of the adult's world. Families required economic capital instead of providing it and lacked the function of transmitting cultural capital; schools increased gaps in cultural capital instead of providing it. In these situations, where significant relationships with the adult world did not provide the necessary resources, the positive influence of youth services could not compensate enough, as clearly stated by the coordinator of the youth service:

> We try to be educational models, a different reference from what they see at home or in the neighbourhood. We try to do a lot of network work; we encourage positive models at school where we try to convince teachers not to be too strict with them but reward small achievements; we try to talk to the social services, because they are always involved in those cases; we involve football coaches, the local parish priest. Sometimes we try to work on the older guys, the leaders of the older group. But it is extremely difficult because we have to fight against a highly chauvinist traditional culture. When on holidays with us we might convince the boys to wash the dishes, but when they are back home the father will never allow them to do it. He might even understand that it is important for them to do it, but he has to defend traditional values, what do you think that his son should actually wash dishes?
>
> (Youth service coordinator #2)

The system of resource distribution across social ties that links the groups within the horizontal and vertical level of both the legal and the illegal worlds is represented in Figure 5.3. Here, the positions of street groups in the illegal youth field that constitutes the horizontal system of *piazza* show the centrality of the groups observed, especially of the boys in charge of dealing and who broker across groups. By being central and well connected, they accumulate more economic resources, in terms of illegal money, and cultural competences, in terms of skills required to succeed in the criminal world. They are also well connected to adults who, when located in the illegal field, occupy central positions and can provide the boys with access to illegal resources, like drug supplies and laundering jobs.

When we look at the interactions that street groups establish with other kinds of young people, like middle-class customers who buy drugs from them or are met in public spaces like bars and pubs, then these social relations provide both economic resources (money that street groups earn in selling drugs), as well as information on fashion trends and styles. Again, the more central the boys are in the illegal field, the more social relations they establish with the youth in the legal field. However, because of their deprived economic and cultural resources, they end up occupying peripheral positions when compared to the better-equipped youth of middle-class families. More important, they relate to adults who themselves occupy peripheral positions in the adult legal world and who often exploit resources from them rather than providing them, whilst in middle-class families the direction of exchange is usually reversed. Middle-class youth acquire, from families and schools, favourable economic and cultural resources that reinforce their centrality and relegate street groups to peripheral and marginalised positions. These groups thus become, in the legal world, the dominated fraction of the dominated class (Bourdieu 1985).

Challenging positions: the fights of symbolic peripheries

The structure of positions within horizontally and vertically embedded social circles was abstracted via the evaluation of the relative meaning and weight that emerged from the composition of economic and cultural resources. To relate this structure back to the empirical realm, I decided to observe Theta's group in public situations, when it was more likely for the boys to engage in relations with youth from other social backgrounds.

From my observations and interviews with the groups and with youth services, it was clear that these street groups were driven by conflicting goals. On the one hand, they aspired to become successful in the criminal world, where they perceived themselves as better located and with an advantage compared to middle-class youth. On the other hand, they knew that, over the long term, it would be better for them to gain more central positions in the legal field. Central positions mean better jobs and better salaries, more objectified signs of cultural capital (where fashion and entertainment are considered the most desired expressions), better contacts and therefore opportunities, and better life trajectories overall.

But conscious of their disadvantaged position in terms of economic resources, the street groups concentrated their investment in leisure symbols, where they could construct an image of accomplishment: appearance was the one area in which they could 'cheat' and try to hide the marks of deprivation. They could consume publicly the material symbols of status and success (e.g. high-end brands of clothing, drugs and drinks, going to expensive clubs). But when they went out to display these symbols, they lacked the *habitus* that develops from the authentic achievement of a central position, and that provides not only the material resources required for occupying that position, but also the cultural conventions for how to handle such resources. In the field of leisure, the street groups are constantly pushed aside, easily recognised for their artificial apparel. In the focus group, for example, they described their experiences when going out clubbing:

LAMBDA: When you go clubbing in Milan you have to know the organisers, or the bouncers, or you have to be with girls, and you have to be well dressed, smart, with a jacket. They work with a specific kind of people. ...
THETA: Yes, they aim and pretend to work only with specific people!
INTERVIEWER: Are you not part of those people?
THETA: We are not, we don't even like to be ... well, it's not that we wouldn't like to be ... well, when I go clubbing I want to be comfortable, a shirt is fine, classic trousers are fine, classic shoes are fine ... but they are fine for one night, then the next I want to wear sneakers and it should be fine as well!

KAPPA: The problem is that they don't know us, if they see good guys they let them in, but because they don't know us they might get the wrong impression. We think it's wrong that we go clubbing on Saturday night and they don't let us in. They come out with bullshit, trivial excuses, and we know they are just excuses, but we still cannot get in … because it doesn't matter that we are all men without girls: they want us to be dressed in a certain way; we come dressed in a certain way. But then they don't have to hassle us at the entrance, because they see us all men, or all from …

The last phrase left unspoken what these young men perceived as the reason for their distinction from 'certain people'. Even when they dress up smartly, their peripheral origins are evident in the slang they use, their dialect and accent, their choice of clothes, and their attitudes. In other words, their positions are evident in the symbolic expression of their *habitus*. Here, *habitus* only exercises its function of signalling position when acted out in front of other people, who can interpret it as a symbolic device that marks distinctions (Bourdieu 1984). This rejection at clubs allows those in central positions to push the boys back to the peripheries, but street youth do not always accept this marginalisation passively. As the boys explained during the focus group, their reaction often implied physical fighting with other youth or bouncers:

INTERVIEWER: You said that even you guys can play by the rules. …
KAPPA: Of course we can play by the rules, but they shouldn't exaggerate. They shouldn't leave a bouncer outside a club who decides to let us in or not.
INTERVIEWER: So what do you do then?
IOTA: Normally we fight! Ah, we end up in fights every Saturday night!
THETA: Oh come on don't exaggerate!
KAPPA: Well most of the time we leave, but sometimes when they really piss us off it might end up in fights; you never know how it will end.
THETA: It always starts from them!
IOTA: The more we are the easier is to end up in a fight. If we are only three of four we might avoid it, but if we are many we feel more like …it's the rule of the herd. We feel protected, covered, we can do whatever we like because we know we have thousands of people on our back, and we know if we fight everyone will step in. But we are not always that many.

Just as the boys came to Mi's defence in the focus group, the adoption of violent reactions was facilitated by the cohesive structure of the groups. In the *piazza*, cohesion did not need to be displayed because the group was in its own territory. However, out of the *piazza*, this territorial affiliation was not immediately visible, and the group found other symbolic ways of displaying its internal cohesion. These symbolic devices reassure the group but also make them highly visible and recognisable and facilitate reactions of discrimination. This emerged in a night out with Theta's group, when we went to a relatively posh nightclub in the city centre.

Inside the club, the group sat together around a table, clustering around and looking out of place. In this way, they attracted the attention of other clients of the club, who both avoided them and stared at them. The avoidance and the whispered comments were picked up by the boys, who reacted by starting a fight and ended up being kicked out of the club. The display of cohesion appeared again when I organised the projection of a movie in the local library and invited Theta's group. I alerted the attendees of the library about the research and the scope of the event, asking them to minimise any kind of judgemental reactions towards Theta and his friends. When I arrived at the venue, the boys were already there, quietly sitting all together in the corner of the room and all wearing the same model of sunglasses, rendering them easily recognisable. The other attendees in the library did not question the group but simply joined it in watching the movie and there was no conflict: however, when out of the *piazza* the group still needed the reassurance of the sunglasses, a sign of belonging that marked their homophilous internal relationships.

Conclusions

Cultural dispositions do not emerge out of a structural vacuum. Urban street gangs are a product of many factors, but almost always involve low educational achievement and lack of job opportunities. In the groups I studied in Milan, a poor educational background is not perceived as discriminatory when everyone in the group is similarly deprived. But it may cause conflicts when people interact with others better educationally equipped, who play out their advantages: in such situations, differences in the composition of symbolic resources become visible and generate distinctions. This is because social worlds, as we saw in Chapter 3, develop particular cultural conventions that reinforce the schema with which people evaluate symbolic resources.

When different social worlds encounter each other, because of overlapping social circles, their systems of classifications encounter each other as well and, if incompatible, eventually clash. This implies that the same resource may assume an opposite meaning in different social worlds. Thus, in the criminal world, being able to steal a motorbike or deal drugs is conventionally evaluated as a profitable skill, and it is worth showing off these skills when interacting with people who belong to criminal networks. In the legal world, the same skill is evaluated negatively, where it should be neither possessed nor displayed.

The young people in the street groups I studied live at the intersection between the legal and the criminal world, and they are caught between the demands of contradictory cultural conventions. The accumulation of symbolic resources and the acquisition of central and powerful positions that help them succeed in the criminal world push them to the margins of the legal world; conversely, like Whyte's college boys (1943), educational achievement pushes the street youth in Milan to the margins of the criminal world. When these contradictions are played out in interactional situations where street groups meet other young people, the clash of cultural conventions becomes evident and can trigger the display of symbolic signs that communicate these contradictions. Such symbolic signs—like wearing the same sunglasses or starting fights—are used as communicative devices that represent the homophilous nature of the groups.

Within a street group, the perception of everyone being on the same team gives the young men confidence that they are not alone in facing adversity, but by displaying their identities they become easily recognisable and increase the risk of marginalisation. A good way to understand these dynamics is the combination of ethnographic and network data. The former make visible the relational displays of cultural conventions, and the latter allows locating these observations within overlapping social worlds, where contradictions and conflicts are more likely to emerge. The networks were abstracted by looking at ties as they unfolded during the ethnographic work: as such, they show the complex nature of embedded stories, of dynamic channels that convey resources whose meaning have a specific symbolic value for the peculiar field in which they are employed, and where the criteria of meaning and value are negotiated.

Notes

1 The study was part of a larger project analysing the condition of youth in Milan. The project 'Trasformare il tempo libero in tempo guadagnato e il consume in produzione' (Transforming leisure time in working time and consumption in production) was commissioned in 2000 by the City Council of Milan to the Centre for the Study of Fashion and Cultural Production, Catholic University of Milan, under the direction of Emanuela Mora and Giancarlo Rovati.
2 All the names of people and places have been changed.
3 The focus group was conducted by another researcher, leaving me the ethnographic role of observing the whole interview process.

6 Scientific communities
Describing social worlds in research collaborations

The last example illustrating the mix of methodological tools uses secondary textual data to explore and analyse the network of collaborations in research projects in philosophy in Italian universities from 1997 to 2006. In a previous project, I conducted a comparative study about sources of funding in physics (Bellotti 2012). In both studies, I collected data on projects, people and universities and analysed the data with a combination of network analysis and statistical tools. In the case of philosophers presented here, the analysis has also been extended to include the content analysis of the topics of research projects.

Although the quantitative analysis of the structure of collaboration allows explaining the success of physicists and philosophers according to the position they occupy within these structures, the subsequent qualitative analysis explores, for the case of philosophers, the narrative strategies used by researchers to solicit funding. The qualitative material is also useful to identify scientific communities and their leaders based on clusters of topics that aggregate sets of projects and people. Finally, it allows observing whether people are aware of their structural position in the network of collaboration and if they explicitly refer to this in the project's description.

In particular, the quantitative component of the analysis identifies some individual, organisational and network properties that may indicate the existence of structural mechanisms that operate underneath the empirical level and favour or hamper the outcome of getting funded. These mechanisms suggest some possible explanations of academic success in research funding and are modelled using regression analysis. In line with the evaluation of regression analysis advanced by critical realism and multilevel social network analysis, the quantitative method is not used here to generalise results from a sample to a reference population but is treated as a tool that allows investigating data and uncovering mechanisms that would not be visible otherwise.

Multilevel analysis adopts the approach of model-based inference rather than the one of design-based inference (Snijders and Bosker 2012). Design-based inference is based on the assumption that it is possible to generalise results obtained for a probability sample to a finite population from which the sample is extracted. Model-based inference, in contrast, postulates a probability model, which, if adequate, means that the inferences based on it are also adequate (Snijders and Bosker 2012: 2–3).

In this study, the generalisation of results is achieved through the analogical and retroductive comparison of the possible mechanisms at work in both physics and philosophy. These fields are similar in that they are based on the same line of funding, and the data in both cases are for the same time period but from quite different disciplines. By replicating the method adopted for physicists to a comparable dataset of the philosophers, I can observe the structural and individual elements at work in both cases, reinforcing the hypothesis that they constitute intransitive mechanisms generating the contextual organisation of research funding in Italy. Results show that in both cases the process of getting funded is facilitated by some individual attributes like rank; by having a national coordinative role in the project; and especially by occupying a brokerage position across different research groups.

Once these underlying mechanisms have been identified, qualitative analysis is employed to examine the results and provide insight in the descriptions that people use to justify their projects. In particular, the detailed account of the content of the philosophers' projects and the distribution of topics within the collaborative network allows overcoming the reductionist approach of categorical analysis, which would consider only individual attributes, like department or disciplinary affiliation, as indicators of scientific communities.

Here, the analysis of the structure of collaborations suggests that people interact not much, and not only, within a base of institutional or disciplinary boundaries, but according to topics of research that can cut across these boundaries. This, in turn, favours the role of brokers who are better positioned to mediate across different research groups. By matching the qualitative descriptions of projects with their structural position, some interesting hypotheses on cultural conventions, symbolic boundaries, and material and immaterial resources exchanges emerge, suggesting that the scientific community of philosophers in Italy can be described as a social world (Becker 1982; Crossley 2011).

Results of the qualitative component explain why some mechanisms are at work in the specific social world of philosophy; they show that structural mechanisms for success can be detected and explained by a combination of network analysis, descriptive statistics, and qualitative data, in the form of narratives. The qualitative approach is employed to investigate the possible reasons that justify the functioning of observed mechanisms, which are not assumed to be the only ones fitting and explaining the empirical data.

One of the advantages in using social network analysis, as we have seen in Chapter 3, is that with this method we can observe and control for structural dependencies in the data. In network studies this structural dependency can be measured and corrected for by adopting a network disturbances model (Dow *et al.* 1983, 1984; White *et al.* 1981), which in the case of physicists and philosophers is done by following one of the solutions proposed by Leenders (2002).[1] In regression analysis, the residuals are defined as the distance of individual measures from the theoretical value for the sampled population. In network disturbance models, specifically the one used here, the values of the residuals are represented by the random errors (as the population is not sampled) calculated for each observation as the weighted sum of the random errors of all the alters a node is linked to, where the weights are typically normalised to sum to one.

When projects are funded, the amount of granted money is often redistributed equally across local units of research. This means that individual researchers collaborating with each other tend to obtain the same amount of funding, and the similarities are reflected in the correlation of residuals, violating the assumption of the independence of the units of analysis. We need, then, to control for the fact that the more people collaborate with someone, the more similar the amount of money will be between them, which is reflected by the similarity of the distances of the estimated coefficients for each actor from the regression line, distances that are represented by the standard error.

Another complementary way of accounting for dependencies is to adopt a multilevel approach (Snijders and Bosker 2012): as we have seen in Chapter 3, within such a perspective the units of analysis at a micro level are nested within higher clusters of affiliation, therefore the variance within groups is expected to be dependent on the characteristics of these groups. In the case presented in this chapter, I consider the networks of collaborations in research projects as systems of interconnections between different actors at different levels, engaging in social interactions where the goal is to make research possible and to gain scientific prestige both for individuals and for the organisations involved. The identification of the levels of interaction depends on the specific research question to be investigated and the peculiarities of the field under analysis.

In the case presented here, and similarly with the case of physicists, academic institutions are identified as the actors at the macro level, corporate actors (Coleman 1975, 1990) that institutionally represent the cluster of academics working in them. They provide the infrastructure and the organisational and intellectual environment for research: universities, departments and research centres exchange people and ideas and they collaborate for production and dissemination of results. They are, to a certain extent, legally responsible for the work of their employees and they produce organisational cultures that define their goals and their practices.

Institutional cultures are reflected, for example, in the stream of research topics that a philosophy department would push forward by appointing scholars with specific research interests. Physicists and philosophers live and work in these environments and interact within the institutional frame that shapes their possibilities and constraints. At the same time, at a micro, individual level, they develop several kinds of relationships with people they meet along the way in their careers: friendship, advice exchange, rivalry, collaboration, conflict and mentorship are social relations that can play an important role in facilitating or hampering the production of knowledge in terms of diffusion and validation of results.

The meso level is conceptualised by following the structural approach of the multilevel analysis of networks (Breiger 1974; Fararo and Doreian 1984; Hedström *et al.* 2000; Lazega *et al.* 2008; Snijders and Bosker 2012), where the macro level of institutional and organisational linkages is connected to the micro level of personal relationship via a meso level of affiliations. In other words, the structural approach is able to connect the organisational structure with the web of personal interactions and observe how the two interconnected levels affect the performances of both institutions and individuals.

As we will see in the next section, the structural approach has emerged as a reaction against several traditions in the sociological studies of science that have ignored and underplayed the importance of observing the concrete networks of interactions between and among scientists in favour of macro or micro approaches. By introducing the analysis of concrete network structures and a meso level of affiliations, the structural approach can take into account the nested nature of social phenomena and link the micro level of individual interactions to the macro level of organisational relations.

The chapter is organised as follows: in the next section, I discuss the reconceptualisation of scientific disciplines in network terms. Then I contextualise the empirical dataset used for this chapter by describing the characteristics of academic research in Italy, the process of obtaining data from archival sources, the coding of textual information, and the univariate analysis that highlights the importance of some individual variables (national coordinator, rank, and sub-disciplines) in the process of obtaining money. Then, as I did for physicists (Bellotti 2012), I describe the micro, macro and meso levels of collaboration on research projects between scholars, between institutions, and a combination of both. Data obtained from this analysis are hierarchically modelled against the total amount of money received by every scientist in the ten years under analysis. Finally, I combine network analysis and content analysis by exploring some possible reasons for individual success, where particular attention is paid to the clustering of research topics and streams of interdisciplinarity, to the brokerage and closure of structural strategies, and to the content and distribution of themes that emerge from the qualitative analysis.

Scientific communities and multilevel network analysis

Much of the work in the sociology of science is dedicated to the influence of social factors in the production of science. Robert Merton (1949) established the debate, insisting on a weak position of sociology, where only cultural aspects of the scientific job could be addressed by sociology, whilst the foundations of the scientific method (empirical verifiability and logic coherence) were left to epistemology of science.

Subsequently, scholars attempted to open the black box of the scientific method and investigate the role of everyday interactions in the construction of the contents of science. They shifted the attention to the analysis of controversies and conflicts that emerged from the contrasts between different scientific communities in specific historical moments (Kuhn 1970). In line with these studies, the Edinburgh School with the work of Barnes and Bloor (1982), and the Bath School with the work of H. Collins (1985), started looking at how specific communities develop local sociocultural norms for the production and validation of scientific results. They did so by looking at the processes of interactions in and through which interests, preferences and beliefs are formed; similarly, laboratory studies (Gilbert and Mulkay 1984; Knorr-Cetina 1992) investigated how scientific objects were culturally constructed, as they were technically built in laboratories and symbolically made up through literary and political discourses, with the aim of establishing alliances and gaining resources.

A departure from previous approaches in the sociology of science can be found in actor–network theory (ANT) developed by Latour and Callon (see, for example, Latour 1987, 2005). Here the concept of network is introduced, where actors can be equally people, objects (actants) and organisations, but network effects tend to be highly deterministic in terms of constraints over actors: once an actor network is stabilised, the possibilities of actions become increasingly narrow (Whittle and Spicer 2008).

ANT also views social network analysis as heavily limited by the fact it accounts only for relationships between humans in informal settings (Callon 2001; Cambrosio *et al.* 2004) and it has not engaged with the wider literature of empirically observed networks. As we saw, the same critique was advanced by Bourdieu, who accused social network analysis of neglecting the study of the underlying structures that shape the field of science, focusing only on 'the analysis of particular linkages (between agents and institutions) and flows (of information, resources, services, etc.) through which they become visible' (Bourdieu 1992: 114).

Whilst these approaches to the sociology of science take social network analysis to task for its focus on concrete relationships, they lack the ability to observe the reciprocal influences of local interactions on organisational structures and vice versa. Laboratory studies and ANT take a micro approach to the study of interactions in which individual strategies to gain prestige are detached from the influence of the overall structure of the field of science. At the other extreme, Bourdieu abstracts the individual features (in terms of combinations of capital required to occupy a structural position) to a macro perspective, without taking into account the level of concrete interactions.

Social network studies on science have tested theories in sociology of science and traced the evolution of various disciplines. In these studies, the nodes have represented individual scientists as well as published articles, or institutions; and the relations have included friendship, mentorship, co-authorship, co-citations, advice and the diffusion of information (Burt 1978/79; Crane 1972; Hummon and Carley 1993; Hummon and Doreian 1989; Liberman and Wolf, 1998; Lievrouw *et al.* 1987).

In particular, the works of Lievrouw *et al.* (1987) and Liberman and Wolf (1998) suggest two interesting elements in the production of science. First, relationships between scientists cannot be reduced to co-authorship and co-citations but involve a wider set of interactions, from competition for research funding to affiliation with different organisations. Second, they make clear the importance of mediating between the micro level of individual relationships and the macro level of exchange between departments, universities, disciplines, specialities, journals or countries.

Social network analysis begins with the assumption that these actors, both individual and aggregate, are simultaneously embedded in everyday micro interactions as well as in affiliations at the higher, macro level. The need for a dual approach in the study of networks, where both individuals and collectivities are taken into account, was first advanced by Breiger (1974)[2] who described the properties of two-mode networks, and then extended to tripartite networks by Fararo and Doreian (1984).

Lazega *et al.* (2008), in their study of the network of the elite of French cancer researchers, applied the principle of linked design (Parcel *et al.* 1991) to structural analysis to study the 'duality' of social life (Breiger 1974), where duality is represented as 'multilevel networks of two systems of superposed and partially interlocked interdependencies, one inter-organizational, the other inter-individual' (Lazega *et al.* 2008: 160). Lazega *et al.* selected the researchers according to the number of articles published in scientific journals between 1996 and 1998 and, moving beyond the traditional analysis of co-citations and co-authorships, map several kinds of relations between individuals and between organisations.

In their analysis, they combine degree centrality measures (at the individual level of network relations) with measures between laboratories, and create four categories according to how central actors are (big fish and little fish) and how important their laboratories are in terms of potential access to resources (big ponds and little ponds). They then regress the production of knowledge—defined as the increase in the impact factor of articles published by actors at two points in time—against the actors' network profiles (big fish in big ponds, little fish in big ponds, big fish in little ponds, and little fish in little ponds), and point out possible strategies for the last three categories to catch up with the big fishes in big ponds. Although it is not necessary to be in a big pond (a large laboratory designated by elites as a central laboratory) to catch up, the position of an organisation in the inter-organisational network is more important than the position of individual members in the network of the elite for attaining a high level of performance (Lazega *et al.* 2008: 174).

The structural models of meso analysis thus allow taking into account actors, their interdependent relationships, their positions, and the interdependent relationships between these positions (Lazega *et al.* 2008: 159). The study by Lazega *et al.* (2008) is another example of a mixed method. They first identified what they call the French elite of cancer researchers as people who had published 25 or more papers in scientific journals in the two and a half years under analysis (although the threshold was lowered to include early career researchers). Next, they interviewed those researchers and laboratory directors, asking specifically about types of relationships that they establish with colleagues and other laboratories and also about their perceptions, performances and opinions in several domains.

By combining name generators together with in-depth narrative accounts, Lazega and colleagues are able not only to account for multiplex relationships and resources exchanges, but also to explain the importance of those relationships for scientists' careers and for laboratories' prestige. Qualitative material suggests how the social context can favour or hamper career trajectories and how individuals develop ad hoc strategies to take advantage of opportunities and overcome obstacles. This information is then formalised into a set of hypotheses that can be tested via statistical analysis.

The database of PRIN projects

The aim of this study is to apply Lazega and colleagues' approach (2008) to the analysis of academic philosophy in Italy and particularly to look at how researchers gain access to institutional lines of funding. Academic fields in Italy are centralised around the Ministry of University and Research (MIUR) that controls the system of recruitment for all disciplines. In philosophy, unlike in physics (Bellotti 2012), MIUR also represents the main source of research funding. Each academic sector in Italy is organised around disciplinary macro areas that are internally divided into sub-disciplines. Philosophy belongs to the macro area of historical, philosophical, psychological and pedagogical sciences.[3]

Within this area, along with the sub-disciplines related to history, psychology and pedagogy, philosophy is itself divided into eight sub-disciplines: theoretical philosophy, logic and philosophy of science, moral philosophy, aesthetics, philosophy and theory of languages, history of philosophy, history of ancient philosophy, and history of medieval philosophy. Philosophers also work in the sub-discipline of philosophy of jurisprudence, which belongs to the macro area of juridical sciences, and in political philosophy and history of political doctrines, which belong to the macro area of social and political sciences. Every sub-discipline enrols scientists via national competitions organised by MIUR, and successful candidates are then appointed by universities according to departments' needs.[4]

In traditional categorical analysis, the sub-disciplines and their attributes would be useful for identifying scientific communities and their subgroups. In social network analysis, by contrast, we want to examine the concrete connections between people, like collaborations, co-authorships, citations, and the like, connections that can be useful to identify scientific communities (Burt 1978/79; Crane 1972; Hummon and Carley 1993; Hummon and Doreian 1989; Liberman and Wolf 1998; Lievrouw *et al.* 1987).

These, then, are the main research questions guiding this chapter. Can we identify scientific communities by looking at concrete research collaborations? Are there some features in the network of collaborations that describe how people aggregate and work together? Do these features depend on characteristics of the actors (rank, disciplinary affiliation, role in research groups) or on structural positions (being part of cohesive and long-term groups, being brokers, working in central institutions)? Do these features favour the process of getting funded? Can scientific communities be identified by looking at the way in which research projects aggregate people with similar or with complementary interests? Can we track visible clusters of topics? And are the structural features of cohesion and connectivity acknowledged by researchers and used as qualitative justifications for collaborations?

In other words, can we identify mechanisms that regulate the circulation of intellectual resources across the network of research collaborations? And is this circulation channelled by cultural conventions that shape symbolic boundaries and define scientific communities? In this way, the field of philosophy in Italy can be conceptualised and analysed as a social world, where structural and cultural configurations concurrently shape opportunities and constrain scientific collaborations and competitions.

These questions are investigated using the case study of the line of funding of Research Projects of National Interests (PRIN), a yearly competition organised by MIUR that represents the main (although not the only) source of funding for philosophy. PRIN projects are inter-organisational collaborations between researchers based in different universities, where each project is led by a national coordinator, and involves a various number of local units. These are normally based in different institutions, although there are some exceptions in which local coordinators all belong to the same department.

The PRIN scheme is a form of co-funding between MIUR and universities: every year, researchers obtain a budget from their universities to cover 30 per cent of a research project's cost, with the other 70 per cent provided by MIUR if the project is selected. Projects must be submitted for a specific area (in this case, the macro area of historical, philosophical, psychological and pedagogical sciences, or jurisprudence, or social and political sciences) but they can be interdisciplinary in terms of researchers involved. Thus, for example, it is possible to have a project where historians of ancient philosophy work with logicians or moral philosophers to analyse certain philosophical constructs in specific historical periods, or where philosophers work with political scientists on the moral foundations of specific political assets.

Operationalisation of archival data

Information on funded projects is available from the MIUR website (www.miur. it). Every funded project for every year (since 1997[5]) is listed in a pdf file containing the name and affiliation of researchers together with their role (national coordinator, local unit coordinator), the amount of funded money for each unit, and the title of the project. This is followed by a general account of the aim of the research, a statement about innovations in the topic of enquiry, a list of criteria for the verifiability of the project's outcomes, and finally a detailed description of each research team's duties.

The rank of scientists (full professor, associate professor and researcher) and the sub-disciplinary affiliation are obtainable from the same MIUR website, together with the full list of all the philosophers working in Italian universities, including those who have never received funding via PRIN projects. The rank refers to the position occupied by every scientist in 2006: to take into account people's promotions, rank was also recorded in 2000, which is the earliest information available from MIUR's website,[6] allowing measuring changes in ranking. People who have not been funded in the ten years under analysis should not be considered unsuccessful as they might not even have entered a bid in this line of funding or they might have been funded elsewhere.

For this analysis, I coded the MIUR archives of PRIN projects. Name of researcher, affiliation, rank, role within the project (as in national or local coordinator), and amount of funding were entered into a data file, along with the rank and the disciplinary affiliation for each researcher. The names of all researchers (with the title of the projects in which they participated) were listed in a linked file and organised in a dataset consisting of ten bipartite networks of 'people by funded projects', one for each year from 1997 to 2006. In other words, the dataset consists of the names of all the units' coordinators (the national and the local ones), where the link represents their collaboration with a specific project.

Every researcher, being national coordinator, local coordinator, or simple équipe member, can only work on one PRIN project per time. The same limit applies to PRIN bids: when a group submits a proposal, all the members must be included only in one bid, so they cannot place their name in several projects in the hope of having more chances to getting funded. All projects are funded for 24 months. Each year's network is thus reduced to a number of disconnected stars (with ties between scientists and the specific project they work on). Summing up the ten bipartite matrices, the resulting network shows the stars' overlap, as researchers move from one project to the next one (and in some cases, from one collaborative group to another) through the years.

Overall, in 2006 there were 1,672 philosophers working in 59 universities: 400 of them (24 per cent), working in 57 universities, have been funded during the ten years under analysis. Seventy-seven of the total number of people funded are not philosophers as they belong to different disciplines, but they are included in the dataset as they were local coordinators in projects led by philosophers. Thus, there were 477 funded people who worked on 173 projects.

Although philosophers may move from one university to another, this is not common in Italy, where people tend to be appointed and spend their entire career in the same university, which often coincides with the place where they obtained their PhD (Beltrame 2008). For example, of the 477 people in this study, only 22 people (4 per cent) changed institution between 2000 and 2006 (similarly to rank, the MIUR database only provides historical information on institutional and disciplinary affiliation from 2000, whilst the archive for research projects goes back to 1997). Therefore, although there are three distinct sets of nodes (people, projects, universities), the data do not form a tripartite network as relations are only defined by individual collaborations on research projects, while institutional affiliation constitutes an attribute of individuals.

Multiple affiliations are not allowed, but it is still possible to apply matrix algebra and extract the university-by-project matrix, moving from the individual to the institutional level of collaboration. This has been done by transforming the university affiliation attribute vector into a two-mode binary university-by-people matrix.

This matrix is multiplied by the two-mode binary people-by-project matrix, obtaining a two-mode valued university-by-project matrix. Transposing both the people by project and the university by project matrices yields a person-by-person valued network (where the cells indicate the number of projects in common), a university-by-university valued network (where the cells indicate the number of projects in common), and a project-by-project valued network (where the cells indicate number of people that projects have in common). All networks are undirected.

The textual information about the projects contained in the pdf files lends itself to content analysis. Content analysis is 'a set of methods for systematically coding and analysing qualitative data' (Bernard and Ryan 2010: 287). It is used to search for textual information whose codes are derived from prior knowledge of the empirical context and for testing theories. In the case presented here, the quantitative analysis of individual and structural characteristics suggests some possible mechanisms for success and content analysis can be used to observe whether these mechanisms are consciously perceived or if they remain latent and covert, producing discrepancies between what actually happens in the network of collaborations and what people think is happening.

Whilst searching for traces of underlying mechanisms, content analysis also lets us identify themes that were not expected in the data, and that can be used to generate further hypotheses. Content analysis is thus applied to the various sections of the projects that describe the aims of the research, its innovation regarding the state of the art, and its verifiability criteria. The emerging themes are aggregated into meaningful categories. I also count the number of projects in which a specific task/topic is mentioned and relate it to the other important characteristics of the network structure (e.g. with the numbers of brokers that connect these projects or with the cohesiveness of the research groups).

When projects are linked by brokers, the same analysis is conducted on the part of the text in which their specific tasks are described: this more focused analysis aims at looking at the brokers' task descriptions to see if there is any reference to their structural position and any justification for it. Although the quantitative analysis has been based on the people-by-people and the university-by-university networks, for the qualitative analysis I look at both the original two-mode people-by-projects network (where it is easier to visually identify brokers who mediate between projects) and the project-by-project matrix (where the link represents the number of people in common). This last, one-mode network allows us to identify independent components and cohesive clusters and to relate them to sub-disciplines and qualitative themes.

Overview of the system of PRIN funding in Italy

Hunting for funding is a highly competitive task in a scientist's life. It is necessary because it is impossible to do research without financial support and because it increases the chances of promotion and of appointing junior staff. In the end, financial support means publication of results, and publications are the measure of job performance in academia. This is true for PRIN projects as

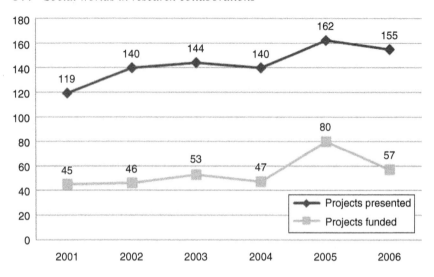

Figure 6.1 Number of research projects proposed and funded in historical, philosophical, psychological and pedagogical sciences from 2001 to 2006

well, where philosophers compete with scientists working not only in philosophical sub-disciplines, but also in other disciplines that belong to the disciplinary macro areas.

For philosophy, the macro area includes historical philosophical, psychological and pedagogical sciences, and their respective sub-disciplines of history, bibliography, palaeography and demo-ethno-anthropology, geography, pedagogy, psychology and sport science. Philosophers who work in juridical disciplines compete against other juridical sciences that include, along with philosophy of jurisprudence, all jurisprudence disciplines and the history of jurisprudence. Finally, philosophers who work in political philosophy and in the history of political doctrines compete against political scientists who work in other disciplines, like sociology.

Although there is no information available on unsuccessful projects, the MIUR website provides data on the number of projects funded and the number of proposals. Figures 6.1, 6.2 and 6.3 show the proportion of funded projects compared to proposed projects in each area between 2001 and 2006. Whilst the PRIN archive for research projects dates back to 1997, the aggregate information on successful and unsuccessful bids only covers the period starting in 2001. For historical, philosophical, psychological and pedagogical sciences, the proportion of funded projects over proposed ones has been steady at around 35 per cent; the exception was 2005, when the percentage rose to 49 per cent because of an increase in money available for that specific area.

For juridical sciences, the proportion of funded projects increased steadily from 43 per cent in 2001 to 57 per cent in 2005, with a drop to 50 per cent in 2006. For social and political sciences, the proportion of funded projects was around 50

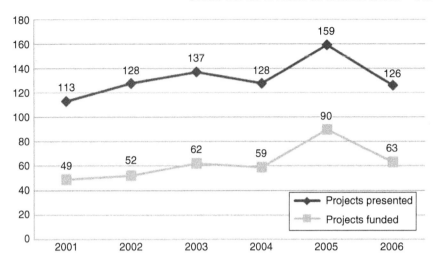

Figure 6.2 Number of research projects proposed and funded in juridical sciences from 2001 to 2006

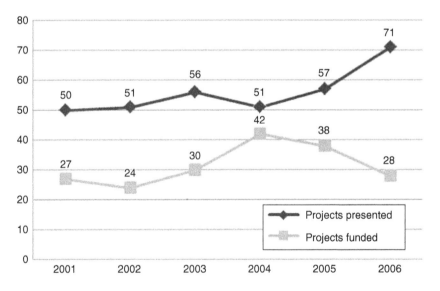

Figure 6.3 Number of research projects proposed and funded in political and social sciences from 2001 to 2006

per cent for the first three years, rising to 82 per cent in 2004 and dropping to 67 per cent in 2005 and to 39 per cent in 2006. One reason for the variation in the success rate for the social and political sciences is that the number of proposed projects was more or less constant for the first three years, but increased dramatically after 2004, following a year of exceptional success, whilst overall funding did not increase accordingly.

The ratio of successful philosophers

Looking at the distribution of philosophers (both funded and non-funded) across sub-disciplines and ranks (Table 6.1), the history of philosophy (including history of ancient and medieval philosophy) appoints the highest number of philosophers (over 300 academics), followed by moral philosophy, philosophy of jurisprudence and theoretical philosophy (all over 200 academics). By comparison, history of political doctrines, logic and philosophy of science, aesthetics, political philosophy and philosophy of languages appoint fewer than 200 academics. The dominance of the historical component is confirmed by the high rate of success in obtaining PRIN funding—over 30 per cent for the three sub-disciplines, followed by political philosophy (27 per cent) and logic and philosophy of science (26 per cent), whereas philosophy of languages, history of political doctrines and philosophy of jurisprudence have less than 20 per cent of their scholars funded.

The total number of people funded in other disciplines in Table 6.1 includes people working in any jurisprudence sub-discipline, who are instead kept separate from the "other" category in the rest of the analysis. This is because here the analysis compares philosophers funded against philosophers not funded; therefore philosophers of jurisprudence would have had to be compared against the whole area of jurisprudence, which is not relevant for the scope of this chapter. In the following analysis, however, which refers only to the people funded under the PRIN scheme, it is interesting to keep jurisprudence scientists in a dedicated category as they represent a fairly large subgroup in the network of collaborations.

Full professors dominate the funded projects with a rate of success of 61 per cent, followed by associate professors (16 per cent) and researchers (4 per cent). The detailed percentage of successful people according to the ranks in individual sub-disciplines reflects this aggregate trend, although researchers in logic and philosophy of science are more successful than their peers in other sub-disciplines, similar to associate professors in philosophy of languages and full professors in aesthetics. Full professors in ancient philosophy have the highest rate of success, with 84 per cent of people funded. The ranking of philosophers in 2006 confirms their rank in 2000.

Comparing 2000 to 2006, 260 (54 per cent) were already full professors; 129 (27 per cent) had moved from researchers to associate, or from associate to full professor; 13 (2 per cent) had jumped two ranks, being promoted from researchers to associate to full professors within the six years, or directly from researchers to full professors (in most cases, these people have been researchers for a very long time, between 15 and 20 years; once they became associate professors, promotion to full professor only took few years, if they were not promoted directly to full professor). Fifty (10 per cent) did not progress, and for 25 the information was not found.

Given that rank is only recorded for two time points, more or less half-way through the years under analysis (2000) and at the end of the ten years (2006) it is not possible to test a hypothesis regarding the direction of causality between funding and promotions. It could be that being funded is the factor that made scientists

Table 6.1 Distribution of funded and non-funded philosophers across sub-disciplines and ranks

Discipline	Total MIUR				Total funded				% of funded over total			
	All	All full professors	All associate professors	All researchers	All funded	Funded full professors	Funded associate professors	Funded researchers	% All	% Full professor	% Associate professor	% Researcher
Philosophy of law	228	94	49	85	44	42	1	1	19%	45%	2%	1%
Theoretical philosophy	209	82	55	72	47	37	6	4	22%	45%	11%	6%
Logic and philosophy of science	112	46	39	27	29	20	6	3	26%	43%	15%	11%
Moral philosophy	232	82	80	70	52	41	8	3	22%	50%	10%	4%
Aesthetics	108	30	36	42	24	20	4	0	22%	67%	11%	0%
Philosophy and theory of languages	104	28	35	41	11	7	4	0	11%	25%	11%	0%
History of philosophy	313	118	80	115	98	82	12	4	31%	69%	15%	3%
History of ancient philosophy	56	19	19	18	22	16	6	0	39%	84%	32%	0%
History of medieval philosophy	50	18	12	20	17	13	4	0	34%	72%	33%	0%
Political philosophy	104	45	26	33	28	23	4	1	27%	51%	15%	3%
History of political doctrines	156	59	41	56	28	25	2	1	18%	42%	5%	2%
Other	na	na	na	na	77	53	18	6	na	na	na	na
Total	1672	621	472	579	477	379	75	23	24%	61%	16%	4%

Table 6.2 Funded money and people across projects: descriptive statistics

	Physics (N projects = 454)		Philosophy (N projects = 173)	
	Amount of money	Number of people	Amount of money	Number of people
Mean	215,719	4.43	111,715	5.32
Median	179,862	4.00	91,000	5.00
Std. deviation	161,456	3.165	78,465	2.264
Skewness	3.312	4.438	1.701	1.001
Std. error of skewness	.115	.115	.185	.185
Minimum	5,000	1	11,877	1
Maximum	1,497,207	34	500,000	14

progress in ranks, rather than being funded because of their high rank. However, the fact that over half of the people were already full professors when they got funded suggests that it is the high rank that attracts funding rather than funding that facilitates promotion. Nevertheless, the dominance in funding of full professors and historical disciplines is clear. Finally, of note is the rate of success among young researchers in philosophy of science and logic. Although the percentage of funded researchers is still very low (11 per cent) and it could be statistically insignificant, it is still worth noticing that it is higher than the ones for other disciplines, with the second-highest value only being 6 per cent for theoretical philosophy.

Descriptive statistics of funding in PRIN projects

Since the amount of funding for each project is often equally distributed across local units, people who collaborate also tend to receive the same amount of funding. This is typical of a discipline like philosophy, where research funding covers only the expenses of participating researchers, as research does not normally require any technical infrastructure. It is different, for example, in physics (Bellotti 2012), where the cost of research may include the rent of laboratory space or the purchase of materials for experiments. In that case, research funding is allocated across local units according to their role in the project: a theoretical physicist may obtain less funding than the experimental unit, as the first does not require the technical support needed for experiments. These differences are shown in Table 6.2—where the funding per project is much higher for physics than for philosophy—together with the standard deviation and the skewness of the measure.

The maximum number of people per project in philosophy is smaller than in physics (14 against 34), although on average projects in philosophy tend to have more units than those in physics, and the overall number of people per project is not as skewed. However, in both disciplines the amount of funding per project is strongly correlated with the number of participating units (0.71 for philosophy

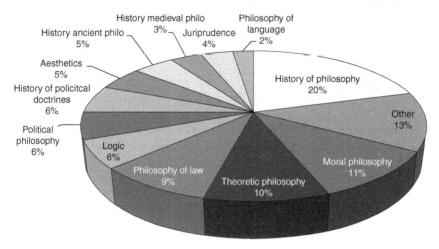

Figure 6.4 Per cent of philosophers in each sub-discipline over the total *N* of funded philosophers

and 0.76 for physics). Unlike physics, units within philosophy projects rarely require much higher budgets compared to other units. Finally, at the individual level the total amount of funding in philosophy is highly correlated with the number of projects in which people participate (0.70), whereas in physics the correlation is much lower (0.32). This means that given the even distribution of money across philosophy projects, the more projects people work on the more money they receive overall, whilst in physics researchers can be working on fewer but more highly funded projects.

In philosophy, of the 477 people who were funded in the ten years under analysis (PRIN archives cover the period 1997–2006), 100 (21 per cent) were national coordinators at least once. Of these, 60 per cent were national coordinators once, 22 per cent two times, 10 per cent three times, 5 per cent four times, and 3 per cent five times. All but two of the 100 are full professors. The other 377 (79 per cent) were never national coordinators but only local coordinators.

The national coordinator usually thinks of and originates a project. The national coordinator also establishes contacts with other local units to work on developing the idea. Because of the role of initiating collaborations, the national coordinator usually receives more money if the project is funded. The ratio of the number of philosophers in every sub-discipline funded via PRIN projects over the total number of funded people indicates which sub-disciplines were best represented in PRIN projects in the last ten years (Figure 6.4). History of philosophy, moral philosophy, theoretical philosophy, and philosophers affiliated with other disciplines (especially jurisprudence) are privileged by MIUR. This possibly suggests some long-term strategies that favour traditional and dominant sub-disciplines as well as a certain degree of interdisciplinarity. Applying the same ratio to the philosophers' rank, 79 per cent of the total number of funded people are full professors,

16 per cent are associate professors, and 5 per cent are researchers, confirming the correlation between high ranks and funding.

The levels of interaction

Sub-disciplines, rank and coordination roles can be considered as individual attributes of philosophers involved in PRIN projects. I now move to analysis of the micro, the macro and the meso levels of interactions. The micro level consists of the network of research collaborations between and among philosophers. The macro level is obtained by combining the micro network with philosophers' institutional affiliations. The outcome is a university-by-university matrix in which the cells contain the number of projects in common. This does not add information to the network itself (in terms of additional links), but it gives a different view of the collaboration process. The meso level is constructed by combining the individuals' number of collaborations (the micro level) with the size of their departments. This gives us a modified version of Lazega *et al.*'s system of classification (2008).

The micro level

The network of collaboration is obtained counting a tie between two researchers every time they are named in the same project. The result is a symmetric and valued square matrix, with actors in rows and columns and cells containing the number of collaborations. Each researcher can collaborate on a maximum of five projects in ten years, as each project lasts 24 months and no one can participate in more than one project at a time. Thirteen people have participated in five projects, 40 in four projects, 80 in three projects, 110 in two projects, and the remaining 234 in only one project. Individual funding ranges from 697€ to 310,278€, with a mean of 40,517€ and a median of 26,758€.

The number of collaborators ranges from 0 (a research project with only one unit, therefore only one philosopher without any collaborations) to 35, with a mean of 7 and a median of 6; this value corresponds to degree centrality, calculated without tanking into accounts the value of the ties. The number of collaborations each researcher has activated (and taking into account that people can collaborate with each other more than once) ranges from 0 to 39, with a mean of 10 and a median of 8; this value corresponds to degree centrality calculated by taking into account the value of the ties. The total number of collaborations can indicate that a philosopher participates in large research projects (with many other researchers) or in several projects. For example, the person with the highest number of collaborations (39) has collaborated with 31 people, indicating that for some collaborators the collaboration has been renewed in more than one project.

The network of individual collaborations has a density of 0.016, and an average distance of 12.3 nodes, which means it is not highly dense. Only six philosophers (one 4-clique and a dyad) have the maximum of five projects in common, meaning they always collaborated with each other over the years. Eleven groups of various sizes (from two to five) have four projects in common, 29 groups (size range from one to eight) have three projects in common, and 41 groups of two to 19 nodes have two projects in common. Twenty-nine groups of sizes ranging from 1 to 235 have at least one project in common (Figure 6.5).

At the minimum level of collaboration, the main component accounts for 49 per cent of philosophers, the second-largest one for only 12 per cent (24 nodes). This structure suggests that there are at least two different structural positions that may increase the chances of getting funded. On the one hand, some research groups tend to collaborate over years, strengthening their mutual relationship. They either

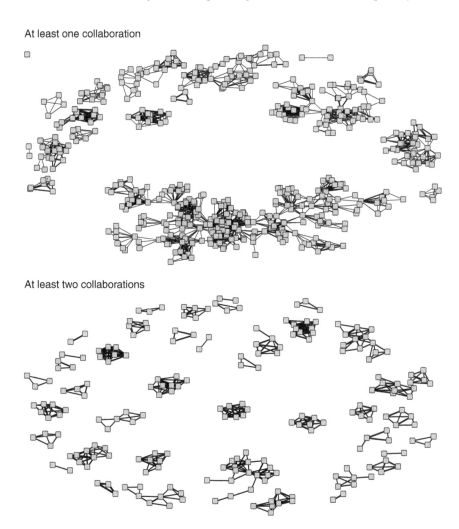

Figure 6.5 Number of collaborations in research projects

At least three collaborations

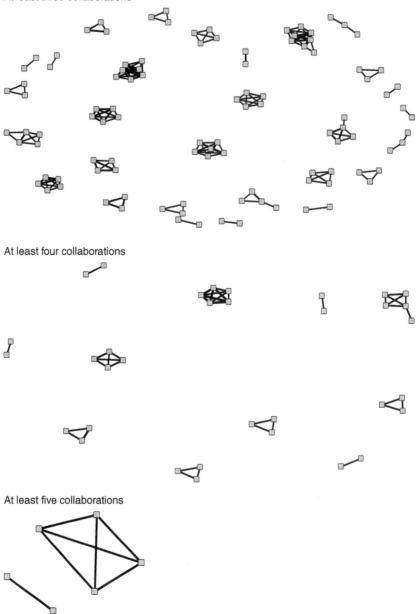

At least four collaborations

At least five collaborations

Figure 6.5 (cont.)

develop long-term research plans, asking for funding for follow-up projects, or they simply decide where to invest their research efforts as a group over the years. Maintaining collaborations can be a good strategy as it creates a successful track record that may favour subsequent funding.

On the other hand, some researchers tend to change the composition of research groups over time: overall, they end up occupying a brokerage position between different sets of people, increasing the number of personal contacts with people who would be otherwise disconnected. A brokerage position is defined as the number of times ego lies on the shortest path between two alters separated by a structural hole (i.e. the number of pairs of alters that are not directly connected). In the regression model presented in the next section, I use the normalised version of this measure, where the number of brokerage opportunities, which is a function of egonetwork size, is taken into account.

Both brokerage and closure may be strategically pursued by researchers, but the network data alone do not allow observing whether the choices of these structural positions are intentional or are the unintentional outcome of structural possibilities and constraints. Philosophers may decide to change the composition of groups because of the unavailability of previous collaborators or because previous collaborations were not satisfactory. They may also switch because they receive more interesting offers or because they want to invest in new topics. In fact, there can be many possible reasons for switching, which will be explored in the analysis of the projects' qualitative descriptions.

Moreover, the mechanisms are not mutually exclusive: someone might collaborate with one group one year, add new people to the original group two years later, and eventually move to collaborate with a third group after another two years. In this case, the researcher would find herself in the position of being the only link between groups 1 and 2 and group 3. These mechanisms resemble those theorised by Burt (2005), who distinguishes between brokerage and closure in organisational settings, where brokerage favours the development of new ideas and closure the delivery of settled projects. In Burt's theory, both mechanisms are valuable. When combined, they maximise the advantage for actors for developing dense egonetworks. This facilitates the development of trust and behavioural control and gives brokers different and exclusive perspectives from otherwise disconnected people.

This is a powerful theory, but the behavioural characteristics linked to specific structural positions need to be tested rather than assumed. Does closure, for example, always imply a higher level of trust and commitment? Does brokerage always favour knowledge transfer? Within the population under study, 267 researchers have a brokerage score equal to 0 (56 per cent out of the 477 philosophers). The remaining 44 per cent have a brokerage score ranging from 0.1 to 0.73; 107 (23 per cent) have a value >0 and <0.33; 84 (18 per cent) have a value ≥0.33 and <0.66; and 7 (1 per cent) have a value ≥0.66 to 0.73, the maximum value for the population.

Closure has been calculated via the measure of density of the egonetworks, taking into account the values of the ties, where the higher the value, the denser the egonetwork. This value ranges from 0 to 4.06, with 101 people (21 per cent) with values ≥0 < 1; 101 (21 per cent) people with values = 1; 207 (43 per cent) with values >1 < 2; and 55 (11 per cent) with values ≥2 and ≤4. For 12 people (2 per cent), brokerage and density cannot be calculated as they are isolates or they belong to dyads (whilst the minimum number of nodes to count brokerage and density is 3).

I model the success of these mechanisms in the next section to test which of the two is more successful for obtaining money. Here I assume a direction of causation from the structure to the level of funding (i.e. brokers attract more funding), but it could also be that a high level of funding attracts new people, resulting in a higher density of collaborations or a higher number of structural holes someone bridges across. Disentangling the direction of causation can only be tested with temporal analysis, where one can see if it is the position in the structure of collaboration that favours the amount of received funding or if it is the amount of funding that stimulates further collaborations. However, this latter direction of causation would imply a higher impact of closure than brokerage over the total amount of money received in the ten years under analysis, as we could expect that successful collaborations favour the establishment of further projects with the same group of people rather than a drastic change of research groups.

Although extremely useful, a longitudinal analysis of the data could not be performed mainly because networks include a completely different set of actors and projects for each year; therefore, dynamic network analysis cannot be applied for the lack of congruence between nodes in each time observation. Some indications of the social mechanisms explaining the roles of these structural positions can be tracked in the qualitative analysis of projects, where brokerage and closure are contextualised within the domain of research topics and the trajectories of national and local coordinators.

Although the picture of the whole network of collaborations between philosophers (Figure 6.6) suggests a tendency for people to aggregate according to similar sub-disciplines, the analysis of homophily, measured via the E-I index (Krackhardt and Stern 1988) tells a different story. The E-I index values measure how much each person is connected to similar or different people, where similarity here is intended as belonging to the same sub-discipline. In other words, it is a ratio of the number of ties linking different nodes over the number of ties linking similar nodes. E-I values range from −1 (all the people belong to the same sub-discipline of the person under observation) to +1 (all the people belong to different sub-disciplines from the person under observation).

By aggregating these values for each sub-disciplines (Table 6.3), we can see that all of them have positive values, indicating the tendency towards interdisciplinary collaboration. The rank of homophilous sub-disciplines closely reflects the rank of successfulness, but only partially reflects the size of the entire sub-disciplines. This indicates that it is probably easier to collaborate with people in the same area of research where these areas are large enough to allow a wide range of choices, although interdisciplinary projects may still be preferred and more successful, as indicated by the high proportion of people working in other disciplines compared to the total number of funded people (see Figure 6.4).

The macro level

Given the redundancy of the universities' network of collaborations and the individual networks, it is not possible to fully apply the approach of multilevel network

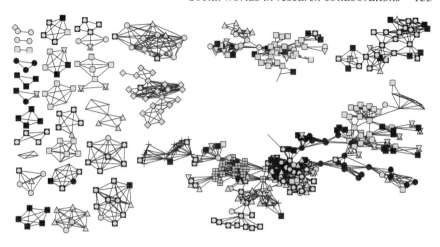

Figure 6.6 The network of individual collaborations
Note: Nodes shaped according to sub-disciplines.

Table 6.3 E-I index for sub-disciplines

	Internal ties	External ties	Total	E-I
History of philosophy	136	603	739	0.632
Other	60	421	481	0.751
Moral philosophy	36	302	338	0.787
Philosophy of law	26	272	298	0.826
Theoretic philosophy	28	385	413	0.864
History ancient philosophy	10	175	185	0.892
Logic	10	224	234	0.915
Political philosophy	8	187	195	0.918
Aesthetics	6	179	185	0.935
History of political doctrines	4	185	189	0.958
History medieval philosophy	2	119	121	0.967
Philosophy of language	0	86	86	1
Law	0	84	84	1

analysis, where different relationships are measured within the micro level, within the macro level, and across them (by linking individuals to the organisations with which they are affiliated; see Lazega *et al.* 2008; Wang *et al.* 2013). To account for the nested nature of data, a multilevel analysis of networks (Snijders and Bosker 2012) is adopted, where the relationships at the micro level are nested within the macro level by taking into account the affiliation with institutions. Although I did not measure any relationship between institutions which is not derivable from the individual level of collaborations, it is still important to include a measure that represents the macro level of institutional prestige, as this might be one of the reasons for selecting research partners.

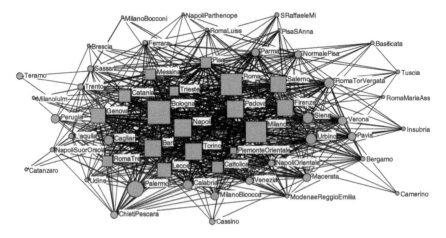

Figure 6.7 Core–periphery structure of the university-by-university network

Out of the possible measures of institutional prestige, the size of the departments in terms of appointed researchers seems to be the most appropriate, as it
still retains a potential network value in terms of the number of colleagues each
philosopher can interact with on a daily basis. Working in a large department can
be an advantage because there are more people from whom to seek advice, or it
could be a disadvantage because in a larger institutional setting people are less
aware of each other (and therefore can count on less potential advice) than in
smaller ones. Also, working in a big department might be counterproductive in
terms of the number of projects funded every year, as MIUR might limit funding
to each institution (the scientific value of the projects being assumed equal) to
guarantee a balance between universities.

Although redundant with the micro level of collaboration, the derived network
of collaborations between institutions (where the link is the number of projects in
common) offers a valuable macro perspective over the positions of universities in
the structure of funding. The network presents a quite distinctive core–periphery
structure, with 18 universities in the core with an average value of 6.77 projects in
common, 39 in the periphery with an average value of 0.36, and average value of
connection between core and periphery of 1.49. Given that the network is valued,
the density within and between core and periphery does not range between 0 and
1, but it shows the average value of connections. In Figure 6.7, the size of the node
represents the number of philosophers working in each university, and the shape
defines core or periphery affiliation.

Core institutions are undoubtedly more successful than peripheral ones, not
only because of the overall higher number of funded projects. In terms of the
amount of received funding, 20 universities obtained more than the median value
for institutions, which is equal to 274,209€ (Figure 6.8). These are mainly core
institutions, as correlation between the total amount of funding and the coreness

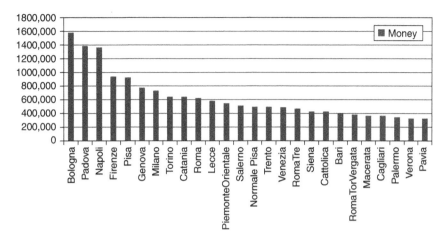

Figure 6.8 Total amount of money received by top-funded universities (over 300,000€)

values is very high (0.914). Coreness is calculated in Ucinet using the continuous core–periphery routine: this routine simultaneously fits a core–periphery model to the data network and estimates the degree of coreness or closeness to the core of each actor (Borgatti and Everett 1999).

In terms of the number of philosophers working in every institution, core institutions are again the ones with the larger number of appointed scientists, with a correlation between the size of department and coreness equal to 0.882. Although as expected the correlation between the numbers of appointed philosophers and the total amount of funding is high (0.81), there is no linear relation between the two variables (Figure 6.9), indicating that working in a big department does not seem to completely determine the process of getting funded.

The analysis of the micro and the macro level of interactions suggests some important properties of the overall network of collaborations. Some sub-disciplines are more powerful and successful than others, as they can count on more affiliated philosophers and more funding from PRIN projects. The history of philosophy, moral philosophy, theoretical philosophy and philosophy of law are not only the disciplines with the highest number of appointed academics, they have also dominated the whole distribution of PRIN funding in the ten years under analysis, with 50 per cent of funded people affiliated with one of them. However, political philosophy and philosophy of science, together with history of philosophy, have a better rate of success in terms of the percentage of funded people over the total number of academics they appoint. This is even more remarkable for philosophy of science, which shows the highest percentage of successful researchers in the lower ranks compared to the other sub-disciplines (although the value is still low and may be statistically insignificant). Apart from philosophy of science, the rest of the funding is indeed distributed mainly to full professors, who seem to monopolise the funding.

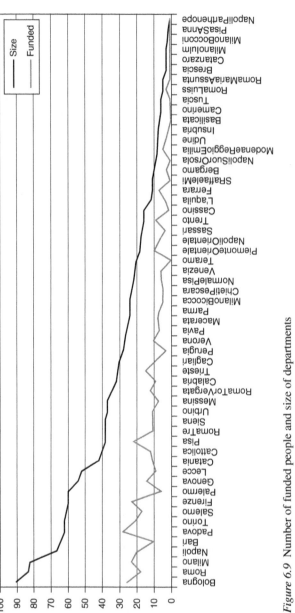

Figure 6.9 Number of funded people and size of departments

When looking at the individual position in the network of collaborations, the strategies of brokerage and closure seem both pursuable and possibly successful. A higher density indicates the tendency to collaborate continually with the same group of people, whereas high brokerage scores indicate the practice of moving from one research group to the other. Nevertheless, as expected, being a broker is highly correlated with the total number of projects in which someone participates because if someone participates in only one project, she or he is connected, by definition, with all the other co-participants. It is only when someone collaborates in more than one project that the possibility of being a broker is available. However, participating in several projects over time, whilst increasing the possibilities of being a broker, does not automatically imply changing research team.

The E-I index values, which measure the tendency of people to collaborate with colleagues from similar or different sub-disciplines, indicate a high level of interdisciplinarity, also confirmed by the fact that 13 per cent of funded people do not belong to philosophical disciplines at all. However, sub-disciplines with lower values of E-I, and therefore with a higher propensity for collaborations within the same sector, are also the most funded. This could be due simply to the fact that they are also the larger ones, where it is easier to find good partners within the same discipline, but it is clear that the potential advantages of interdisciplinarity need further investigation. Finally, there are indications that core departments tend to be more successful, as they can count on a higher number of appointed philosophers, funded projects and amounts of money.

The meso level: fishes and ponds in Italian philosophy

In the previous section I analysed the micro and the macro level separately; here I combine the two together to observe the meso level of interaction, which allows for a multilevel analysis. This is done by adapting Lazega *et al.*'s (2008) method of classification. The authors create four categories, two for people and two for institutions, using centrality degree values as the threshold. Actors and institutions with degree values above the median are big fishes and big ponds; those with degree values below the median are little fishes and little ponds. Combining them, Lazega *et al.* establish four categories: big fish in a big pond, little fish in a big pond, big fish in a little pond, and little fish in a little pond.

Similarly, here I consider big fish philosophers with a valued degree above the median = 8 (as the distribution is skewed): within the 477 philosophers, 232 are big fish, 245 little fish. As the network of universities is redundant with the network of individuals, it does not make sense to use degree values to distinguish between ponds. Therefore, the distinction is calculated on the number of philosophers working in every institution, regardless of being funded or not, the assumption being that an organisation with a higher number of philosophers offers a larger potential pool of contacts. I consider big ponds universities with a number of appointed philosophers above the mean = 28.75 (the distribution is not

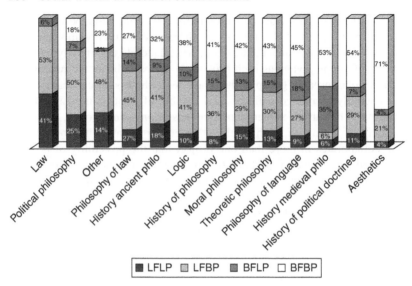

Figure 6.10 Distribution of fish and pond categories across sub-disciplines

skewed). Of the 57 universities that obtained PRIN funding from 1997 to 2006, 24 are big ponds and 33 are little ponds. Combining information about fish and ponds, I derive the same four categories of Lazega *et al.* (2008), obtaining 177 big fish in big ponds (BFBP), 174 little fish in big ponds (LFBP), 55 big fish in little ponds (BFLP), and 71 little fish in little ponds (LFLP).

If we look at the distribution of fish and pond categories in every sub-discipline (Figure 6.10), we find that aesthetics, history of political doctrines and history of medieval philosophy are dominated by BFBP, which represent over 50 per cent of their affiliates. The lower the number of BFBP the higher the number of LFBP, with the exception of history of medieval philosophy where the percentage of LFBP is down to 6 per cent and is compensated by a higher percentage of BFLP. Overall, little ponds are not well represented, given the low number of people working there. Finally, law disciplines do not have any BFBP, possibly because the affiliates are big fish in their own disciplines.

Regarding rank (Figure 6.11), LFBP accounts for 48 per cent of researchers, followed by LFLP (30 per cent). Associate professors are mainly LFBP (44 per cent) and BFBP (35 per cent), whereas full professors are mainly BFBP (39 per cent) and LFBP (34 per cent). There is little difference in the distribution of full and associate professors in these roles; the main gap is in funding achievements between researchers and professors. Overall, the meso level indicates that better-connected philosophers tend to work in large departments and that there is a correlation between rank and the position of philosophers in the meso level of connections, with BFBP decreasing in numbers in subsequent lower ranks.

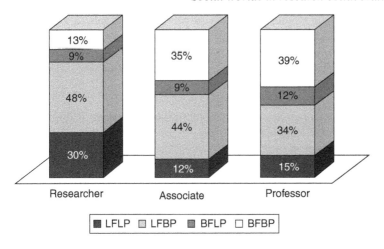

Figure 6.11 Distribution of fish and pond categories across ranks

Modelling funding achievements

Academic success is usually measured in number of publications and the impact factor of journals. Here, success is represented by the total amount of funding a researcher achieved from 1997 to 2006. So far, I have analysed the network characteristics in terms of getting connected with other researchers, without taking into account the amount of money received for every project scientists get involved with. Participating in a large number of projects increases the total amount of money received by each researcher (correlation 0.70). But establishing a higher number of collaborations does not necessarily mean receiving more funding, as someone can participate in fewer, but larger projects, where the total amount of money has to be distributed across a higher number of participants. In such situations, a researcher will show a high number of collaborations, but a lower amount of money than a researcher participating in a smaller number of projects with an overall better budget.

In the last part of this chapter, I model the amount of money obtained by every researcher in the last ten years against the variables that emerged as important at the individual, micro, macro and meso levels of analysis. I model each level hierarchically, to measure its influence separately from the other levels. At the individual level, I expect national coordinators and full professors to be more successful in obtaining money for research as well as the affiliation with specific sub-disciplines like history of philosophy, moral philosophy, theoretical philosophy, as well as other disciplines, which are overall the best funded.

The direction of causality must be taken with caution, as it could be that previous successful national coordination increases individuals' credibility and facilitates their convincing other people to join their projects in subsequent years. Similarly, the ability of obtaining funding might contribute to career advances, although, as discussed before, this is unlikely. The inverse direction of causality is less likely for sub-disciplines, as it is difficult for a scientist to change his or her discipline affiliation to invest in more successful fields.

H1. On average, national coordinators obtain a larger amount of money for research than people who only lead local units.

H2. On average, full professors obtain a larger amount of money for research than do scholars in other ranks.

H3. On average, people working in the history of philosophy, moral philosophy, theoretical philosophy and other disciplines obtain more money than do people in other sub-disciplines.

At the micro level, I expect projects with a higher level of interdisciplinarity to be more successful. This is represented by the E-I index values calculated for sub-disciplines. Again, direction of causality cannot be robustly tested, because it is possible that people who received funding for interdisciplinary collaborations will continue in the same direction. I also want to measure the success rate of researchers occupying a brokerage position or being involved in dense egonetworks. Following Burt (2005), I expect both brokerage scores and egonetwork density (which, for valued networks, is equal to the average value of ties) to impact on the total amount of funding. If the direction of causality is reversed, I would expect closure (as in density) to be the most successful strategy.

H4. On average, people with higher E-I index values for sub-disciplines obtain a larger amount of money for research than do people with lower values.

H5. On average, people with higher ego brokerage scores and/or higher egonetwork density obtain a larger amount of money for research than do people with low values on one or both measures.

At the macro level, given that core institutions are the largest ones and the ones getting more funding, I expect scientists working in them to be more successful than those working in peripheral universities. Here, the direction of causality is more robust, because given the low level of mobility of Italian researchers, it is very unlikely that a scientist will decide to move to a core institution attracted by the higher level of funding received by core departments.

H6. On average, people working in core institutions obtain a larger amount of money for research than do people working in peripheral ones.

At the meso level, which combines the size of the egonetworks (degree) with the size of universities in which philosophers work (number of appointed philosophers), I expect BFBP to be more successful than the other categories, given that to be big fish philosophers must have activated more collaborations than the median and that big ponds might be considered more prestigious institutions, thereby attracting a higher level of funding. The direction of causality for the size of the fish could be partially affected by the previous amount of funding, because previous successful projects can be one of the criteria for evaluation for future bids; it is more robust for the size of the pond due to the lack of mobility in Italian universities, making it unlikely that researchers change their institutional affiliation on the basis of their successful funding tracks.

H7. On average, big fish in big ponds (BFBP) obtain a larger amount of money for research than little fish in big ponds (LFBP), big fish in little ponds (BFLP), and little fish in little ponds (LFLP).

In all the models, the log of money values (the sum of all funding granted to each researcher over the ten years) is the dependent variable. I use the log of the money as the distribution is skewed. I also do not include, as an independent variable, the one measuring the number of projects each researcher participates in because it is highly correlated to the dependent variable and therefore hides all the possible effects of the other independent variables.

In the first model, I introduce the variable of being a national coordinator (no roles as national coordinator as constant). In the second model, I introduce variables related to rank (full professor as constant, associate professor and researcher). In the third model, I introduce variables related to sub-disciplines (theoretical philosophy as constant, logic, moral philosophy, aesthetics, philosophy of language, history of philosophy, history of ancient philosophy, history of medieval philosophy, jurisprudence, philosophy of law, political philosophy, history of political doctrines, and other disciplines). In the fourth model, E-I values for sub-disciplines (ranging from −1 to +1), brokerage scores (ranging from 0 to 0.73) and egonetwork valued density (ranging from 0 to 4.06) are introduced (−1 scores for E-I and 0 values for brokerage and closure being constant). In the fifth model, I take into account core values, being in the periphery is constant. In the sixth and final model, the meso categories are introduced (BFBP as constant, BFLP, LFBP, LFLP).

The summary of variables' values is presented in Table 6.4. Outputs of the models are displayed in Table 6.5, which reports the values for R, R^2 and standard errors, and in Table 6.6, which reports coefficients for every variable. I correct for potential lack of independence between cases using the network disturbances model (Leenders 2002). As expected, there is a very large network correlation: the estimate of the feedback parameter is 0.5 and the standard error is 0.05. The diagnostics show that there are some very large residuals but there are no alarming departures from model assumptions (see Note 1 above).

The first model, which takes into account how many times scientists have been in the role of national coordinators, explains 16.8 per cent of the variance: being a national coordinator increases the total amount of money from an average of 21,114€ to an average of 35,062€, and values are significant. Therefore,

Table 6.4 Descriptive statistics of variables

Variable	Abs. values	%	Average value	Range
National coordinator	100	21%	1.69	1/5
Of which 5 times national coordinator	3	3%		
Of which 4 times national coordinator	5	5%		
Of which 3 times national coordinator	10	10%		
Of which 2 times national coordinator	22	22%		
Of which 1 time national coordinator	60	60%		
Professor	379	80%		
Associate	75	15%		
Researchers	23	5%		
Theoretical philosophy	47	10%		
Logic	29	6%		
Moral philosophy	52	11%		
Aesthetic	24	5%		
Philosophy of language	11	2%		
History of philosophy	98	20%		
History of ancient philosophy	22	5%		
History of medieval philosophy	17	3%		
Jurisprudence	17	4%		
Philosophy of law	44	9%		
Political philosophy	28	6%		
History of political doctrines	28	6%		
Other	60	13%		
E-I			0.88	−1/1
Normalised broker			0.14	0/0.73
Egonet-valued density			1.27	0/4.06
Core	292	61%		
BFBP	177	37%		
BFLP	55	12%		
LFBP	174	36%		
LFLP	71	15%		

Note: See Bellotti (2012: 225) for the descriptive statistics of variables in physics.

Hypothesis 1 is confirmed: this can be considered as a control variable, as the national coordinator is in most of the cases the one who sets up the project and obtains the largest part of the funding.

The second model, which includes the philosophers' ranks, does not explain much of the variation in the amount of funding (R^2 rises only to 19.2 per cent) but it is significant: full professors have gained on average 23,358€ over the ten years under analysis compared to 16,245€ earned by associate professors and 12,843€ by researchers. Therefore, Hypothesis 2 is confirmed.

Table 6.5 Model summary. Dependent variable: Logmoney

Model	R	R^2	Adjusted R^2	Std. error of the estimate
1	0.412	0.170	0.168	0.93925
2	0.444	0.198	0.192	0.92538
3	0.498	0.248	0.223	0.90763
4	0.643	0.414	0.391	0.80373
5	0.643	0.414	0.390	0.80460
6	0.690	0.475	0.450	0.76365

1. Predictors: (Constant), Sum of national coordinator
2. Predictors: (Constant: Full professor), Sum of national coordinator, Researcher, Associate
3. Predictors: (Constant: Full professor, Theoretical philosophy), Sum of national coordinator, Researcher, Associate, Politicalphilo, Politicaldoctrines, Philolanguage, Aesthetic, Jurisprudence, Historymedieval, Historyancient, Logic, Moral, Philolaw, Other, Historyphilo
4. Predictors: (Constant: Full professor, Theoretical philosophy, E-I disciplines = −1, Normalized broker and Egonetwork density = 0), Sum of national coordinator, Researcher, Associate, Politicalphilo, Politicaldoctrines, Philolanguage, Aesthetic, Jurisprudence, Historymedieval, Historyancient, Logic, Moral, Philolaw, Other, Historyphilo, E-I disciplines few, Density, nBroker
5. Predictors: (Constant: Full professor, Theoretical philosophy, E-I disciplines = −1, Normalized broker and Egonetwork density = 0, Coreness = 0), Sum of national coordinator, Researcher, Associate, Politicalphilo, Politicaldoctrines, Philolanguage, Aesthetic, Jurisprudence, Historymedieval, Historyancient, Logic, Moral, Philolaw, Other, Historyphilo, E-I disciplines few, Density, nBroker, Coreness
6. Predictors: (Constant: Full professor, Theoretical philosophy, E-I disciplines = −1, Normalized broker and Egonetwork density = 0, Coreness = 0, BFBP), Sum of national coordinator, Researcher, Associate, Politicalphilo, Politicaldoctrines, Philolanguage, Aesthetic, Jurisprudence, Historymedieval, Historyancient, Logic, Moral, Philolaw, Other, Historyphilo, E-I disciplines few, Density, nBroker, Coreness, BFLP, LFBP, LFLP

In the third model, sub-disciplines are included: a significant increase is visible for theoretic philosophy (27,184€), whereas academics working in jurisprudence or other disciplines receive significantly less funding than other philosophers (13,475€ and 16,680€). Also, the overall explanation only increases to 22.3 per cent. Hypothesis 3 is thus only confirmed for theoretical philosophy, but it is not confirmed for history of philosophy, moral philosophy, and especially other disciplines, which, contrary to the hypothesis, are less successful.

The fourth model adds the network variables of the micro level of interactions, and it explains, like in the case of physics (Bellotti 2012) much more of the variance (R^2 is now up to 39.1 per cent). On average, professors with −1 E-I values, 0 brokerage scores, and 0 density obtain 12,892€. But although the E-I index calculated for disciplines is not significant, a brokerage role is highly significant and accounts for a substantial increase in the amount of funding. For example, having a brokerage score of 0.2 increases the average amount of obtained funding to 21,951€, having a brokerage score of 0.4 increases it to 37,375€, and having a maximum brokerage score of 0.73 increases it to 89,936€. At the same time, egonetwork valued density is also positively significant. Having a density of 0.5 increases the average amount of funding to 14,695€, a density of 1.5 increases it

Table 6.6 Coefficients' values

Model	1		2		3		4		5		6	
Variables	B	Std. error	B	Std. error	B	Std. error	B	Std. error	B	Std. error	B	Std. error
(Constant)	9.9577***	0.0467	10.0587***	0.0514	10.2104***	0.0527	9.4644***	0.173646	9.4654***	0.177857	9.8112***	0.193763
Sum of national coordinator	0.5072***	0.0514	0.4647***	0.0518	0.4245***	0.0518	0.3117***	0.046018	0.3118***	0.046195	0.3213***	0.044368
Associate			-0.3631**	0.1190	-0.3204**	0.1192	-0.20501	0.104753	-0.20482	0.105136	-0.2153**	0.100894
Researcher			-0.5981**	0.2000	-0.5657**	0.1981	-0.31004	0.173552	-0.31024	0.173909	-0.25182	0.167119
Logic					-0.1122	0.2148	-0.25206	0.187135	-0.25181	0.187581	-0.15895	0.180552
Moral					-0.2370	0.1827	-0.23425	0.158933	-0.23414	0.159162	-0.22767	0.152804
Aesthetics					-0.1993	0.2283	-0.4619**	0.200069	-0.4615**	0.20078	-0.4650**	0.19284
Philolanguage					-0.1610	0.3056	-0.13612	0.266178	-0.13621	0.266489	-0.17309	0.255652
Historyphilo					0.1085	0.1618	0.001936	0.141497	0.001946	0.141652	0.057811	0.136227
Historyancient					-0.3402	0.2356	-0.24487	0.205252	-0.24476	0.205517	-0.17269	0.197632
Historymedieval					0.2693	0.2585	0.00258	0.226161	0.002454	0.226459	-0.09325	0.218294
Jurisprudence					-0.7054**	0.2572	-0.41533	0.224812	-0.41548	0.225128	-0.221	0.218884
Philolaw					-0.0352	0.1918	-0.03003	0.167125	-0.02978	0.167568	0.076876	0.162223
Politicalphilo					-0.3656	0.2171	-0.35786	0.189042	-0.35778	0.189273	-0.16956	0.184372
Politicaldoctrines					-0.0717	0.2171	-0.17206	0.189386	-0.17176	0.189917	-0.15442	0.18225
Other					-0.4884**	0.1775	-0.3213**	0.155011	-0.3212**	0.155203	-0.19442	0.150451
Density							0.2618***	0.062173	0.2618***	0.062245	0.1748**	0.0613
nBroker							2.6609***	0.217371	2.6608***	0.217621	1.8601***	0.242954
E-I disciplines few							0.091444	0.119554	0.091584	0.119803	0.122053	0.115611
Coreness									-0.00199	0.075428	0.068379	0.110319
BFLP											0.136392	0.149843
LFBP											-0.5522***	0.097351
LFLP											-0.4768**	0.151413

*** = <0.001

** = <0.05

to 19,093€, a density of 2.5 increases it to 24,807€, and a maximum density of 4 increases it to 36,739€.

Thus, Hypothesis 4 is not confirmed, whilst Hypothesis 5 is: brokers gain much more advantage than their colleagues in terms of funding, but closure is a valuable strategy too, even if not as successful as brokerage. Interestingly, brokerage roles and closure reduce the influence of individual characteristics, like being a full professor working in theoretical philosophy (the constant), and the disadvantages for other ranks, where researchers are not as penalised against full professors and values for associate professors lose significance. Similarly, they reduce the disadvantage of working in other disciplines, although it disfavours academics working in aesthetics for whom the structural position of the broker, or being embedded in highly cohesive groups, are not successful strategies.

The fifth model considers working in a core institution. This is not significant, and it does not explain any more variance (R^2 slightly drops to 39.0 per cent). Therefore, Hypothesis 6 is not confirmed.

The sixth and final model takes into account the meso level network variables, which produces another increase in the amount of variance explained (R^2 is 45 per cent). Big fish in big ponds (BFBP) obtain on average significantly more funding (18,236€) than little fish either in big ponds (LFBP) (10,498€) or in little ponds (LFLP) (11,320€) and the values are significant, but values for big fish in little ponds (BFLP) are not significant. Therefore, Hypothesis 7 is only partially confirmed. It is interesting to note that little fish are generally penalised against the big fish, but LFBP are more penalised than LFLP, as the former gain, on average, less funding than the latter. Moreover, the meso level variables diminish the positive effect of brokerage and closure and delete the disadvantages of other disciplines, indicating the importance of taking into account the size of the institutions.

The analysis of the influence of micro, macro and meso factors on the rate of success of gaining research funding indicates some interesting elements that suggest the possible existence of an underlying mechanism. The roles of national coordinators and of brokers are extremely important in obtaining money, and these results are very similar to the ones obtained for the physicists (Bellotti 2012: 226). Along with individual attributes, which together explain 22.3 per cent, what makes a difference for Italian physicists and philosophers is their ability to establish research collaborations, either by attracting people under their coordination or by attracting people who do not otherwise collaborate with each other.

The importance of the structural position of researchers in relation to colleagues and competitors is shown by the further 22.7 per cent of the variance explained by the micro and meso structural factors. It is also confirmed by the lack of influence of dominant disciplines like history of philosophy, which do not attract, on average, a higher amount of funding compared to other sub-disciplines. Further, the fact that micro structural elements diminish the influence of individual attributes like the rank and affiliation with specific sub-disciplines like aesthetics suggests the existence of an underlying structural mechanism.

Finally, the meso level indicates that the number of collaborations produces more advantages than the size of institutions where philosophers work, although similar to the physicists, working in a big pond without having a large number of collaborators may imply facing the competition of the big fish who belong to the same institution. Controlling the degree with the size of the department thus improves the understanding of the data and diminishes the effect of micro network variables, showing that whilst the position of individuals in the network is an important element in predicting the amount of funding, the size of institutions also play a crucial role. This is also evident in the lack of effects at a macro level. Core universities that activate more PRIN projects gain more money overall, but this is not reflected at an individual level: the fact that a department is successful in getting funded does not mean that its researchers will obtain, on average, more money than the ones who work in institutions with fewer projects.

Although the numerical data show the impact of the individual positions in the network, the meaning of these positions, in terms of what flows in the network, cannot be extracted from this kind of analysis. A structural hole does not automatically mean a powerful position in controlling information flow; indeed, there may not be the need for such control. Similarly, closure cannot be automatically considered the result of positive relationships, because people may be constrained to stick with a research group by other collaborators or by the lack of alternative opportunities. The underlying structural mechanisms appear likely to influence participants' behaviour as they partially shape opportunities and constraints in terms of possibilities of research collaborations. The numerical data, however, do not indicate if people are aware of their structural location within the network or if they consciously exploit network positions to increase the chances of getting funded.

Qualitative analysis of projects' content: chasing economic resources

To answer these questions, I now turn to content analysis of the projects' descriptions. My first objective is to see if researchers are aware of the various structural advantages and use them to solicit funding, or if the structural effects operate as intransitive mechanisms and individuals use different narratives to describe their work. I will look at the projects' descriptions and see if there are any mentions of structural characteristics of interdisciplinary, of cohesiveness of the group based on previous successful collaborations and of brokers' specialisations and expertise. Subsequently, I also code further emerging themes and connect them to these main topics. The first goal of the analysis is thus to observe if projects aggregate according to sub-disciplinary clusters.

We already know, by looking at the E-I index, that individual researchers tend to favour interdisciplinary collaborations, although the strategy is not successful in terms of increasing the chances of getting funded. However, by looking at the one mode network that links projects together via the number of researchers in common and reading the descriptions, it is possible to identify the general philosophical areas to which projects belong—for example, distinguishing between projects focused on some specific historical aspects (history of ancient, medieval, modern and contemporary philosophy), projects in ethics, aesthetics, logic and philosophy of sciences, political doctrines, philosophy of law, and the like. In particular, I will look at components of different sizes to see if streams of topics aggregate in independent clusters, possibly building structural barriers around research groups working on specific topics.

The second goal of the analysis is to see if there is any reference to the complementary structures of brokerage and closure. To do this, I counted the number of projects in which a broker is present and then analysed the descriptions of the brokers' tasks in each specific project they work on. Next, I observed whether there was any reference to the opposite but complementary strategy of closure, where researchers play the card of previous successful PRIN collaboration to solicit continued funding. To do that, I looked at the bipartite network that links people to projects, where it is easier to identify cohesive sub-clusters and people in brokering positions.

The identification of brokers based on the two-mode network follows stricter criteria than the ones used for the quantitative analysis. This is because the algorithm that calculates brokerage scores identifies people who are brokers within their egonetwork and normalises the number of times they link two otherwise disconnected people relative to the size of their local neighbourhood. There may be more than two people brokering between projects, but given that the value for brokerage scores is calculated for each egonetwork, redundant roles are not taken into account. Here, instead, I only consider as brokers people who are actual cut points between projects, which means that if they are removed, the network will disconnect. This makes the task of analysing the content of the project descriptions of brokers' duties more manageable, because instead of looking at 198 people with a value of normalised brokerage > 0, I only looked at the 104 cut points in the two-mode network whose role is not equivalent to anyone else's.

Finally, I coded every topic that emerged from reading the projects descriptions and I looked at the distribution of these topics in projects where there are brokers and where there is a reference to cohesiveness. This last part of the analysis adds depth to the content of the projects, especially in relation to possible reasons for brokers to change groups and for groups to strengthen collaborations.

Clusters of projects and disciplinary boundaries

The analysis of the project-by-project network with number of researchers in common reveals a structure of several independent components, with variously cohesive clusters embedded in them (Figure 6.12). Apart from 12 isolates (indicating projects that do not share any researcher with any other project), there are five dyads (two projects linked together), three triads (three linked projects), five

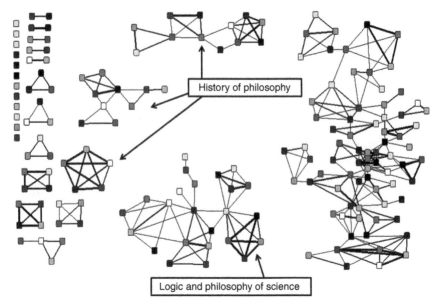

Darkness of color: oldest projects
Thickness of ties: number of researchers in common

Figure 6.12 Project-by-project network

four-sized components (four cliques and one triad with a pendant), one five-sized clique (with five projects all connected to each other), one 10-sized component, one 12-sized component, one 24-sized component, and one 71-sized component (where the size of the components represent the number of projects in them).

Smaller components (<10) represent highly cohesive research groups working repetitively on projects, normally focused on specific topics and led by a dominant professor who always acted as national coordinator. For example, Full Professor Gallini led three projects working on unpublished letters and field notes of the philosophical anthropologist Ernesto de Martino, who had been Professor Gallini's teacher. The research group Professor Gallini led involved the same people for six years. Similarly, Vescovini led three projects on Spinoza, managing two other people. After the first collaboration, one of the researchers left the group (possibly to retire) and was substituted by his research assistant. The other collaborator, Vinti, led a subsequent project involving other people, for whom he acted as a broker with Vescovini's group: this last project is not dedicated as much to medieval history as to theoretical philosophy.

Whilst the smaller components (<10) and the 71 component aggregate topics from various sub-disciplines, the five, 10, and 12 components are completely dominated by the history of philosophy, and the 24 component is dedicated to projects on logics and philosophy of science. This does not mean that every researcher working in these projects belongs to a unique sub-discipline, as projects may involve people from different affiliations, but that the topics of projects are related to specific philosophical themes.

For example, the 24 component includes a highly cohesive 4clique of projects all led by different people, dedicated to analytical philosophy and the relationship between mind and language, reasoning and representation, knowledge and cognition. Another highly cohesive 4clique, led by Chiereghin, includes projects on classic German philosophy and its role in the development of the debate around the relationship between ethos and nature, science, knowledge and action. Researchers working in these two cliques have subsequently merged together in a project investigating the architecture of theoretical and practical knowledge, which also attracted researchers coming from another 4clique of projects, led by Pizzi and specifically dedicated to the role of reasoning and logic in scientific discoveries.

This clique merged with another 4clique, led by Carsetti, on knowledge construction, complex cognitive systems, and the theory of semantic information, and with a dyad on the importance of information and causal relations in science and technology advancements. Pendant projects on the concepts of equality and freedom and their implications for political science are also attached. Researchers working on these projects were mostly affiliated with the subdisciplines of theoretical philosophy (nine) and logic and philosophy of science (22), although three of them worked in philosophy of language (for the projects related to analytical philosophy and semantic theories) and two in political philosophy.

In the case of the components dominated by history of philosophy, the 5clique is dedicated to the study of modern and contemporary German philosophy, and involves a highly cohesive research group led by Poggi, a Florentine professor who specialised in this specific philosophical area. The 10 component is dedicated to Aristotelian and Platonism philosophy, where a 4clique led by Berti and his student Natali is connected to a methodological dyad led by Leszl. Berti's group is also connected to a more recent project led by Casertano on the rise of European identity and the problem of individuality that mediates between Berti's projects and a dyad on Hellenism. Apart from Berti's group, the rest of the people involved in this component do not seem to have built up a highly cohesive research group, but the three main components instead are loosely linked by two brokers (Casertano and Calvini). The brokers moved from the original groups they worked with to a more recent Casertano project, that aggregated people not highly involved in any other group by merging them with part of Berti's group.

A similar loose structure characterises the 12 component. A highly cohesive 5clique of projects dedicated to Bruno and Spinoza is led by Ciliberto, a professor at Pisa and a leading expert in Renaissance philosophy. This group is linked via a broker to a triad of projects on Descartes, Galileo and the emergence of a scientific culture from Renaissance to Enlightenment. The two groups also involve some people coming from an old project on Bruno and Campanella, whereas the Descartes and Galileo triad is connected via a broker to a triad on Schopenhauer

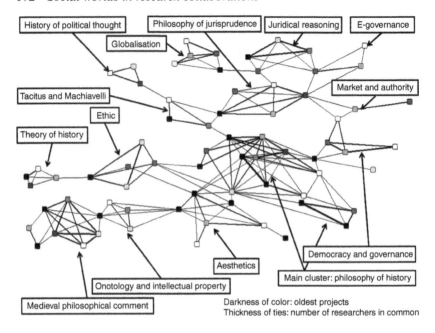

History of political thought Philosophy of jurisprudence Juridical reasoning E-governance

Globalisation

Tacitus and Machiavelli

Ethic

Theory of history

Market and authority

Democracy and governance

Aesthetics

Main cluster: philosophy of history

Onotology and intellectual property

Medieval philosophical comment

Darkness of color: oldest projects
Thickness of ties: number of researchers in common

Figure 6.13 The 71 component in the project-by-project network

and Nietzsche. These last two groups do not show a cohesive structure, as they are not continuously led by the same coordinators but seem to aggregate a circle of people who move around various collaborations. Whilst the 10 component is composed only by people affiliated with the disciplinary area of ancient philosophy, the 12 component involves only researchers affiliated with the general area of history of philosophy.

In both the logic and the history of philosophy components, there seem to be some highly cohesive groups, led by a few professors who aggregate people around them in continuous collaborations: these core groups add and drop peripheral collaborators who jump across groups over the years, ending up in brokering positions. The next analysis section looks specifically at these 'free riders' and their role in research projects. It is worth noting that the stream of research in logic and philosophy of science that showed up as especially successful in the quantitative analysis cluster together in the second-largest component of the network, indicating the important position it occupies within the overall direction of research in philosophy.

The 71 component shows an interesting configuration (on the right in Figure 6.12 and in more detail in Figure 6.13). A main core cluster is led by three dominant professors (Cantilla and Cacciatore from Naples and Bianco from Rome) and some minor leaders, and they all work with a large group of researchers participating in several projects. They mainly work at the University of Naples, with a smaller group coming from the University of Rome, and they mainly belong to the sub-disciplines of moral philosophy and history of philosophy. All the projects focus on philosophy of history.

Around this main cluster are two fairly cohesive groups working on ethics and aesthetics and led by several people: these groups mediate with other cohesive groups dedicated to mediaeval philosophical commentaries (led by Fioravanti), ontology and intellectual property (led by Ferraris), and theory of history (without a single leader). Also around the main cluster are groups working on philosophy of jurisprudence (led by Faralli), juridical reasoning (led by Guastini), the role of authority in market regulation (led by Sartori) and e-governance (led by Pattaro). Other groups focus on applications of philosophical concepts in politics and governance, studying history of political thought, the influence of Tacito and Machiavelli on political science, issues related to globalisation (led by Cerutti) and contemporary democracy and governance (led by Conti).

The interesting aspect of this component is that, on the one hand, it is composed of fairly independent groups, with few brokers connecting various projects. Groups are dominated by a few full professors who aggregate researchers over the years. Again, it is interesting to look at the role of brokers who connect them and investigate the possible reasons why they move across projects and, ultimately, gain more success. On the other hand, the loose connections that brokers establish across disciplines indicate broad applications of classic philosophical themes, especially in the area of ethics and its implications for juridical frameworks and political assets.

Despite the dominance of some sub-disciplines in Italian academia, like the history of philosophy, this analysis seems to confirm the relative power of traditional studies in terms of setting up the research agenda and the importance of linking the philosophical work to applied fields. These observations are in line with the results of quantitative analysis, where we saw that once the micro level of network structure is taken into account, the significant differences between traditional disciplines and applied ones are washed out.

Brokerage and closure as strategic configurations

For the analysis of brokerage roles, I searched the overall description of the projects and the detailed description of the specific tasks of brokers for emerging themes, particularly looking for any textual script that refers to possible characteristics of the brokers or of their positions. Not all the descriptions contain a reference to the brokerage structure: often the text illustrates the local units' duties in very general terms by simply listing the tasks to be performed. Also, the topics often occur together or are included in other emerging themes, so it is difficult to exclusively count the times individual themes appear in projects' descriptions.

When references to peculiar tasks of the brokers are made, these normally describe a particular expertise of the broker, who specialises in either studying a specific author or school of thought or in focusing on the investigation of a specific topic. For example, some brokers are involved in various projects due to their expertise on the philosophy of Bruno, Campanella, Descartes, Mach,

Hussler, Suarez, or more specifically on the development of philosophy of science in Aristotle's thought or in medieval philosophy. Some others specialise in the study of different kinds of logic or on teleological structures; in some cases, the attention to a specific type of topic also favours the link between different disciplines and its application in peripheral fields. The description of the tasks of Signore, who brokers between a 2001 project led by Bianco on the ethical aspects of responsibility and a 2006 project led by Cacciatore on the concept of interculturality, exemplifies the interdisciplinary potential of specialised knowledge that can be transferred and applied to the study of various concepts:

> The contribution of the research group working at the University of Lecce is characterised by the attention to the socio-economic dimension of the problem of responsibility. The group can count on the collaboration between philosophers and economists, who extend the work on the concept of values to the one of responsibility, where the latter is not only seen in ethical terms but also in its economic implications.
>
> (Signore in Bianco's project 2001)

> In the task of the local unit of University of Lecce there are various and differentiated competences: philosophical, historical, scientific, political, economic and ethical-religious. The goal is to focus on the new Weltanschauungen that appear covertly or explicitly within the debate over interculturality and their possible outcome for the embracement of multiculturalisms in contemporary times.
>
> (Signore in Cacciatore's project 2006)

While the reference to the mechanism of brokerage does not often explicitly emerge in the projects' descriptions, the mechanism of closure is widely acknowledged and strategically used in the proposals. In all cases where high density is measured, the qualitative content of the project that explicitly refers to the structural mechanism of closure adopts the narrative of the need to consolidate previously established relationships between researchers belonging to the group. It is also differentiated in a series of sub-themes: some groups make direct references to the continuation of previously funded PRIN research projects. In some cases, they claim the need to build up and expand on previous significant results (not necessarily from PRIN projects); in other projects, they want to reinforce relationships developed through conferences, affiliations with philosophical societies and inter-university research centres.

> The research presented here has been made possible by an antecedent funded PRIN project (Ioppolo 1998) on the cynic and stoic tradition from the Hellenism to the period of the Empire, and it can be understood as its continuation.
>
> (Brancacci's project 2001)

The various local units involved in this project constitute a community that has been active for several years through conferences, seminars, and other forms of systematic contact, often facilitated by the Italian Society of Analytic Philosophy.

(Parrini's project 1999)

We want to continue to pursue a shared stream of research that started in the biannual PRIN project funded in 2002. The aim is to promote the collaboration between all the Italian philosophers that, although from different perspectives, have looked at the theme of scientific discoveries by using logic, cognitive and computational instruments. In order to do so we also want to keep organising international conferences, following the ones organised in 1998–2001–2004.

(Pizzi's project 2004)

Some of the results obtained by the national coordinator in a previously funded PRIN project (2000) on the measurement of freedom and social mobility seem to suggest that some statistical indexes, like the Spearman index, can be extremely useful also for the analysis of belief-revision and theoretical change.

(Giorello's project 2002)

Overall, it seems that the strategy of cohesiveness is more overtly recognised by researchers, who explicitly advocate previously successful collaborations as a reason for obtaining more funding. Brokerage is less explicitly recognised and seems to emerge as an intransitive mechanism due to the specialised expertise of researchers who use them to collaborate in various projects.

Emerging topics

The last section of the content analysis looks at topics that emerge from projects' descriptions, aggregates them in general categories, and observes the frequency in which these categories occur, either combined with topics of brokerage and closure or combined with other themes. This analysis is done by simply counting the occurrence of topics, and then by looking at how many times the descriptions also contain references to brokerage and closure narratives (Table 6.7). Finally, the two-mode, project-by-topic affiliation matrix is converted to a one-mode, topic-by-topic matrix. This matrix is visualised in Netdraw (Figure 6.14), where nodes represent topics, and lines the number of projects that mention these topics. The visualisation is made with a spring embedder, a method in which the nodes in a graph are like springs that push and pull on each other. Nodes similar to one other tend to pull each other close, while nodes different from one other push each other apart. Spring embedders arrange the nodes in a way that reduces the stresses of pulling and pushing (Freeman 2000).

Table 6.7 Occurrence of topics and relations with brokerage and closure

Topics	Number of mentions	In projects with brokers	In projects claiming cohesion
Studying a specific concept	131	49	15
Linking different philosophical traditions	119	54	16
Studying a specific author	83	40	9
Interdisciplinarity	62	17	10
Critical editions and translations	53	19	11
Previous publications	46	9	10
Impact and applicability	44	19	5
Organising a conference	37	13	4
International collaborations	35	7	7
Density (cohesion)	30	4	NA
e-publication	29	6	8
European and global issues	27	9	2
Groups' expertise	24	5	7
Unpublished material	23	4	7

As indicated in Table 6.7, the most frequently occurring topic is the one describing a specific concept that is the focus of a research project. This category includes, for example, studies on rationality, its definition and implications for the philosophy of knowledge and scientific inference and explanation; the aesthetic relationship between image, perception, memory and ideas; the problem of subjectivity, agency and intentionality, and their ethical implications for the relationship between individuals and communities; medieval philosophical lexicon and translating techniques; juridical reasoning, theory of rights, but also privacy and copyright issues; public sphere, conflict, authority and individual freedom.

Another very common topic relates to the study of specific schools of thought, like analytic philosophy; classic German philosophy of Hegel and Leibniz; together with the study of the philosophy of authors like Nietzsche, Schopenhauer, Heidegger, Bruno, Campanella, S. Tommaso, Descartes, Husserl and Scheler.

Apart from these two topics, the other most frequent description relates to projects that link different philosophical traditions, either by looking at evolutions of school of thought and reciprocal influences, or at philosophical controversies and debates. For example, a project led by Egidi aims to

> Investigate, by reinterpreting some Kantian proposals, the relationship between apparel and experience as it was first advanced in the conflicting positions of Newton and Mach.
>
> (Egidi's project 2005)

Several projects mention interdisciplinarity, either as the main aim of the project, or as verifiability criteria. For example, a 2004 project led by Cavalla aims to

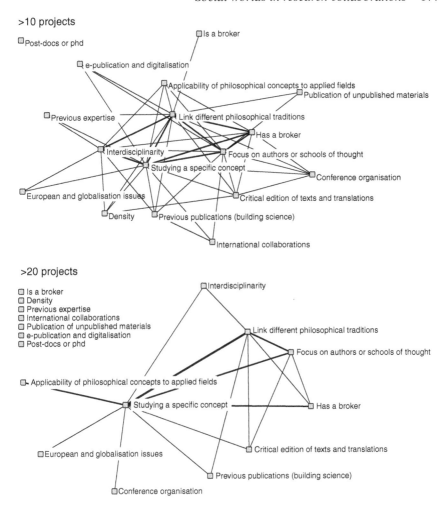

Figure 6.14 Affiliation network topic-by-topic with number of projects in common

Identify the path of stratification of the main systematic models of juridical reasoning (historical level), their effective diffusion (sociological level), their rational justifications (theoretical level).

(Cavalla's project 2004)

Similarly, a project led by Galli (2006) is described as

A research project that gathers various competences and overcomes disciplinary boundaries by cross analysing common themes.

(Galli's project 2006)

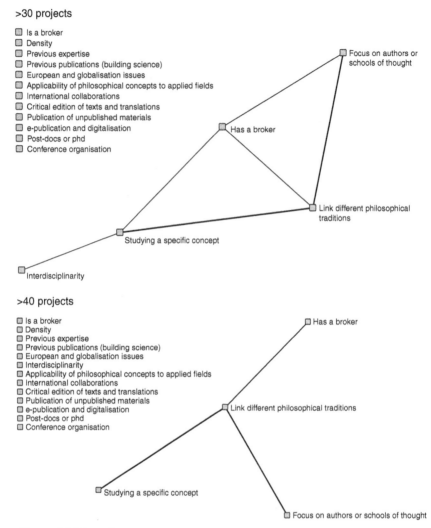

Figure 6.14 (cont.)

Other common themes describe the aim of the projects by publishing critical editions and Italian translations of philosophical works, or by updating previous works published by the research groups. Other themes are the possible applicability of philosophical studies to other fields (e.g. in developing training modules for professional sectors of secondary schools), the intention of organising conferences, publishing material online, and studying unpublished texts. International relationships are often mentioned to indicate the importance of the study. Finally, some projects refer explicitly to European or global emerging issues (such as the problem of inequality, civil and human rights, multiculturalism, immigration and the like) and to the specific expertise of the research group, for example by mentioning previous works that have been successful both at national and international levels.

Within these topics, the reference to closure is more common in ones referring to publications (either in terms of future publications of critical editions, e-publications, unpublished materials or updating previous publications) and to international collaborations or group expertise. Brokers are scattered around all topics, but dominate especially the ones referring to studying specific concepts or authors and to linking different traditions. These links emerge more clearly by looking at the network of topics' co-occurrences (Figure 6.14): with up to ten projects in common, the topics of focusing on a single author or concept, of linking different traditions, of applicability, interdisciplinarity and brokerage cluster together in a highly dense core, whilst the remaining topics are peripherally located and only link with topics in the core.

By raising the number of projects in common up to at least 20, the topic of studying a specific concept becomes highly central and remains connected in a clique including the focus on a specific author, the link of different traditions, and the brokerage structure even when the number of projects in common rises to 30. Interestingly, the concept of interdisciplinarity is also still connected to these core topics. Finally, at a level of up to 40 projects in common, the main central topic becomes the one linking different traditions, which is still connected to both studying a specific concept and focusing on a single author, but also to the brokerage structure.

The content analysis of projects' descriptions seems to indicate that closure is a strategy that is more likely to be advocated by researchers who focus on the traditional philosophical tasks of archival work on philosophical texts and publication of this material. Brokerage structures are more likely be found for researchers with a specialised expertise, who are involved in projects for studying particular authors, topics, and especially for linking different traditions of studies. Interdisciplinarity is widely used as a narrative strategy for advocating for funding (with 62 mentions, it is the fourth most common topic), but it is not pursued in practice, as indicated by the clustering of disciplines around topics, confirming its lack of success in increasing the chances of getting funded at an individual level.

Conclusion

In this chapter, I have used archival data to describe and analyse the relations of research collaborations between philosophers in Italy. Whilst archival data have been widely used in network research, the main limit of this kind of textual source is that the information is not created for the purpose of the research but pre-exist before the data collection process (Marsden 2005). Therefore, not all the required data are available for the analysis. In the case of philosophers, the database of PRIN projects does not include any information on collaborations before 1997. More important, it does not include data on unsuccessful projects, which would reinforce the evidence of the structural mechanisms that favour or hamper the process of getting funded. Despite their limits, archival data are a rich source of information: they can be coded and then analysed for formal network characteristics. They can also be analysed qualitatively, providing contextual depth to the formal structure of research collaborations.

Although it makes use of statistical analysis, the quantitative modelling of individual and network characteristics is different from classic variable analysis. Variable analysis, specifically regression analysis, would look at the distribution of funding against the distribution of ranks, disciplines and institutional affiliation. It would assume that researchers represent independent units of analysis and explain the variance of funding by correlating it with their individual characteristics. It would then try to generalise results to some reference population (e.g. all the philosophers in Italy), given the fairly good distribution of funded philosophers compared to non-funded philosophers.

In the case presented in this chapter, the analysis of distribution of individual characteristics, which explains 22.3 per cent of the variance, is modelled together with network dependencies at micro, meso and macro levels, which explain a further 22.7 per cent of the variance. These results confirm that interdependencies of actors and structural positions are important. Coordinating roles, ranks, brokerage and closure, and the type of institution where philosophers work are all crucial elements that increase the chances of getting funded. They represent the underlying intransitive mechanisms ($M_{1...n}$) that generate specific outcomes (O) within the context (C) of Italian philosophy.

The peculiarities of this context are investigated by looking at the narratives that researchers utilise to advocate for money: closure and interdisciplinarity are popular cultural conventions; brokerage is not explicitly mentioned as a successful mechanism but indicates the importance of specialised knowledge. Therefore, content analysis investigates the empirical level of people's perceptions that are not perfectly congruent with the multiple underlying mechanisms that generate the structural outcomes. Generalisation of results is not obtained via inferring similar mechanisms for a wider population but by transferring the analysis to comparable case studies. In this case, the same mechanisms have been detected for the research collaborations in physics (Bellotti 2012), although some contextual elements indicate important difference. Further content analysis of physicists' projects could reveal different cultural conventions that shape the collaborative work and other types of asymmetries that hide the structural mechanisms regulating the process of getting funded.

Notes

1 I thank Johan Koskinen for advising me on the network disturbance models and for running the regression models presented here and in Bellotti (2012).
2 Fararo and Doreian (1984) acknowledge that the same formalisation was proposed by Wilson (1982) in a paper written in the 1960s but not published until later.
3 For a detailed description of the field of physics, see Bellotti (2012).

4 The system of recruitment has recently been reformed: whilst data here refer to a period in which recruitment was organised around sub-disciplines, it is now organised around disciplines' macro areas. This means that the baseline for competition is now larger, as academics have to compete with people in the whole disciplinary area of reference (e.g. the macro area of historical, philosophical, psychological and pedagogical sciences) to get jobs and obtain promotions, whereas in the past they competed with experts in their specialised areas (e.g. history of ancient philosophy, or logic and philosophy of science).

5 Years were selected according to the availability of data at the time of the research from the Ministry of Italian University and Research website, www.miur.it.

6 While for collaborations to research projects the information dates back to 1997, for rank, disciplinary and institutional affiliations data are only available from 2000 onwards.

7   Coda

I started this book with a discussion about the historical rise of a paradigm war between quantitative and qualitative methods: I showed how paradigms should not be considered as ontologically and epistemologically incompatible perspectives, but, following Kuhn (1970), should be seen as scientific communities that share a defined set of problems considered worthy to investigate and that agree on the appropriate research techniques with which to conduct investigations. I conclude now by reflecting on network science in paradigmatic terms.

Although I discussed in some detail the foundational elements that characterise network science in Chapter 3, I do not believe that the study of networks should be seen as a recognisable paradigmatic field, given the wide variety of areas in which it has been applied. And, far from being a limit, this lack of paradigmatic stance should be seen as an advantage in network studies. Because of its essential interdisciplinarity, it is difficult to identify a set of problems that network scientists would agree to prioritise in their research: within each discipline, it is more likely that there will be several substantive questions that the study of networks could address.

Network science, as sketched in the important contributions of Borgatti and colleagues (2009), Brandes and colleagues (2013) and Kadushin (2012) provide the ontological, epistemological and methodological foundations that are to be used when addressing substantive questions, regardless of the discipline. Therefore, when discussing network science, instead of looking at common topics, it is possibly more useful to shift the attention from substantive problems to general network mechanisms, which are more likely to be found across various contexts of research.

In the three empirical cases presented in this book, some common structural features have emerged: homophily (e.g. in terms of similarities in age, geographical location, social class and cultural background) has been detected in friendship structures and in street groups, the latter to be considered as a specialised type of friendship network. Homophily also plays a role in the social world of philosophers: here the content analysis of projects indicates the tendency of some topics to aggregate in cohesive clusters, like in the case of the study of logic and philosophy of science. However, in philosophy, interdisciplinarity is also highly evaluated, as it clearly emerges from the qualitative analysis.

The case of interdisciplinary projects is an example of how some mechanisms may play a structural role beneath people's perceptions. Although researchers use the narrative of interdisciplinarity to advocate for funding, at a network level the strategy does not pay off and is contradicted by the tendency of creating cohesive sub-clusters that aggregate philosophers around some specific substantive areas. The combination of qualitative analysis with the formalisation of network structures allows us to observe some recurrent mechanisms and to contextualise them in specific settings where they may be more or less consciously played out by actors and may assume different meanings.

Similarly, the structure of brokerage has been detected across the three case studies. In the case of friendship, it indicates the embeddedness of individuals in various friendship circles, which are intentionally or unintentionally kept separated, either to give people the possibility of playing different identity roles, or because the circles simply do not overlap. In street groups, brokers are people located across overlapping networks, who can therefore better access different types of material and immaterial resources. In the case of philosophers, brokers are highly specialised people who, by moving across research groups, are favoured in the process of obtaining research funding. Again, the mechanism of brokerage assumes different meaning not only depending on the context in which it is activated, but also when the magnifying lens of structural analysis focuses on different levels of granularity.

In the various empirical examples analysed here, brokers' advantages at the micro level of personal relationships include the freedom from social control and from the stereotypical evaluations of someone's identity that it is commonly shared in a closed and cohesive group. When social circles overlap, brokers can benefit from bridging across different networks, but they can also be exposed to cultural contradictions and conflicting norms. At the macro level of social worlds, given the complexity of the community structure and the sometimes mismatching cultural conventions, people may not be fully aware of the advantages of brokerage positions and therefore develop misaligned narratives that privilege the structure of closure.

This mechanism of closure has also emerged as relevant across the case studies. In friendship networks and street groups, it seems to facilitate, alongside the mechanism of homophily, the development of shared group identities and of cultural conventions; in the social world of philosophy, it is the outcome of long-established collaborations that tend to be dominated by some powerful full professors, and, although not as efficient as the structure of brokerage, it still favours the process of obtaining funding. The detection of these peculiar structural mechanisms and the observation of the sometimes matching, sometimes mismatching cultural norms and conventions that regulate and contextualise them in the empirical realm suggest that such mechanisms may be a fruitful area to direct further research efforts in network science.

To continue with the rhetoric of paradigms, I offer some final notes on methodological approaches. In all the cases presented here, the mix of social network analysis and qualitative methods has been fruitful in the investigation of empirical contexts that can be defined as open systems. That is, the cases under analysis all represented situations in which network boundaries could not be robustly identified. When networks represent closed systems, some powerful statistical techniques can be applied. In such cases, given a specified set of actors at one (or more) points in time, statistical modelling can detect the micro mechanisms that regulate social interactions. What these models do is compare an observed network with all the possible configurations that a network with similar characteristics may assume: in this way, it is possible to statistically infer the mechanisms that influence the formation of specific network structures (Robins *et al.* 2007) or its dynamic evolutions over time (Snijders *et al.* 2010).

Although powerful, these statistical approaches work better in contexts where actors in networks are fully identified and endogenous and exogenous mechanisms fully described: furthermore, in dynamic models, the assumption is that the network at various points in time is always constituted by the same actors. Such specifications are more likely to be respected in closed systems, where all the parameters that define them can be robustly set, and where data can be collected from all the actors involved. But in the empirical cases presented in this book, like in most natural occurring social phenomena, it is unlikely that the requirement of closure will be respected. This means that in empirical research, it is often very difficult to robustly define the number of actors who belong to a network and to gain information from all of them. Furthermore, boundaries are more likely to be artificially set by methodological choices (as in the case of friendship), by some contextual limits of the research settings (as in the case of street groups, where, for example, some relationships with the criminal world could not be directly observed), or by the availability of data (as in the case of philosophers, where archival material was available only for the decade under analysis, and only for successful projects).

Similarly, structural mechanisms are difficult to define a priori; a limit that also affects the methodological strategy of agent-based modelling discussed in Chapter 3. Although there are now some interesting attempts to resolve the various issues related to missing data (see, for example, Koskinen *et al.* 2013; Pattison *et al.* 2013), the mixture of formal network analysis with qualitative material is useful for observing the contextual traces that underlying mechanisms leave in the scripts of the empirical domain. This allows us to detect mechanisms and to observe their emergence across different contexts and in different case studies. This exploratory strategy does not allow us to generalise results to any wider population because it is not formulated in terms of probability models. What this strategy can do is to help us to observe structural and cultural configurations across cases using the logic of retroduction, and to deduce postulates and analogies that qualitatively describe and explain the interwoven nature of social phenomena.

Qualitative methods are valuable in exploring the thick nature of identities, stories and social structures, because they can follow the unfurling processes of interactional work that defines actors, social relations and overlapping networks. Social network analysis abstracts contingent elements and formalises them so that they can used to detect and compare the partially stabilised aspects of interactions.

In open systems, these aspects produce the demi-regularities that make the empirical world meaningful and account for the social aspects of structural and cultural configurations. Quantitative analysis, on the other hand, intended as statistical and mathematical techniques, should not be marginalised. On the contrary, they are extremely useful for observing phenomena from a perspective not reachable with qualitative data.

Intransitive mechanisms belong to the real domain not directly accessible by individuals in everyday life. The contingency of events in the actual domain confound the perceptions of the interlocking patterns of social phenomena, and quantitative analysis has the power of reveal these underneath patterns which are otherwise hidden to individuals' observation. As Kadushin says (2012: 4), it is like being stuck in a traffic jam: we can only see cars and trucks around us, but the helicopter can observe beyond our immediate surroundings and find a route to extricate the jam. When we aggregate the elements that constitute the thread of social phenomena in everyday life, the advantages of using quantitative methods that reveal intricate patterns is indubitable.

In conclusion, I hope I communicated in this book the importance of dropping the boundaries between methods in social sciences. We all know that methods are simply tools that we can use to do some specific types of jobs. Each job requires its own tools, and as researchers we can only improve the robustness of our results if we adopt the right tool at the right time. The coherence of science does not depend on the exclusivity of methods, and theories and disciplines should not cast out the richness of the tools that we have on hand. The coherence is rooted on the logical consistency between the questions addressed, the theoretical assumptions that guide an enquiry, the congruency of the methods adopted, and the robustness of the analysis. An approach that integrates various tools can better explore, describe and explain the features that characterise a social world, both in its structural and in its cultural aspects. Dividing the two only means we end up with the view of one side of the coin and lose the strength of a mixed method approach. Instead, we should use the tools at our disposal to formalise the structure and understand the content of social worlds and observe under which conditions they can be found in the social realm.

References

Abbott, A. (1992) 'What do cases do? Some notes on activity in sociological analysis', in C. C. Ragin and H. S. Becker (eds) *What Is a Case? Exploring the Foundations of Social Inquiry*, Cambridge: Cambridge University Press.

Abell, P. (2008) 'History, case studies, statistics, and causal inference', *European Sociological Review* 25: 561–7 (first published online 2008; printed in 2009).

Adams, R. G. and Allan, G. (eds) (1998) *Placing Friendship in Context*, Cambridge: Cambridge University Press.

Allan, G. (1979) *A Sociology of Friendship and Kinship*, London: George Allen & Unwin.

Ansell, C. K. (1997) 'Symbolic networks: the realignment of the French working class, 1887–1894', *American Journal of Sociology* 103: 359–90.

Azarian, R. (2003) 'The general sociology of Harrison White', Stockholm: Department of Sociology, Stockholm University.

Baert, P. (2005) *Philosophy of the Social Sciences: Towards Pragmatism*, Cambridge: Polity Press.

Baldassarri, D. and Bearman, P. (2007) 'Dynamics of political polarization', *American Sociological Review* 72: 784–811.

Barnes, B. and Bloor, D. (1982) 'Relativism, rationalism and sociology of knowledge', in M. Hollis and S. Lukes (eds) *Rationality and Relativism*, Oxford: Blackwell.

Barnes, J. A. (1972) 'Social networks', in J. B. Casagrande, W. Goodenough and E. Hammel (eds) *Module 26*, Boston: Addison-Wesley.

Bartels, C. and Ketellapper, R. (eds) (1979) *Exploratory and Explanatory Statistical Analysis of Spatial Data*, The Hague: Martinus Nijhoff.

Bauman, Z. (2003) *Liquid Love: On the Frailty of Human Bonds*, Cambridge: Polity Press.

Bearman, P. S. (1995) *From Relations to Rhetorics*, New Brunswick, NJ: Rutgers University Press.

Bearman, P. S., Moody, J. and Stovel, K. (2004) 'Chains of affection: the structure of adolescent romantic and sexual networks', *American Journal of Sociology* 1101: 44–91.

Beck, U. and Beck-Gernsheim, E. (1995) *The Normal Chaos of Love*, Cambridge: Polity Press.

Becker, H. S. (1982) *Art Worlds*, Berkley: University of California Press.

Bellotti, E. (2008a) 'What are friends for? Elective communities of single people', *Social Networks* 30: 318–29.

——(2008b) *Amicizie. Le reti social dei giovani single*, Milan: Franco Angeli.

——(2010) 'Comment on Nick Crossley/1', *Sociologica* 1.

——(2012) 'Getting funded: multi-level network of physicists in Italy', *Social Networks* 34: 215–29.

Bellotti, E. and Mora, E. (2014) 'Networks of practices in critical consumption', *Journal of Consumer Culture*, published online before print, May 26, 2014, doi: 10.1177/1469540514536191.

Beltrame, L. (2008) 'La struttura del campo scientifico: una geografia delle traiettorie dei fisici delle particelle', in E. Bellotti, L. Beltrame and P. Volontè (eds) *Il campo sociale della fisica particellare in Italia. Uno studio sociologico*, Bolzano: Bolzano University Press.

Berger, P. L. (2002) 'Whatever happened to sociology?', *First Things*, October.

Bergman, M. M. (2008) 'The straw men of the qualitative–quantitative divide and their influence on mixed method research', in M. M. Bergman (ed.) *Advances in Mixed Methods Research: Theories and Applications*, London: Sage.

Berg-Schlosser, D. and De Meur, G. (2009) 'Comparative research design: case and variable selection', in B. Rihoux and C.C. Ragin (eds) *Configurational Comparative Methods: Qualitative Comparative Analysis (QCA) and Related Techniques*, Thousand Oaks, CA: Sage.

Berg-Schlosser, D., De Meur, G., Rihoux, B. and Ragin, C. C. (2009) 'Qualitative comparative analysis (QCA) as an approach', in B. Rihoux and C. C. Ragin (eds) *Configurational Comparative Methods: Qualitative Comparative Analysis (QCA) and Related Techniques*, Thousand Oaks, CA: Sage.

Bernard, H. R. (2000) *Social Research Methods: Qualitative and Quantitative Approaches*, Thousand Oaks, CA: Sage.

Bernard, H. R. and Killworth, P. D. (1977) 'Informant accuracy in social network data II', *Human Communications Research* 4: 3–18.

Bernard, H. R. and Ryan, G. W. (2010) *Analyzing Qualitative Data: Systematic Approaches*, Thousand Oaks, CA: Sage.

Bernard, H. R., Killworth, P. D. and Sailer, L. (1979/80) 'Informant accuracy in social network data IV', *Social Networks* 2: 191–218.

——(1981) 'Summary of research on informant accuracy in network data, and on the reverse small world problem', *Connections* 4: 11–25.

——(1982) 'Informant accuracy in social network data V', *Social Science Research* 5: 30–66.

Bernard, H. R., Killworth, P. D., Kronenfeld, D. and Sailer, L. (1984) 'The problem of informant accuracy: the validity of retrospective data', *Annual Review of Anthropology* 13: 495–517.

Bernard, H. R., Killworth, P. D., Johnsen, E., Shelley, G. and McCarty, C. (2001) 'Estimating the ripple effect of a disaster', *Connections* 24: 18–22.

Bernard, L. L. (1930) 'Schools of sociology', *Southwestern Political and Social Science Quarterly* 11: 117–34.

Bernardi, L., Keim S. and von der Lippe H. (2007) 'Social influences on fertility: a comparative mixed methods study in Eastern and Western Germany', *Journal of Mixed Methods Research* 1: 23–47.

Bhaskar, R. (1978 [1975]) *A Realist Theory of Science*, Brighton: Harvester.

——(1998 [1979]) *The Possibility of Naturalism*, Brighton: Harvester.

Bidart, C. (1991) 'L'amitié, les amis, leur histoire. Représentations et récits', *Sociétés Contemporaines* 5: 21–42.

——(1997) *L'amitié: un lien social*, Paris: La Découverte.

Bidart, C. and Lavenu, D. (2005) 'Evolution of personal networks and life events', *Social Networks* 27: 359–76.

Blau, P. M. (1955) *The Dynamics of Bureaucracy*, Chicago: University of Chicago Press.

Blau, P. M. and Duncan, O. D. (1967) *The American Occupational Structure*, New York: Free Press.

Bodin, Ö and Tengö, M. (2012) 'Disentangling intangible social–ecological systems', *Global Environmental Change* 22: 430–9.

Borgatti, S. P. (2002) *NetDraw: Graph Visualization Software*, Harvard, MA: Analytic Technologies.

Borgatti, S. P. and Everett, M. G. (1999) 'Models of core/periphery structures', *Social Networks* 21: 375–95.

Borgatti, S. P., Mehra, A., Brass, D. J. and Labianca G. (2009) 'Network analysis in the social sciences', *Science* 13: 892–5.

Borgatti, S. P., Everett, M. G. and Johnson, J. C. (2013) *Analyzing Social Networks*, London: Sage.

Boswell, D. M. (1969) 'Personal crisis and the mobilization of the social network', in J. C. Mitchell (ed.) *Social Networks in Urban Situations*, Manchester: Manchester University Press.

Bott, E. (1956) 'Urban families: the norms of conjugal roles', *Human Relations* 9: 325–42.

Bottero, W. and Crossley, N. (2011) 'Worlds, fields and networks: Becker, Bourdieu and the structures of social structures', *Cultural Sociology* 5: 99–119.

Bourdieu, P. (1984) *Distinction: A Social Critique of the Judgement of Taste*, London: Routledge.

——(1985) 'The social space and the genesis of groups', *Theory and Society* 14: 723–44.

——(1986) 'The forms of capital', in J. G. Richardson (ed.) *Handbook of Theory and Research for the Sociology of Education*, New York: Greenwood Press.

——(1992) *An Invitation to Reflexive Sociology*, Cambridge: Polity Press.

Boutroux, É. (1916 [1874]) *The Contingency of the Laws of Nature*, Chicago: Open Court Publishing.

Braithwaite, R. B. (1968) *Scientific Explanation: A Study of Function of Theory Probability and Law in Science*, Cambridge: Cambridge University Press.

Brandes, U., Robins, G., Mccranie, A. and Wasserman, W. (2013) 'What is network science?', *Network Sciences* 1: 1–15.

Breiger, R. (1974) 'The duality of persons and groups', *Social Forces* 53: 181–90.

Bridges, W. P. and Nelson R. L. (1989) 'Markets in hierarchies: organizational and market influences on gender inequality in a state pay system', *American Journal of Sociology* 95: 616–58.

Brint, S. (1992) 'Hidden meanings: cultural content and context in Harrison White's structural sociology', *Sociological Theory* 10: 194–208.

Broadbent, J. (2003) 'Movement in context: thick networks and Japanese environmental protest', in M. Diani and D. McAdam (eds) *Social Movements and Networks: Relational Approaches to Collective Action*, Oxford: Oxford University Press.

Brotherton, D. C. (2008) 'Beyond social reproduction: bringing resistance back in gang theory', *Theoretical Criminology* 12: 55–77.

Bryant, C. (1985) *Positivism in Social Theory and Research*, New York: St Martin's Press.

Bryman, A. (2006) 'Integrating quantitative and qualitative research: how is it done?', *Qualitative Research* 6: 97–113.

——(2007) 'Barriers to integrating quantitative and qualitative research', *Journal of Mixed Methods Research* 1: 1–18.

——(2008) 'Of methods and methodology', *Qualitative Research in Organizations and Management* 3: 159–68.

Bryman, A., Becker, S. and Sempik, J. (2008) 'Quality criteria for quantitative, qualitative and mixed methods research: a view from social policy', *International Journal of Social Research Methodology* 11: 261–76.

Burk, W. J., Steglich, C. E. G. and Snijders, T. A. B. (2007) 'Beyond dyadic interdependence: actor-oriented models for co-evolving social networks and individual behaviors', *International Journal of Behavioral Development* 31: 397–404.

Burt, R. S. (1978/9) 'Stratification and prestige among elite experts in methodological and mathematical sociology circa 1975', *Social Networks* 1: 105–58.

——(1984) 'Network items and the general social survey', *Social Networks* 6: 293–339.

——(2005) *Brokerage and Closure: An Introduction to Social Capital*, Oxford: Oxford University Press.

Callon, M. (2001) 'Les méthodes d'analyse des grands nombres peuvent-elles contribuer à l'enrichissement de la sociologie du travail?', in A. Pouchet (ed.) *Sociologies du travail: quarante ans après*, Paris: Elsevier.

Cambrosio, A., Keating, P. and Mogoutov, A. (2004) 'Mapping collaborative work and innovation in biomedicine', *Social Studies of Science* 34: 325–64.

Campbell, D. T. and Fiske, D. W. (1959) 'Convergent and discriminant validation by the multitrait-multimethod matrix', *Psychological Bulletin* 56: 81–105.

Coleman, J. (1975) 'Social structure and a theory of action', in P. Blau (ed.) *Approaches to the Study of Social Structure*, New York: Free Press.

——(1990) *The Foundations of Social Theory*, Cambridge, MA: Harvard University Press.

Collins, H. (1985) *Changing Order: Replication and Induction in Scientific Practice*, Chicago: University of Chicago Press.

Collins, R. (1981) 'On the microfoundations of macrosociology', *American Journal of Sociology* 86: 984–1014.

Comte, A. (1907 [1830–42]) *Cours de philosophie positive*, 5th edn, Paris: Rouen.

Cordaz, D. (2011) *Dati e processi. sull'integrazione tra metodi quantitativi e metodi qualitativi nelle scienze sociali*, Milan: Franco Angeli.

Crane, D. (1972) *Invisible Colleges*, Chicago: University of Chicago Press.

Creswell, J. W. and Tashakkori, A. (2007) 'Editorial: differing perspectives on mixed methods research', *Journal of Mixed Methods Research* 1: 303–8.

Crossley, N. (2008) 'Pretty connected: the social network of the early UK punk movement', *Theory, Culture and Society* 25: 89–116.

——(2009) 'The man whose web expanded: network dynamics in Manchester's post-punk music scene 1976–1980', *Poetics* 37: 24–49.

——(2010) 'The social world of the network: combining quantitative and qualitative elements in social network analysis', *Sociologica* 1.

——(2011) *Towards Relational Sociology*, London: Routledge.

Curtis, R., Friedman, A., Neaigus, B., Jose, B., Goldstein, M. and Ildefonso, G. (1995) 'Street-level drug markets: network structure and HIV risk', *Social Networks* 17: 229–49.

Czymoniewicz-Klippel, M. T. (2011) 'Bad boys, big trouble: subcultural formation and resistance in a Cambodian village', *Youth & Society*, published online before print, 23 November.

Davies, A. (2008) *The Gangs of Manchester*, Preston: Milo Books.

Davies, K. and Heaphy, B. (2011) 'Interactions that matter: researching critical relationships', *Methodological Innovations Online* 6: 5–16.

Davis, J. A. and Leinhardt, S. (1972) 'The structure of positive interpersonal relations in small groups', in J. Berger (ed.) *Sociological Theories in Progress*, vol. 2, Boston: Houghton Mifflin.

Dellinger, A. B. and Leech, N. L. (2007) 'Toward a unified validation framework in mixed methods research', *Journal of Mixed Methods Research* 1: 309–32.

Denscombe, M. (2008) 'Communities of practice: a research paradigm for the mixed methods approach', *Journal of Mixed Methods Research* 2: 270–83.

Denzin, N. K. (1978) *The Research Act: A Theoretical Introduction to Sociological Methods*, New York: McGraw-Hill.

Di Nicola, P. (ed.) (2003) *Amici Miei: fenomenologia delle reti amicali nella società del benessere*, Milan: Franco Angeli.

Doreian, P. (1980) 'Linear models with spatially distributed data: spatial disturbances or spatial effects?', *Sociological Methods and Research* 9: 29–60.

Dow, M. M., White, D. R. and Burton, M. L. (1983) 'Multivariate modeling with interdependent network data', *Behavior Science Research* 17: 216–45.

Dow, M. M., Burton, M. L., White, D. R. and Reitz, K. P. (1984) 'Galton's problem as network autocorrelation', *American Ethnologist* 11: 754–70.

Dow, S. C. (2010) 'Structured pluralism', in W. Olsen (ed.) *Realist Methodology*, vol. 2, London: Sage.

Downward, P. and Mearman, A. (2010) 'Retroduction as mixed methods triangulation in economic research: reorienting economics into social sciences', in W. Olsen (ed.) *Realist Methodology*, vol. 2, London: Sage.

Downward, P., Finch, J. H. and Ramsay, J. (2010) 'Critical realism, empirical methods and inference: a critical discussion', in W. Olsen (ed.) *Realist Methodology*, vol. 2, London: Sage.

Dunbar, R. I. M. (1992) 'Neocortex size as a constraint on group size in primates', *Journal of Human Evolution* 22: 469–93.

Durkheim, E. (1964a [1893]) *The Division of Labour in Society*, New York: Free Press.

——(1964b [1895]) *The Rules of Sociological Method*, New York: Free Press.

Edmonds, B. (2012) 'Context in social simulation: why it can't be wished away', *Computational and Mathematical Organization Theory* 18: 5–21.

Edwards, G. (2010) 'Mixed-method approaches to social network analysis', Review paper, ESRC National Centre for Research Methods, http://eprints.ncrm.ac.uk/842/ (accessed August 2013).

Edwards, G. and Crossley, N. (2009) 'Measures and meanings: exploring the ego-net of Helen Kirkpatrick Watts, militant suffragette', *Methodological Innovations Online* 4: 7–61.

Elias, N. (1978 [1970]) *What is Sociology?*, New York: Columbia University Press.

Emirbayer, M. (1997) 'Manifesto for a relational sociology', *American Journal of Sociology* 103: 281–317.

Emirbayer, M. and Goodwin, J. (1994) 'Network analysis, culture, and the problem of agency', *American Journal of Sociology* 99: 1411–54.

Emirbayer, M. and Mische, A. (1998) 'What is agency?', *American Journal of Sociology* 103: 962 1023.

Entwisle, B., Faust, K., Rindfuss, R. R. and Kaneda, T. (2007) 'Networks and contexts: variation in the structure of social ties', *American Journal of Sociology* 112: 1495–533.

Epstein, A. L. (1969a) 'The network and urban social organization', in J. C. Mitchell (ed.) *Social Networks in Urban Situations*, Manchester: Manchester University Press.

——(1969b) 'Gossip, norms and social networks', in J. C. Mitchell (ed.) *Social Networks in Urban Situations*, Manchester: Manchester University Press.

Erickson, B. (1978) 'Some problems of inference from chain data', in K. F. Schuessler (ed.) *Sociological Methodology*, San Francisco: Jossey-Bass.

Esbensen, F.-A., Winfree, L.T., Jr., He, N. and Taylor, T. J. (2001) 'Youth gangs and definitional issues: when is a gang a gang, and why does it matter?', *Crime and Delinquency* 47: 105–30.

Everett, M. G. and Borgatti, S. P. (1994) 'Regular equivalence: general theory', *Journal of Mathematical Sociology* 19: 29–52.

Fararo, T. J. and Doreian, P. (1984) 'Tripartite structural analysis: generalizing the Breiger–Wilson formalism', *Social Networks* 6: 141–75.

Faust, K. (1988) 'Comparison of methods for positional analysis: structural and general equivalence', *Social Networks* 10: 313–41.

Festinger, L., Back, K. Schachter, S., Kelley, H. H. and Thibaut, J. (eds) (1950) *Theory and Experiment in Social Communication*, Ann Arbor: Research Center for Dynamics, University of Michigan.

Fielding, N. (2005) 'The resurgence, legitimation and institutionalization of qualitative methods', *Forum Qualitative Sozialforschung/Forum: Qualitative Social Research* 6.

Fischer, C. S. (1982a) *To Dwell among Friends: Personal Networks in Town and City*, Chicago: University of Chicago Press.

——(1982b) 'What do we mean by "friend"? An inductive study', *Social Networks* 3: 287–306.

Flyvbjerg, B. (2010) 'Five misunderstandings about case-study research', in W. Olsen (ed.) *Realist Methodology*, vol. 2, London: Sage.

Freeman, L. (2000) 'Visualizing social networks', *Journal of Social Structure*, www.cmu.edu/joss/content/articles/volume1/Freeman.html (accessed 20 December 2013).

——(2004) *The Development of Social Network Analysis: A Study in the Sociology of Science*, Vancouver: Empirical Press.

Fuhse, J. and Mützel, S. (2011) 'Tackling connections, structure, and meaning in networks: quantitative and qualitative methods in sociological network research', *Quality & Quantity* 45: 1067–89.

Gambetta, D. (1998) 'Concatenations of mechanisms', in P. Hedrström and R. Swedberg (eds) *Social Mechanisms: An Analytical Approach to Social Theory*, Cambridge: Cambridge University Press.

Giddens, A. (1992) *The Transformation of Intimacy: Sexuality, Love and Eroticism in Modern Societies*, Cambridge: Polity Press.

Gilbert, N. (2008) *Agent-Based Models* (Quantitative Applications in the Social Sciences), London: Sage.

Gilbert, N. and Mulkay, M. (1984) *Opening Pandora's Box: A Sociological Analysis of Scientists' Discourse*, Cambridge: Cambridge University Press.

Glaser, B. G. and Strauss, A. L. (1967) *The Discovery of Grounded Theory: Strategies for Qualitative Research*, New York: Aldine de Gruyter.

Gluesing, J., Riopelle, K. and Danowski, J. A. (forthcoming) 'Innovation networks in global organizations: understanding network practices and dynamics by mixing ethnography and information technology data', in S. Dominguez and B. Hollstein (eds) *Mixed-Methods in Studying Social Networks*, New York: Cambridge University Press.

Goffman, E. (1959) *The Presentation of Self in Everyday Life*, New York: Doubleday.

Goodman, L. A. (1949) 'On the estimation of the number of classes in a population', *Annals of Mathematical Statistics* 20: 572–9.

——(1961) 'Snowball sampling', *Annals of Mathematical Statistics* 32: 148–70.

Gordon, R. (2000) 'Criminal business organisations, street gangs and "wanna be" groups: a Vancouver perspective', *Canadian Journal of Criminology and Criminal Justice* 42: 39–60.

Gould, R. (1995) *Insurgent Identities: Class Community and Protest in Paris from 1848 in the Commune*, Chicago: University of Chicago Press.

Gouldner, H. (1987) *Speaking of Friendship: Middle-Class Women and their Friends*, Westport, CT: Greenwood Press.

Granovetter, M. S. (1973) 'The strength of weak ties', *American Journal of Sociology* 78: 1360–80.

Guba, E. G. and Lincoln, Y. S. (1994) 'Competing paradigms in qualitative research', in N. K. Denzin and Y. S. Lincoln (eds) *Handbook of Qualitative Research*, Thousand Oaks, CA: Sage.

Hagedorn, J. M. and Macon, P. (1988) *People and Folks: Gangs, Crime, and the Underclass in a Rustbelt City*, Chicago: Lake View Press.

Halaby, C. N. and Weakliem, D. L. (1989) 'Worker control and attachment to the firm', *American Journal of Sociology* 95: 549–91.

Hall, P. (1987) 'Interactionism and the study of social organisation', *Sociological Quarterly* 28: 1–22.

Hallinan, M. T. (1978/79) 'The process of friendship formation', *Social Networks* 1: 193–210.

Hallsworth, S. and Young, T. (2004) 'Getting real about gangs', *Criminal Justice Matters* 55: 12–13.

Heath, S. (2004) 'Peer-shared households, quasi-communes and neo-tribes', *Current Sociology* 52: 161–79.

Heath, S. and Cleaver, E. (2003) *Young, Free and Single? Twenty-Somethings and Household Change*, New York: Palgrave Macmillan.

Heath, S., Fuller, A. and Johnston, B. (2009) 'Chasing shadows: defining network boundaries in qualitative social network analysis', *Qualitative Research* 9: 645–61.

Hedström, P. (2005) *Dissecting the Social*, Cambridge: Cambridge University Press.

Hedström, P., Sandell, R. and Stern, C. (2000) 'Mesolevel networks and the diffusion of social movements: the case of the Swedish Social Democratic Party', *American Journal of Sociology* 106: 145–72.

Heisenberg W. (1989) *Physics and Philosophy*, Harmondsworth: Penguin.

Hennig, M., Brandes, U., Pfeffer, J. and Mergel, I. (2012) *Studying Social Networks: A Guide to Empirical Research*, Frankfurt: Campus Verlag.

Hodgson, G. M. (2000) 'What is the essence of institutional economics?', *Journal of Economic Issues* 34: 317–29.

Hogan, B., Carrasco, J. A. and Wellman, B. (2007) 'Visualizing personal networks: working with participant-aided sociograms', *Field Methods* 19: 116–44.

Holland, P. W. and Leinhardt, S. (1970) 'A method for detecting structure in sociometric data', *American Journal of Sociology* 70: 492–513.

Hollstein, B. (2011) 'Qualitative approaches', in J. Scott and P. J. Carrington (eds) *The Sage Handbook of Social Network Analysis*, London: Sage.

——(forthcoming) 'Fuzzy set analysis of network data as mixed method. Personal networks and the transition from school to work', in B. Hollstein and S. Dominguez (eds) *Mixed-Methods Social Network Research*, New York: Cambridge University Press.

Homans, G. (1958) 'Social behavior as exchange', *American Journal of Sociology* 63: 597–606.

——(1961) *Social Behavior: Its Elementary Forms*, New York: Harcourt Brace Jovanovich.

Hummon, N. P. and Doreian, P. (1989) 'Connectivity in a citation network: the development of DNA theory', *Social Networks* 11: 39–63.

Hummon, N. P. and Carley, K. (1993) 'Social networks as normal science', *Social Networks* 15: 71–106.

Husserl, E. (1960) *Cartesian Meditations: An Introduction to Phenomenology*, The Hague: Martinus Nijhoff.

Jack, S. L. (2005) 'The role, use and activation of strong and weak network ties: a qualitative analysis', *Journal of Management Studies* 42: 1233–59.

James, W. (1907) *Pragmatism: A New Name for Some Old Ways of Thinking*, Cambridge, MA: Harvard University Press.

——(1976) *Essays in Radical Empiricism*, Cambridge: Cambridge University Press.

Johnson, E. C. (1986) 'Structure and process: agreement models for friendship formation', *Social Networks* 8: 257–306.

Johnson, J. C. (1990) *Selecting Ethnographic Informants*, Newbury Park, CA: Sage.

Johnson, J. C. and Orbach, M. K. (2002) 'Perceiving the political landscape: ego biases in cognitive political networks', *Social Networks* 24: 291–310.

Johnson, J. C., Boster, J. S. and Holbert, D. (1989) 'Estimating relational attributes from snowball samples through simulation', *Social Networks* 11: 135–58.

Johnson, R. B., Onwuegbuzie, A. J. and Turner, L. A. (2007) 'Toward a definition of mixed methods research', *Journal of Mixed Methods Research* 1: 112–33.

Kadushin, C. (1966) 'The friends and supporters of psychotherapy: on social circles in urban life', *American Sociological Review* 31: 786–802.

——(1976) 'Networks and circles in the production of culture', *American Behavioral Scientist* 19: 769–84.

——(2012) *Understanding Social Networks: Theories, Concepts and Findings*, Oxford: Oxford University Press.

Kahn, R. L. and Antonucci, T. C. (1980) 'Convoys over the life course: attachment, roles, and social support', in P. B. Baltes and O. G. Brim (eds) *Life-span Development and Behavior*, New York: Academic Press.

Kapferer, B. (1969) 'Norms and manipulation of relationships in a work context', in J. C. Mitchell (ed.) *Social Networks in Urban Situations*, Manchester: Manchester University Press.

Kemp, S. and Holmwood, J. (2010) 'Realism, regularity and social explanation', in W. Olsen (ed.) *Realist Methodology*, vol. 2, London: Sage.

Killworth, P. D. and Bernard, H. R. (1976) 'Informant accuracy in social network data', *Human Organization* 35: 269–96.

——(1979/80) 'Informant accuracy in social network data III', *Social Networks* 2: 19–46.

Kirke, D. (2010) 'Comment on Nick Crossley/2', *Sociologica* 1.

Klein, M. W. (1995) *The American Street Gang: Its Nature, Prevalence, and Control*, New York: Oxford University Press.

——(2001) 'Resolving the Eurogang paradox', in M. W. Klein, H.-J. Kerner, C. L. Maxson and E. G. Weitekamp (eds) *The Eurogang Paradox: Street Gangs and Youth Groups in the US and Europe*, Dordrecht: Kluwer Academic.

Knecht, A., Snijders, T. A. B., Baerveldt, C., Steglich, C. E. G. and Raub, W. (2010) 'Friendship and delinquency: selection and influence processes in early adolescence', *Social Development* 19: 494–514.

Knorr-Cetina, K. (1992) 'The couch, the cathedral and the laboratory: on the relationship between experiment and laboratory in science', in A. Pickering (ed.) *Science as Practice and Culture*, Chicago: University of Chicago Press.

Knox, H., Savage, M. and Harvey, P. (2006) 'Social networks and the study of relations: networks as method, metaphor and form', *Economy and Society* 35: 113–40.

Kogovšek, T. and Ferligoj, A. (2005) 'Effects on reliability and validity of egocentered network measurements', *Social Networks* 27: 205–29.

Koskinen, J. H., Robins, G. L., Wang, P. and Pattison, P. E. (2013) 'Bayesian analysis for partially observed network data, missing ties, attributes and actors', *Social Networks* 35: 514–27.

Krackhardt, D. (1998) 'Simmelian tie: super strong and sticky', in R. Kramer and M. Neale (eds) *Power and Influence in Organizations*, Thousand Oaks, CA: Sage.

Krackhardt, D. and Stern, R. N. (1988) 'Informal networks and organizational crises: an experimental simulation', *Social Psychology Quarterly* 51: 123–40.

Kuhn, T. S. (1970) *The Structure of Scientific Revolutions*, 2nd edn, Chicago: University of Chicago Press.

Latour, B. (1987) *Science in Action: How to Follow Scientists and Engineers through Society*, Cambridge, MA: Harvard University Press.

——(2005) *Reassembling the Social: An Introduction to Actor-Network-Theory*, Oxford: Oxford University Press.

Laumann, E. O., Marsden, P. Y. and Prensky, D. (1983) 'The boundary specification problem in network analysis', in R. S. Burt and M. J. Minor (eds) *Applied Network Analysis: A Methodological Introduction*, Beverly Hills, CA: Sage.

Lawson, T. (1997) *Economics and Reality*, London: Routledge.

Lazega, E., Jourda, M. T., Mounier, L. and Stofer, R. (2008) 'Catching up with big fish in the big pond? Multi-level network analysis through linked design', *Social Networks* 30: 157–76.

Leenders, T. T. A. J. (2002) 'Modeling social influence through network autocorrelation: constructing the weight matrix', *Social Networks* 24: 21–47.

Lewis, D. M. G., Conroy-Beam, D., Al-Shawaf, L., Raja, A., DeKay, T. and Buss, D. M. (2011) 'Friends with benefits: the evolved psychology of same- and opposite-sex friendships', *Evolutionary Psychology* 9: 543–63.

Liberman, S. and Wolf, K. B. (1998) 'Bonding number in scientific disciplines', *Social Networks* 20: 239–46.

Lievrouw, L. A., Rogers, E. M., Lowe, C. U. and Nadel, E. (1987) 'Triangulation as a research strategy for identifying invisible colleges among biomedical scientists', *Social Networks* 9: 217–48.

Lin, N. (1999) 'Building a network theory of social capital', *Connections* 22: 28–51.

Lin, N. and Dumin, M. (1986) 'Access to occupations through social ties', *Social Networks* 8: 365–85.

Lin, N., Ensel, W. M. and Vaughn, J. C. (1981a) 'Social resources and strength of ties: structural factors in occupational status attainment', *American Sociological Review* 46: 393–405.

Lin, N., Vaughn, J. C. and Ensel, W. M. (1981b) 'Social resources and occupational status attainment', *Social Forces* 59: 1163–81.

Lincoln, Y. S. and Guba, E. G. (1985) *Naturalistic Inquiry*, Beverly Hills, CA: Sage.

Lonkila, M. and Salmi, A. (2005) 'The Russian work collective and migration', *Europe-Asia Studies* 57: 681–703.

Lorrain, F. and White, H. C. (1971) 'Structural equivalence of individuals in social networks', *Journal of Mathematical Sociology* 1: 49–80.

Lubbers, M., Molina, J. L., Lerner, J., Brandes, U., Avila, J. and McCarty, C. (2010) 'Longitudinal analysis of personal networks: the case of Argentinean migrants in Spain', *Social Networks* 32: 91–104.

Luce, R. and Perry, A. (1949) 'A method of matrix analysis of group structure', *Psychometrika* 14: 95–116.

Lusher, D., Koskinen, J. and Robins, G. (2012) *Exponential Random Graph Models for Social Networks*, Cambridge: Cambridge University Press.

Lykken, D. (1970) 'Statistical significance in psychological research', in R. E. Herkel and D. E. Morrison (eds) *The Significance Test Controversy*, London: Butterworth.

McCarty, C. (2010) 'Comment on Nick Crossley/3', *Sociologica* 1.

MacDonald, J. S. and MacDonald, L. D. (1964) 'Chain migration ethnic neighborhood formation and social networks', *The Milbank Memorial Fund Quarterly* 42: 82–97.

McDonald, S. (2005) 'Studying actions in context: a qualitative shadowing method for organizational research', *Qualitative Research* 5: 455–73.

McEvoy, P. and Richards, D. (2010) 'Critical realism: a way forward for evaluation research in nursing?', in W. Olsen (ed.) *Realist Methodology*, vol. 2, London: Sage.

McPherson, M., Smith-Lovin, L. and Cook, J. M. (2001) 'Birds of a feather: homophily in social networks', *Annual Review of Sociology* 27: 415–44.

McRobbie, A. (2000) *Feminism and Youth Culture*, London: Routledge.

Manzo, G. (2009) *La spirale des inégalités. choix scolaires en France et en Italie au XXe siècle*, Paris: Presses de l'Université Paris-Sorbonne.

——(2013) 'Educational choices and social interactions: a formal model and a computational test', *Comparative Social Research* 30: 47–100.

Marinoff, L. (2003) *The Big Questions*, London: Bloomsbury.

Marsden, P. V. (2005) 'Recent developments in network measurements', in P. J. Carrington, J. Scott and S. Wasserman (eds) *Models and Methods in Social Network Analysis*, Cambridge: Cambridge University Press.

Martinez, A., Dimitriadis, Y., Rubia, B., Gomez, E. and de la Fuente, P. (2003) 'Combining qualitative evaluation and social network analysis for the study of classroom social interactions', *Computers and Education* 41: 353–68.

Masterman, M. (1970) 'The nature of paradigms', in I. Lakatos and A. Musgrave (eds) *Criticism and the Growth of Knowledge*, Cambridge: Cambridge University Press.

Matthews, R. B., Gilbert, N. G., Roach, A., Polhill, J. G. and Gotts, N. M. (2007) 'Agent-based land-use models: a review of applications', *Landscape Ecology* 22: 1447–59.

Mauss, M. (1954) *The Gift*, London: Cohen and West.

Mead, G. H. (1932) *The Philosophy of the Present*, Chicago: University of Chicago Press.

——(1934) *Mind, Self and Society*, Chicago: University of Chicago Press.

Menjivar, C. (2000) *Fragmented Ties: Salvadoran Immigrant Networks in America*, Berkeley: University of California Press.

Merton, R. K. (1949) *Social Theory and Social Structure*, New York: Free Press.

Mesa, D. (2003) 'Il genere come risorsa comunicativa nelle relazioni amicali e nel tempo libero', in E. Besozzi (ed.) *Il genere come risorsa comunicativa. maschile e femminile nei processi di crescita*, Milan: Franco Angeli.

Milgram, S. (1977) The familiar stranger: an aspect of urban anonymity', in S. Milgram, *The Individual in a Social World*, Reading, MA: Addison-Wesley.

Mill, J. S. (1967 [1843]) *A System of Logic: Ratiocinative and Inductive*, Toronto: University of Toronto Press.

Miller, W. B. (1982) *Crime by Youth Gangs and Groups in the United States*, Washington, DC: US Department of Justice.

Mische, A. (2003) 'Cross-talk in movements: reconceiving the culture-network link', in M. Diani and D. McAdam (eds) *Social Movements and Networks*, Oxford: Oxford University Press.

——(2008) *Partisan Publics: Communication and Contention across Brazilian Youth Activist Networks*, Princeton and Oxford: Princeton University Press.

Mische, A. and White, H. (1998) 'Between conversation and situation: public switching dynamics across network-domains', *Social Research* 65: 295–324.

Mitchell, J. C. (ed.) (1969) *Social Networks in Urban Situations*, Manchester: Manchester University Press.

——(1983) 'Case and situational analysis', *Sociological Review* 31: 187–211.

Mizruchi, M. S. (1996) 'What do interlocks do? An analysis, critique, and assessment of research on interlocking directorates', *Annual Review of Sociology* 22: 271–98.

Mok, D., Wellman, B. and Basu, R. (2007) 'Did distance matter before the Internet? Interpersonal contact and support in the 1970s', *Social Networks* 29: 430–61.

Morgan, D. L. (2007) 'Paradigms lost and pragmatism regained: methodological implications of combining qualitative and quantitative methods', *Journal of Mixed Methods Research* 1: 48–76.

——(2009) *Acquaintances: The Space between Intimates and Strangers*, Maidenhead: Open University Press.

Murray, C. (1990) *The Emerging British Underclass*, London: Institute of Economic Affairs.

Naroll, R. (1961) 'Two solutions to Galton's problem', *Philosophy of Science* 28: 15–39.

——(1965) 'Galton's problem: the logic of cross-cultural analysis', *Social Research* 32: 428–51.

Neaigus, A., Friedman, S. R., Curtis, R., Des Jarlais, D. C., Terry Furst, R., Jose, B., Mota, P., Stepherson, B., Sufian, M., Ward, T. and Wright, J. W. (1994) 'The relevance of drug injectors' social and risk networks for understanding and preventing HIV infection', *Social Science and Medicine* 38: 67–78.

O'Connor, P. (1992) *Friendship between Women: A Critical Review*, Indianapolis: Prentice Hall.

——(1998) 'Women's friendships in a post-modern world', in R. G. Adams and G. Allan (eds) *Placing Friendship in Context*, Cambridge: Cambridge University Press.

Ogburn, W. F. (1930) 'The folk-ways of a scientific sociology', *Publication of the American Sociological Society* 25: 1–10.

Olsen, W. (ed.) (2010) *Realist Methodology*, vol. 2, London: Sage.

Onwuegbuzie, A. J. and Leech, N. L. (2007) 'Validity and qualitative research: an oxymoron?', *Quality & Quantity* 41: 233–49.

Opp, K. (1999) 'Contending conceptions of the theory of rational action', *Journal of Theoretical Politics* 11: 171–202.

Ord, K. (1975) 'Estimation methods for models of spatial interaction', *Journal of the American Statistical Association* 70: 120–6.

Padgett, J. F. and Ansell, C. K. (1993) 'Robust action and the rise of the Medici, 1400–1434', *American Journal of Sociology* 98: 1259–319.

Paine, R. (1969) 'In search of friendship', *Man* 4: 505–24.

Parcel, T. L., Kaufman, R. L. and Leeann, J. (1991) 'Going up the ladder: multiplicity sampling to create linked macro-to-micro organizational samples', in P. Marsden (ed) *Sociological Methodology*, Oxford: Basil Blackwell.

Pattison, P., Robins, G., Snijders, T. A. B. and Wang, P. (2013) 'Conditional estimation of exponential random graph models from snowball and other sampling designs', *Journal of Mathematical Psychology* 57: 284–296.

Pavalko, E. K. (1989) 'State timing of policy adoption: workmen's compensation in the United States, 1909–1929', *American Journal of Sociology* 95: 592–615.

Pawson, R. (2006) *Evidence-based Policy: A Realist Perspective*, London: Sage.

Pearson, M. and Michell, L. (2000) 'Smoke rings: social network analysis of friendship groups, smoking, and drug-taking', *Drugs: Education, Prevention and Policy* 7: 21–37.

Peirce, C. S. (1931–58) *Collected Papers of Charles Sanders Peirce*, ed. C. Hartshorne, P. Weiss and A. Burks, Cambridge, MA: Harvard University Press.

Pih, K. K.-H., De La Rosa, M., Rugh, D and Mao, K. 2008 'Different strokes for different gangs? An analysis of capital among Latino and Asian gang members', *Sociological Perspectives* 51: 473–94.

Pitts, J. (2008) *Reluctant Gangsters: The Changing Face of Youth Crime*, Cullompton, UK: Willan Publishing.

Plummer, K. (1997) *The Chicago School*, London: Routledge.

Podolny, J. M. (2001) 'Networks as the pipes and prisms of the market', *American Journal of Sociology* 107: 33–60.

Prell, C. (2011) *Social Network Analysis: History, Theory and Methodology*, London: Sage.

Putnam, R. D. (2000) *Bowling Alone*, New York: Simon & Schuster.

Ragin, C. C. (1987) *The Comparative Method: Moving beyond Qualitative and Quantitative Strategies*, Berkeley: University of California Press.

——(1992) 'Introduction: cases of "What Is a Case?"', in C. C. Ragin and H. S. Becker (eds) *What Is a Case? Exploring the Foundations of Social Inquiry*, Cambridge: Cambridge University Press.

——(1994) *Constructing Social Research: The Unity and Diversity of Method*, Thousand Oaks, CA: Pine Forge Press.

——(2006) 'Systematic cross-case analysis with small-Ns', ESRC Research Methods Festival, 17–20 July, Oxford: St Catherine's College.

——(2008) *Redesigning Social Inquiry: Fuzzy Sets and Beyond*, Chicago: University of Chicago Press.

Ragin, C. C. and Becker, H. S. (eds) (1992) *What Is a Case? Exploring the Foundations of Social Inquiry*, Cambridge: Cambridge University Press.

Renouvier, C. B. J. (1859) *Essais de critique générale. Premier (deuxième) essai*, Oxford: Oxford University Press.

Rihoux, B. and Ragin, C. C. (eds) (2009) *Configurational Comparative Methods: Qualitative Comparative Analysis (QCA) and Related Techniques*, Thousand Oaks, CA: Sage.

Robins, G., Pattison, P., Kalish, Y. and Lusher, D. (2007) 'An introduction to exponential random graph (p*) models for social networks', *Social Networks* 29: 173–91.

Robinson, S. E., Everett, M. G. and Christley, R. M. (2007) 'Recent network evolution increases the potential for large epidemics in the British cattle population', *Journal of the Royal Society Interface* 4: 669–74.

Ron, A. (2010) 'Regression analysis and the philosophy of social science: a critical realist view', in W. Olsen (ed.) *Realist Methodology*, vol. 2, London: Sage.

Roseneil, S. and Budgeon, S. (2004) 'Cultures of intimacy and care beyond "the family": personal life and social change in the early 21st century', *Current Sociology* 52: 135–59.

Rossi, P. H. (1994) 'The war between the quals and the quants: is a lasting peace possible?', *New Directions for Program Evaluation* 61: 23–36.

Ryan, J. W. (2013) 'Network hubs and opportunity for complex thinking among young British Muslims', *Journal for the Scientific Study of Religion* 52: 573–95.

Sailer, L. D. (1978) 'Structural equivalence: meaning and definition, computation and application', *Social Networks* 1: 73–90.

Saleh, N. (2009) 'Philosophical pitfalls: the methods debate in American political science', *Journal of Integrated Social Sciences* 1: 141–76.

Sanchez-Jankowski, M. (1991) *Islands in the Street: Gangs in American Urban Society*, Berkeley: University of California Press.

Sawyer, R. K. (2002) 'Durkheim's dilemma: toward a sociology of emergence', *Sociological Theory* 20: 227–47.

Sayer, A. (1992) *Method in Social Science: A Realist Approach*, London: Routledge.

——(2000) *Realism and Social Science*, London: Sage.

Schaefer J. (ed.) (1974) *Studies in Cultural Diffusion: Galton's Problem*, New Haven, CT: HRAFlex Books.

Scheibelhofer, E. (2008) 'Combining narration-based interviews with topical interviews: methodological reflections on research practices', *International Journal of Social Research Methodology* 11: 403–16.

Schutz, A. (1954) 'Concept and theory formation in the social sciences', *Journal of Philosophy* 51: 257–72.

——(1966) *Collected Papers*, vol. 3, The Hague: Martinus Nijhoff.

——(1972) *The Phenomenology of the Social World*, Evanston, IL: Northwestern University Press.

Scott, J. (1991) *Social Network Analysis: A Handbook*, London: Sage.

——(1997) *Corporate Business and Capitalist Classes*, New York: Oxford University Press.

Scriven M. (1964) 'Views of human nature', in T. Wann (ed.) *Behaviorism and Phenomenology: Contrasting Bases for Modern Psychology*, Chicago: University of Chicago Press.

Shibutani, T. (1955) 'Reference groups as perspectives', *American Journal of Sociology* 60: 562–9.

Short, J. F., Jr. (1996) *Gangs and Adolescent Violence*, Boulder: Institute of Behavioral Science, Regents of the University of Colorado.

Shove, E., Pantzar, M. and Watson, M. (2012) *The Dynamics of Social Practice: Everyday Life and How it Changes*, London: Sage.

Simmel, G. (1921) 'Fragment über die liebe dem nachlass Georg Simmels', *Logos* 9: 1–54 (English translation: 'A fragment on love', in G. Simmel, *On Women, Sexuality and Love*, New Haven, CT: Yale University Press, 1984).

——(1955 [1922]) *Conflict and the Web of Group Affiliations*, Glencoe, IL: Free Press.

——(1976a [1903]) 'The metropolis and mental life', in *The Sociology of Georg Simmel*, New York: Free Press.

——(1976b [1903]) *The Sociology of Georg Simmel*, New York: Free Press.

Simon, H. A. (1957) *Models of Man: Social and Rational*, New York: Wiley.

Skvoretz, J. and Faust, K. (2002) 'Relations, species, and network structure', *Journal of Social Structure* 3.

Smart, C. (2007) *Personal Life: New Directions in Sociological Thinking*, Cambridge: Polity Press.

Smart, C., Davies, K., Heaphy, B. and Mason, J. (2012) 'Difficult friendship and ontological insecurity', *Sociological Review* 60: 1–19.

Smith, S. S. (2005) '"Don't put my name on it": social capital activation and job finding assistance among the black urban poor', *American Journal of Sociology* 111: 1–57.

Snijders, T. A. B. and Bosker, R. J. (2012) *Multilevel Analysis: An Introduction to Basic and Advanced Multilevel Modelling* (2nd edn), London: Sage.

Snijders, T. A. B., Steglich, C. E. G. and Van de Bunt, G. G. (2010) 'Introduction to actor-based models for network dynamics', *Social Networks* 32: 44–60.

Spencer, L. and Pahl, R. (2006) *Rethinking Friendship: Hidden Solidarities Today*, Princeton, NJ: Princeton University Press.

Spradley, J. P. (1979) *The Ethnographic Interview*, New York: Holt, Rinehart & Winston.

——(1980) *Participant Observation*, Orlando, FL: Harcourt Brace Jovanovich.

Stanford Encyclopedia of Philosophy (2010) ed. E.N. Zalta, http://plato.stanford.edu/ (accessed August 2013).

Strauss, A. (1973) 'Social world perspective', *Studies in Symbolic Interaction* 1: 119–28.

Sullivan, M. L. (1989) *"Getting Paid": Youth Crime and Work in the Inner City*, Ithaca, NY: Cornell University Press.

——(2005) 'Maybe we shouldn't study "gangs": does reification obscure youth violence?', *Journal of Contemporary Criminal Justice* 21: 170–90.

Tashakkori, A. and Teddlie, C. (1998) *Mixed Methodology: Combining Qualitative and Quantitative Approaches*, London: Sage.

Thornberry, T. P., Krohn, M. D., Lizotte, A. J. and Smith, C. A. (2003) *Gangs and Delinquency in Developmental Perspective*, New York: Cambridge University Press.

Thrasher, F. M. (1963 [1927]) *The Gang: A Study of 1,313 Gangs in Chicago*, Chicago: University of Chicago Press.

Tilly, C. (2002) *Stories, Identities and Political Change*, New York: Rowman & Littlefield.

Van de Bunt, G. G., Van Duijn, M. A. J. and Snijder, T. A. B. (1999) 'Friendship networks through time: an actor-oriented dynamic statistical network model', *Computational & Mathematical Organization Theory* 5: 167–92.

Van der Gaag M. and Snijders, T. A. B. (2003) *Social Capital Quantification with Concrete Items*, Groningen, Netherlands: University of Groningen Press.

Wad, P. (2001) 'Critical realism and comparative sociology', Draft paper for the 5th IACR conference, 17–19 August.

Wang, P., Robins, G., Pattison, P. and Lazega, E. (2013) 'Exponential random graph models for multilevel networks', *Social Networks* 35: 96–115.

Warde, A. (2005) 'Consumption and the theory of practice', *Journal of Consumer Culture* 5: 131–54.

Wasserman, S. S. and Faust K. (1994) *Social Network Analysis: Methods and Applications*, Cambridge: Cambridge University Press.

Watters, E. (2003) *Urban Tribes: A Generation Redefines Friendship, Family and Commitment*, New York: Bloomsbury.

Weber, M. (1978) *Economy and Society: An Outline of Interpretative Sociology*, Berkeley: University of California Press.

——(2004 [1917]) *The Vocation Lectures*, Indianapolis: Hackett Publishing.

Weeks, J., Heaphy, B. and Donovan, C. (2001) *Same Sex Intimacies: Families of Choice and Other Life Experiments*, London: Routledge.

Weerman, F. M., Maxson, C. L., Esbensen, F., Aldridge, J., Medina, J. and van Gemert, F. (2009) *Eurogang Program Manual: Background, Development, and Use of the Eurogang Instruments in Multi-Site, Multi-Method Comparative Research*, University of Missouri at St Louis: Eurogang.

Wellman, B. (1979) 'The community question: the intimate networks of east Yorkers', *American Journal of Sociology* 84: 1201–31.

——(1990) 'Different strokes from different folks: community ties and social support', *American Journal of Sociology* 96: 558–88.

——(1993) 'An egocentric network tale: comment on Bien et al. "An account of the origin and design of the East York studies"', *Social Networks* 15: 423–36.

Wellman, B., Carrington, P. J. and Hall, A. (1988) 'Networks as personal communities', in B. Wellman and S. D. Berkowitz (eds) *Social Structures: A Network Approach*, Cambridge: Cambridge University Press.

Werking, K. (1997) *We Are Just Good Friends: Women and Men in Nonromantic Relationships*, New York: Guilford Press.

Weston, K. (1998) *Longslowburn: Sexuality and Social Science*, New York: Routledge.

Wheeldon, P. D. (1969) 'The operation of voluntary associations and personal networks in the political processes of an inter-ethnic community', in J. C. Mitchell (ed.) *Social Networks in Urban Situations*, Manchester: Manchester University Press.

White, D. R. and Reitz, K. P. (1983) 'Graph and semigroup homomorphisms on networks of relations', *Social Networks* 5: 193–234.

White, D. R., Burton, M. L. and Dow, M. M. (1981) 'Sexual division of labor in African agriculture: a network autocorrelation analysis', *American Anthropologist* 83: 824–49.

White, H. C. (1973) 'Everyday life in stochastic networks', *Sociological Inquiry* 43: 43–9.

——(2008 [1992]) *Identity and Control*, Princeton, NJ: Princeton University Press.

White, H. C., Boorman, S. and Breiger, R. (1976) 'Social structure from multiple networks: blockmodels of roles and positions', *American Journal of Sociology* 81: 730–80.

Whittle, A. and Spicer, A. (2008) 'Is actor network theory critique?', *Organization Studies* 29: 611–29.

Whyte, W. F. (1943) *Street Corner Society: The Social Structure of an Italian Slum*, Chicago: University of Chicago Press.

Williams, M. (2000) *Science and Social Science: An Introduction*, London: Routledge.

Williamson, H. (1997) 'Status zero youth and the "underclass": some considerations', in R. MacDonald (ed.) *Youth, the 'Underclass' and Social Exclusion*, London: Routledge.

Wilson, T. P. (1982) 'Relational networks: an extension of sociometric concepts', *Social Networks* 4: 105–16.

Wong, S.-L. and Salaff, J. W. (1998) 'Network capital: emigration from Hong Kong', *British Journal of Sociology* 49: 358–74.

Woo Park, H. and Kluver, R. (2009) 'Trends in online networking among South Korean politicians: a mixed-method approach', *Government Information Quarterly* 26: 505–15.

Wright, P. (1982) 'Men's friendship, women's friendship and the alleged inferiority of the latter', *Sex Roles* 8: 1–20.

Zachary, W. (1977) 'An information flow model for conflict and fission in small groups', *Journal of Anthropological Research* 33: 452–73.

Znaniecki, F. (1934) *The Method of Sociology*, New York: Farrar & Rinehart.

Index

Page numbers shown in *italics* refer to figures and tables.